# PROMISE
## I'll Stay for Mother's Day

SHIRLEYANNE THOM

## ACKNOWLEDGMENTS

*I could not have written this book*
*without the contributions of*
*Mabel Thompson Knosp and Lois Thompson Wilson.*
*Their recollections of growing up*
*in Eastern Oregon provided the foundation*
*for the telling of this story.*

Promise I'll Stay for Mother's Day © 2013 Shirleyanne Thom
All rights reserved.

ISBN: 0615913121
ISBN-13: 978-0615913124
LCCN: 2013920872

COVER AND INTERIOR DESIGN: Elizabeth Watson

CREDITS FOR POEMS AND SONGS: Pages 18, Little Brown Church in the Vale, William S. Pitts, 1857; 19, Home Sweet Home, Henry Bishop and John Howard Payne 1823; He's in the Jailhouse Now, Recorded by Jmmy Rogers 1920s; 62, I'm Thinking Tonight of M Blue Eyes © Carter Family 1929; 165, The Shooting of Dan McGrew, Robert W. Service 1907; Trees, Joyce Kilmer 1914; Oh Captain, My Captain, Walt Whitman, Leaves of Grass 1900, (also page 196); Charge of the Light Brigade, Alfred Lord Tennyson; 176 and 178, original poems, Cliff Perry 1985;* 178, My Grandfather's Clock, Henry Clay Work 1876; Old Joe Clark, Sung by WW1 Soldiers, printed 1918, 90 stanzas; Little Annie, Old Bluegrass tune, author unknown (also page 205); 196, excerpt from the 23rd Psalm, Holy Bible; 206, Gathering Flowers in the Master's Bouquet, Marvin E. Baumgardner 1947; 208, The Doodle Bug Song, many variations traced back to Mark Twain writings about lion ants.

*1986 Cliff Perry and Laurel Bliss recorded a CD called "Old Pal", a collection of Old Timey tunes; it was dedicated to Lois Wilson, and is available Online. Laurel is seen playing the Dobro in the photo on page 7 and Cliff is singing in the photo on page 176.

## DEDICATION

*How can I begin to thank the family and friends*
*who traveled the long road with me to live the story of our lives.*
*Rebecca Anderson Suryan and Shannon Anderson Archer,*
*two daughters who somehow survived my ever-changing path of raising them;*
*Gene Wilson, Texanna Casey Thompson, and Cliff Perry,*
*brother, cousin, family friend, who helped care for the amazing woman we loved;*
*Heidi Koster, Taylor Hayes and Judith Strand,*
*three friends who encouraged my writing of this memoir;*
*Thomas Henry Wilson,*
*our quiet, steady, loving Father who left us too soon;*
*And to my Mother, Lois Thompson Wilson,*
*middle child of the very special Thompson Clan I am privileged to call family,*
*what a remarkable journey you chartered for us all.*
*This is your story.*

*Preface* 7

1  *The Rough-Hewn Country Patriarch* 9

2  *The Poetic Patriarch* 17

3  *Divided by Death and Ambition* 20

4  *Middle Child on Her Own* 30

5  *Romance Turns Deadly* 33

6  *Husband to the Rescue* 39

7  *The Matriarch Steps Forward* 43

8  *It's a Fun War* 51

9  *Lois Goes to Work* 57

10  *Dad Fills In* 61

11  *We Yield to Tradition* 67

12  *The Arranged Marriage Begins* 74

13  *We Lose Dad* 83

14  *A New Generation Arrives* 91

15  *The Arranged Marriage Ends* 95

16  *A New Family Order* 102

17  *Messing With the Order   107*

18  *Summer Celebrations Turn Cold   119*

19  *A Tough Diagnosis   125*

20  *Medical Decisions   133*

21  *Sandwiched   139*

22  *Christmas Past and Present   145*

23  *Another Damn Divorce   154*

14  *Today I Marry My Friend   159*

25  *Easter Deliverance   164*

26  *Traveling Handicapped   169*

27  *Crossing the Pass Leaves Spring Behind   175*

28  *Awakened By a Loud Thud   180*

29  *I'll Stay for Mother's Day   191*

30  *Our Separate Journeys Begin   198*

31  *Promise Fulfilled   203*

# *Preface*

*This is the story of a young woman*

*Who left the dirt roads of her country upbringing*

*To travel the opportunistic streets of the city*

*Only to return to her roots*

*'Neath the boughs of a fragrant lilac tree*

A YOUNG WOMAN'S road to independence is not a smooth one, even today. It is important that we lay a family foundation sturdy enough to support homecomings when we need rest and comfort, and to offer a final return home at the end of our journey.

—ST

*Annie 1903, West Virginia.*

CHAPTER 1

## *The Rough-Hewn Country Patriarch*

BRESLEY EDMUND THOMPSON was your basic shiftless bloke, turning to easy tricks to get by and ornery as all get out if anyone tried to push him into altering his dithering ways. He had no desire to continue his education beyond his neighborhood's generally accepted eighth grade level, nor did he see a reason to develop working skills that would upgrade his common rank. Bress liked his uncomplicated status and wasn't about to change it for anyone for any reason.

He managed to get enough work to support his needs and habits, and that was all he expected of himself. His needs were simple enough, limited to a couple of rooms, a bag of groceries, and a change of clothes. His habits were equally plain. Booze was his escape and loose women his entertainment. As long as both were available and easy to lay his hands on, he saw no need to alter the framework for his version of a good life.

Bress' perspective worked for a while, but shiftless behavior sooner or later brings consequences, and Bress' day of reckoning arrived sooner rather than later. His easy life came to an unsettling end with a knock on the door when he was but twenty years old. He opened the door to one of his loose women who wanted a more permanent kind of arrangement. She wanted a relationship with ties—ties that bind, to be exact. This particular playmate came to him in a family way, demanding that he elevate his regard for her.

"Bress, I'm havin' your baby and I want you t' marry me," she said, standing in the doorway, looking him straight in the eye.

Bress decided on the spot he didn't want to marry at the tender age of twenty, and even if he did, it wouldn't be to this irresponsible loose woman who managed to get herself pregnant. Never mind the folly of his mind set. It served him well to blame her for his bothersome predicament.

He told himself he had to get out of this mess fast, but he needed time to figure out how to do it. With his brain racing around weighing a variety of options, his body fashioned an ignorant pose, standing there on the doorstep, nodding and mumbling a load of mindless nonsense, belying his big, strong, red-headed machismo.

"I gotta figger out what t' do . . . you gotta gimme time t' figger what t' do..." he said to this female intrusion while he played his delay game.

She could tell she'd made a big mistake throwing herself at him like she'd done. She whirled around and tromped down the stairs, tossing back her departing words, "You go ahead n' figger all you want, Bress Thompson, but you better get it figgered out, 'cause I'll be back. It's yer kid I'm havin' an' I'm goin' t' need your help t' take care of it. I ain't goin' t' do it all by m'self." She left him grumbling at the door.

Bress sat himself down to think about this unwanted invasion into his effortless life. *The only sure way fer me t' keep from havin' t' marry that woman, he thought, is fer me t' find m'self another wife. Don't really want t' marry, but th' law says you can't have more 'n one wife, so I have t' git me a wife before she claims me. I'm goin' t' find me a strong decent woman who'll take care a' me like a good woman should, one who won't be thinkin' she can tell me what t' do. Then I'll tell that floozy I can't marry her b'cause, I already have a wife. That ought a' get rid a' her.*

Having a plan that suited his needs, Bress went looking for a more permanent kind of woman. It was easy enough. Good women of little means and few options weren't hard to find in this early twentieth century small-town environment. With no moral compunction holding him back, he set out to take advantage of their plight.

Bress found an acre of women to choose from on a nearby farm. Filled with his usual intake of liquid courage to get him there, he stood at the edge of the field looking over the female prospects. They didn't look too bad through his squinty, likkered up eyes. He noticed one fair-haired woman bending over a row of taters, with a hoe in her hand.

*There's one, over thar on th' far side a th' field, he observed. I seen that woman b'fore, even talked to 'er once r' twice. Fine, sturdy-lookin; woman. But not so fine lookin' as t' give me problems down the road. Kind of a sensible look. As I recall, she talks nice too, refined, if ya' will. Yep. That's the one. That's the woman I'm goin' t' marry. Think I'll go over 'n talk t' her agin, an' git m'self a hard-workin' wife who knows her place.*

Bress crossed the field to where this fine lookin' woman was a' hoein'.

"Woman", he said, "I b'lieve we met b'fore, an' I b'lieve we could have a fine life together. If you'd come with me, we could talk it over an' git married, an' you wouldn't have to stay here in this field an' hoe them taters no more."

The women in the fields were good marriage material for men like Bress. They were amenable to any kind of marriage proposal; subservient, hard-working women who wanted only a roof over their heads and food in their bellies, not far from the basic needs of their births. They were willing to trade their bodies and unknown freedoms for the guarantee of a life-long dwelling place. No questions asked, Louisa Ann Bowyer put down her hoe and followed Bresley Edmund Thompson out of the tater field into his marriage bed.

Even with a fine, sturdy woman as his wife, Bress either didn't understand that marriage was supposed to bring responsibilities along with the convenience of a marriage bed, or he didn't care. Sidestepping one hasty near marriage and entering into the shelter of the real thing did nothing to stop his taste for philandering. He got himself out of the first escapade unscathed. Why not others? Even as he continued to seek out playmates and sire at least one more child outside of marriage, he and Louisa produced three children of their own in short order. With help from Louisa's family, they managed to get by. Life for them was, well, what life was.

> The women in the fields were good marriage material ... they were amenable to any kind of marriage proposal; subservient, hard-working women who wanted only a roof over their heads and food in their bellies.

It was the imminent birth of another bastard child that prompted their move west. This unborn child's mother, unlike the impulsive woman who tried to secure a marriage without family back up, was threatening to make what Bress thought were unreasonable demands on his time and resources. After all, he had a wife and his own offspring to support. How could she think he'd leave them to go off with an immoral woman like her?

But he knew her demands could cause trouble between him and his wife, Louisa Ann, now endearingly called Annie, a wife he'd come to respect and care about in his own limited way. And he was crazy about his kids, again with the limitations related to a call of the flesh. Bress came to be called "Pop" in deference to his talent for attracting the pleasures of his kids as well as the woman who bore him these young saplings.

There'd been whispers about a possible bastard child before his marriage, but only whispers. This second one was about to become town news. Pop knew he had to do something drastic and quick to spare himself and his family the shame of his recklessness.

Escape had become his standard answer to problems he didn't know how to fix, and he didn't think he could fix this latest quandary by keeping himself in the middle of it. With his luck still running one step ahead of disaster, he found another way out. Pop had heard about a group of people moving west to the state of Oregon where land was available once again to would-be homesteaders.

The Thompsons were not alone, nor were they among the first group of folks leaving their eastern homes to begin new lives in new places. The Homestead Act of 1862 enticed many families to head west believing that a move away from their East Coast roots would automatically improve their lot. The sad fact is, many of these folks moved their shortcomings with them.

Whatever caused them to fail in their eastern abodes traveled with them to their new homes, leaving these ill-fated wanderers in much the same dark hole they'd lived in before they took off in their search for new horizons. Their difficulties were tied not so much to a particular community as to an inherent lack of talent and know-how to help them overcome everyday problems, wherever they lived. These people made their way west with suitcases full of pitiful belongings, hearts full of hopeful anticipation, and not a whole lot more.

Although many of the original Homesteaders did well, some did not. Those who couldn't make it in their new surroundings abandoned their properties, creating vacant land with opportunities for a new wave of hopeful transplants.

As usual, Pop was short of money and didn't have much to sell in an attempt to raise the cash to support their move. But he thought he could put together enough for the train ride, and he knew he could borrow from his in-laws to secure the acreage and purchase basic supplies for settling his family on the new land. He believed they'd give it to him to keep scandal from their door, even if it meant never seeing their daughter again. And he was right. Having secured the anticipated financial help from his in-laws, Pop knew he could get to Oregon and at least claim his plot of ground. The rest he'd figure out once they got there. He was ready to join the western migration.

*We have enough to go with 'em, n' git the land, an' we can live in a tent once we get there, 'til a house can be built. 'S all I can do. Can't wait for more. Gotta go. Gotta tell Annie we're movin' to a better place. Time t' move on.*

In the summer of 1910, Bresley Thompson and his wife, Louisa Anne, along with their three children, Herb, born in 1904, Mabel, born in 1906 and Edith, born in 1908, left their home in Fayette, West Virginia, and headed west to the Blue Mountains of Eastern Oregon. They traveled mostly by rail to a place called Promise, where they hoped to find a life more prosperous than the meager existence they'd left behind.

Promise is located at the top of the Blue Mountains, thirty miles up the one-lane dirt road from Wallowa, the nearest registered Oregon township. With cold weather fast approaching, the young family had just enough time and money to purchase a large tent, a horse and wagon, seeds for a garden, and the bare necessities for running a household. They pitched their tent, planted their garden, and settled in for winter on their new piece of land.

Edith, nicknamed Teeny for her frail appearance, passed away in the diphtheria epidemic of 1910-11, barely surviving the trip west. She lived only three years.

Neither relentless poverty nor the short life of their third child dissuaded Bress and Annie from continuing to plant more family seeds. Every two-to-three years another infant was born into their small home. Eb was the first born in Promise, in 1911. Lida, 1913, and Lon in 1915, were numbers five and six. Lois, who was to become my mother, was their seventh born, arriving July 17, 1918, followed by Hazel in 1921, Dick in '24 and Jack in '26; ten kids over twenty-two years. Funny, isn't it? What we do well, we keep on doing. Bress and Annie made beautiful, robust children and the family grew and grew.

"They kept havin' 'em and we kept tryin' to figure a way to take care of 'em," Mabel, the eldest female child, said. "We never seemed to be able to keep the table completely full or have clothes that really fit, but we survived, and I guess that's the main thing. I don't recall every bein' real hungry or walkin' around stark nekkid," she recalls with a wry grin.

Due to his drinking, Pop had a hard time keeping jobs in the logging camps. Absence doesn't play well on a two-man saw. He wasn't a consistent presence at home either. Supplies that were not produced on the homestead could be bought in Wallowa. The round trip took more than a day in their horse-drawn wagon. It was a long trek and a rough ride and Pop conveniently saw no need to subject his wife and kids to what he deemed to be unnecessary exertion on their part. "I can take care of it m'self," he said.

With Annie's list of essentials and money taken from the household bag of cash, Bress made the supply trips alone. The frequency of his outings increased as he got to know the people in and around town. Many times he spent more than a day or two away from home. There was an unspoken family understanding that where he stayed was not to be a topic for discussion.

"We didn't really want to know," Mabel said, "and we knew he wouldn't tell us if we did. He always answered our questions with questions right back. 'You don't 'spect me t' tell ya everything I do, do ya?' he'd say."

When he was home, Pop was more a nuisance than a guiding light. Having been raised to believe that men set up housekeeping to have a place to eat, sleep, give orders, rest awhile, and have baby-making sex, either all in one day, or one day at a time, Pop's grown-up behavior for the most part, remained true to his upbringing.

He was tougher on Annie and Mabel than on the rest of the family. Women were meant to serve their men folk. And if they didn't serve the man the way it was meant to be, it was the man's job to teach them how it was to be done. Pop's demands on Annie and Mabel were often unreasonable and sometimes bordering on cruel.

> "We should 'a known it wouldn't be right. He was just lookin' for an excuse to stomp out of the house and go off to town so he could pick up some floozy to give him his bath."

"Pop ordained that he would be the first to get anything and have the best of everything, such as it was," Mabel told me.

"Saturday night was bath night, and of course Pop's bath came first. After dinner, Annie'd haul out the tub and put it in the middle of the kitchen, where it was warm. We put a screen around it for privacy. It was my job to go to the well and bring in the buckets of water for Annie to heat up and pour into the tub. None of the boys even thought about helping. Fixin' Pop's bath was woman's work. At least they didn't think it was our job to do their baths too. Prob'ly a modesty thing," she says grinning, "or they found more satisfyin' places to get their bath water heated.

"Pop would take off his shoes and stick his foot in the tub after every bucket, to make sure the temperature was just how he liked it.

'That's good . . . that's good,' he'd say, right up to the top.' When we'd pour the last bucket in, sometimes he'd holler . . . 'It ain't right . . . it ain't right!' Then he'd turn the whole thing over, just to be mean, after all the haulin' and pourin' we'd done to make it just right.

"We should 'a known it wouldn't be right. He was just lookin' for an excuse to stomp out of the house and go off to town so he could pick up some floozy to give him his bath, and spend the rest of the weekend with her, rather than us. Once in a while, he took his pleasure in stayin' to watch us clean up the mess and start all over, fixin' him his damn bath. I guess he figured watchin' us serve him twice was worth stickin' around for.

"Or maybe the floozies were as sick of him as we were, and it was just our turn with him." She pauses for reflection before continuing with her reminiscing.

"He pulled stupid stunts like that", she says, "to make sure we knew he was the boss. Annie never made a move to stop him. Once in a while she'd get bold enough to say, 'Oh Bress now look at what you done.' The only thing

## The Rough-Hewn Country Patriarch

I could ever fault her for was makin' us put up with his belligerent nature. She accepted her trade off for a roof over her head, but her personal bargain covered us too, and I'm not so sure she understood that."

Mabel's tone has a bitter ring to it as she tells me of her early years. Like most women raised by disrespectful fathers, when she grew up she was vulnerable to the men who handed her the garbage she felt she deserved.

But unlike most women, she didn't marry them. When all her siblings were raised and living away from home she got a full-time job at the local pea cannery. She eventually saved enough money to move into a house of her own, which she rented from a garbage kind of man. His name was Eddie. There were rumors as to what she had to do to stay in the house, and he said many times he was going to marry her. But they never married. She strung him along to keep the house, and he strung her along with talk of marriage. It was their kind of trade off, and it worked for as long as it needed to. And there were no kids dependent on their agreement.

When Mabel was forty-four, a very nice farming man, named Carl Knosp, came to town. They were introduced and he soon was smitten with this woman who had all of a sudden given birth to a pretty glow on her face and acquired a new, infectious giggle that was hard to resist. Carl offered Mabel a real marriage and a permanent home, without having to play the see-how-far-I-can-string-you-along kind of game.

Knowing how long Mabel had waited for a good man, town folk were jubilant for her. I was present when Aunt Mamie and Uncle Carl were surprised with what is called a shivaree, where relatives and neighbors kidnap a newly-married couple in their pajamas in the middle of the night and parade them through town on a hay wagon, with everyone laughing and dancing to the music of local musicians on board the wagon.

To be fair, Pop's history just told with Mabel's recollections for embellishment is not the total story of Pop. The Aunt Mamie I came to know wouldn't have stored up the giggles she shared with Carl or known how to dance to the music of the hay wagon if that were Pop's whole story.

I don't propose that we excuse either his cowardice or his orneriness in dealing, or not dealing, with things not to his liking. But there was another side to Pop that bears telling. Pop's other side, seldom seen but there just the same, had as much influence on his succeeding generations as all the orneriness he could muster and dish out to his immediate family.

We can fault him in so many ways, but we can never know the pressures he felt trying to keep his life and family together, mired in eternal poverty.

His plans for an easy life were disrupted at a very early age. Heading across the country with a family of five, before reaching the age of thirty was a heavy burden. We can claim that others did what he tried to do without succumbing to booze, and we can say others did it without running away. But how many of us are heroes? And how many of us are average blokes, just like Pop, who have only moments of satisfaction tucked inside weeks, months, and years of seemingly hopeless struggle?

I'll venture to say there are some among us who have thrown back a shot or two of liquor to settle jangled nerves and aching brains for a few moments of respite from the daily grind. I might even suggest that a stolen weekend away from unrelenting labors has kept more than one family together for the long haul.

Reputations and resulting family lore are spared somewhat by the fact that kids and grand kids will naturally seek out and remember the softer side of their parents and grand parents. We have an inherent need to believe in our family's goodness. Pop did have his ornery, dark side, and we don't deny that. But he also had a bright and a sunny side, and that's the Pop we choose to remember.

CHAPTER 2

## *The Poetic Patriarch*

WHEN POP WAS GOING to school in West Virginia, young people were exposed to a broader range of subject material in their early school years than what kids receive today.

There was more academic learning in the eight years of the late nineteenth century school house than the curriculum offered in twelve years of today's frenetic searches for a relevant education. Schools in previous generations didn't serve as baby sitters for working parents. Nor did children go to school to receive structure, discipline and breakfast. Primary care was the responsibility of the home no matter how poor. Parents were still parenting and teachers had time to teach a full slate of scholarly subjects.

Students, even in their early years, heard classical music and read fine literature before they hit the streets of hard-core reality. In the early American school rooms, Beethoven's Fifth Symphony sounded out familiar notes—"Bum-Bum-Bum-Buuum!" And Shakespeare's histories of kings shouted out well-recognized words . . . "A horse! My kingdom for a horse! . . . "

While these elegant subjects may not have struck a permanent chord in the value structure of every young student, they at least had the opportunity to sample and discern the long-lasting qualities of classical learning. Some were fortunate enough to continue these lessons inside their homes because their mothers and fathers had experienced such art through generations of family traditions.

The love of music and poetry had permanently woven its way into the fiber of the Thompson clan through the heritage of their European ancestors before children began their formal New World educations. The music and literature these descendants from Scotland and Ireland heard at home was enhanced by the learning they received in their American schools.

Because they had limited financial resources for entertainment outside their home, the family gathered inside the parlor almost daily to share stories, poetry and music. Each family member contributed their special talents for readings, recitations, and instrumental and vocal renditions of familiar European tales and tunes. Adding newly learned English and American classics to their own cultural repertoire allowed the refinement of artistic pleasures to set the tone of the family home in spite of their material indigence.

It was the tough neighborhoods surrounding their residences that forced a seedy reality into the impressionable second and third generations of these new Americans. Music and literature had no place on the small-town streets of Fayette, West Virginia, and Bress wasn't strong enough to assert his bent for the more scholarly side of his life born at home. He succumbed to the lore of the streets, the sounds of spit hittin' the sidewalks, and fists meeting the chins of adversaries. Crude conformity won out over the grace of the parlor.

I can't help but wonder how many modern day Mozarts, Homers and Michaelangelos are lost to the bashfulness of poverty, and how many poets are trapped inside their cloaks of orneriness. It's not easy to buck the expectations of our urban surroundings once we leave the sanctity of our homes. The temptations of the streets will always produce conflict with the securities of home. Whether or how we resist temptation ultimately is for each of us to decide for ourselves.

The more time Bress spent on the streets, the more bad-tempered he was. The more time he spent at home, the more gentle he was. Unfortunately, as he grew older, the street captured more of his time than the home, and the negative influence of the streets continued throughout most of his adult life. We simply must find a way to court the more genteel side of our natures by encouraging families to spend more time together at home, even as one generation gives way to another.

Years later when Pop was in his own family home for a stretch of time, either from lack of funds for philandering or a rare absence of inclination, he'd recall his childhood home and give in to the calming influence of poetry and the joyful memories of his musical past.

After dinner Pop would sit down with his little kids to recite the literature of his younger years and tell his stories from more innocent times. Once the readings and recitations began, Pop couldn't resist singing a few simple songs. Pretty soon the sound of his music drew the rest of the family out of their solitary refuges from his ranting into the fellowship of the parlor. Instruments appeared from under beds and backs of closets—fiddle, banjo, guitar—and music magically filled the spaces of their sparse surroundings.

"There's a church in the valley by the wildwood,
No lovelier place in the dell . . . "

## The Poetic Patriarch

"Mid pleasures and palaces tho' we may roam,
Be it ever so humble, there's no place like home . . . "

Following poetry recitations with tunes played and sung in sweet hillbilly harmony, evenings turned to song and Pop turned tender toward his wife and older kids, as well as his younger kids.

How do you live with a man like Pop? Mired in physical and emotional poverty, he was a typical mountain patriarch, feared by some, revered by others, loved and hated at the same time. People living in this kind of environment either elected to stay with it and pass its influence on to yet another generation of mountain families or they sucked in their bellies and got the hell out.

Telephones, radios and cars lured many people out of the mountains by making cities and towns seem closer and more familiar than they were. Adult males who couldn't make up their minds where they wanted to live, or hadn't the financial resources to make other choices, joined the armed forces. In the first half of the Twentieth Century, two World Wars afforded men the opportunity to leave home and explore a greater world.

It was the Second World War that gave women more options. In addition to joining the Services themselves, they increasingly took over jobs that men abandoned as they went overseas to fight for American liberties. Thus began the independence of women and the two-income households. With each generation, fewer offspring remained in the hills to live within their mountain legacies of patriarchal supervision and suppression.

We have choices; we always have. People who are perpetually unhappy choose to hold on to the comfort of their misery rather than opting for the more difficult task of searching for solutions to end their discontent. People who choose to fight for more optimistic outcomes eventually find a way out. I believe it is choice more than fate that determines our destinies.

Lois Thompson, seventh born Thompson sibling, made an enormous choice to secure her personal destiny. She chose to not wait for adulthood to leave home. She and her Pop couldn't live with each other that long. They declared their own personal war to hurry the process of her leave taking. Pop saw for her a future that would keep her at home, living her life as her mother and older siblings lived theirs. It was what he regarded as a decent life for a woman.

Lois couldn't imagine settling for a life of unquestioned patriarchal dominance, doomed by the whims of ignorance and resulting poverty. She'd heard just enough about the world outside their personal experience to envision a more expansive future for herself. Lois knew her dreams would require change on her part. At age fourteen she elected to get the hell out.

CHAPTER 3

## *Divided by Death and Ambition*

UNDERSTANDING THAT POP's lack of full-time work was the primary cause of the Thompson family's economic distress, the people of Promise appointed him to the position of Postmaster. In that position he could work from home and earn a steady income without having to conjure up excuses not to go to work or wander off to feign a search for work.

The appointment didn't work out the way people had hoped it would. Pop still went off on his alcoholic toots, and Annie covered the Postmaster duties. Annie now not only ran the house, she also provided the income. Community assistance had unwittingly placed new responsibilities onto her. But it was steady income, which they sorely needed.

Unfortunately, the application of the income was not so steady. Since the work technically was his position and therefore his earnings, Pop decided it was his money to do with as he chose. In his care, the every day necessities were covered, but the small amounts left over for taxes and a rainy day were not. The choice of buying booze overrode the choice of paying taxes. As the family home headed for foreclosure Pop once again did the only thing he knew to do. In the middle of a winter's night in 1922, he packed up his family and a few household items, and fled. The Thompson family abandoned their home in Promise.

Fortunately, they were not left to manage the move completely on their own. With the help of people who knew of Pop and his weaknesses, the destitute family found a temporary place in Wallowa. Within a few days, by pooling their resources and obtaining promissory notes of employment, Pop and his oldest sons, Herb and Eb, came up with enough resources to obtain a rental contract on a small house just outside of town. The three of them went to work in the paper mill nearby, and together they earned enough money to establish a decent living.

To add to the money they earned at the mill, and put a little money in their own pockets, Herb and Eb took to prize fighting. Boxing relieved boredom

## Divided by Death and Ambition

for many young men of that era and provided much needed extra income for those who were good enough to consistently win their bouts. The Thompson boys were tough and cunning and soon earned wide-spread reputations as the pair to beat in the competition between the mills and logging camps.

Herb was the first to establish the Thompson name. Eb followed Herb and earned a greater renown over time. He became a three-state Welter Weight Champion, the states being Oregon, Washington, and Idaho. But it was Herb, after a long string of decisive victories, who delivered the most fabled punch.

> Annie's body, that had carried nine children to full term without benefit of medical care, was growing weary.

One champion fighter from a mill in another town thought he could beat Herb. The two towns began bragging about their knock-out champions. A date and place were set to decide who was to be the real champion. The wagering began. The furor of this bout stirred up a roar of emotions between the two towns. Before long, it became a grudge match advertised as a fight to the death. No one took the death part seriously, but it made for good press.

The two men stood toe-to-toe pummeling each other bare knuckled for round after round. Nine, ten, eleven, twelve... sweat and blood dripping down their bodies and flying into the air around them until they could barely lift their fists to punch or defend. Then one last desperate bloody fist flew toward Herb's opponent who hadn't the strength left to cover his face... and the hype hit home.

In the 18th round, Herb's bare, raw knuckles literally smashed his opponent's teeth down his throat, blocking his wind pipe, cutting off his ability to breathe. Herb's opponent did not live through the night. That night's take went to the family of the man who didn't survive. It was Herb's last fight, but he'd claimed his mark of infamy.

Eb's championships never quite matched Herb's fatal knock-out punch, but he did continue to bring in money with his fists. Pretty soon Lon came along and took up the family's boxing banner, and with his jarring left hook he took down opponents as consistently as did his brother Eb. The extra money the two of them brought in proved to be more necessary than anyone could have imagined when the boxing began.

Annie's body, that had carried nine children to full term without benefit of medical care, was growing weary. Their tenth child delivered her own villainous opponent. Her body nearly succumbed to its over-extended labors. The post partum flow of blood continued and Annie grew weaker.

Although she tried to hide it, the fact of her physical pain became evident to the family who lived with her. Primitive home remedies of hot packs, bed rest, and hand-wringing prayers had run their course. Annie needed to have professional medical attention. The Thompson men again pooled their cash resources to seek help for their family's expanded needs.

Dr. Anderson had Annie inside his examination room for nearly an hour. When the door finally opened he nodded for Pop to follow him into his office.

"Mr. Thompson, I need to do more tests. I'd like to put Mrs. Thompson in the hospital for a few days.'

"What kind 'a tests?" Pop asked suspiciously.

"We need to look at a biopsy," Dr. Anderson replied.

Even a backwoods patriarch understands the significance of the word biopsy.

Pop's heart thundered inside his chest in useless protest. He wanted to say no, but he couldn't.

"All right. Do yer biopsy."

The biopsy revealed a dreadful disease. There was no question as to the diagnosis.

"Mr. Thompson," Dr. Anderson said, "I'm very sorry. Your wife has an advanced case of cervical cancer, and her widespread pain indicates it has spread to other parts of her body. It would be of no use to operate. There's too much. It is too late."

I know what we're all thinking here. Cervical cancer caused by too many pregnancies without medical care? Or cervical cancer caused by too much booze, leading to a husband cavorting with diseased women? But it really doesn't matter what we think, does it.

Annie has cancer. Pop's Annie has cancer. Nine kids' mother, nine kids' mainstay, has cancer. And it's too late. "There's no need to operate. It's too late," the Doctor said. Pop could hear the words in his head but his heart wouldn't believe it and he couldn't totally accept it.

I wish I could say that Pop took on this added responsibility and mended his likkered up ways. But he couldn't and he didn't. He just didn't have the mettle to meet heavy challenges without his habitual crutches. But this time he didn't immediately bolt across the country. Time with Annie was short. He couldn't leave knowing she'd be gone if and when he returned. Unable to make decisions on his own other than flight, he went along with family decisions that concerned Annie's medical care, and he stayed around to see that they were applied.

*Family photo 1933, Wallowa, Oregon.*

The biggest family decision involved another move. A year into Annie's diagnosis, they moved again, to be closer to the Hot Springs Medical Facility near La Grande. It also brought them closer to fields of wheat, peas and onions, and orchards of apple and cherry trees. In the summer of 1928, the five kids who were old enough and not otherwise occupied with work and household duties, took to the fields and orchards, hoeing and picking the aforementioned crops to bring in family revenues. Annie wasn't hoein' them taters no more, but her kids were hoeing and picking darn near everything else.

Late 1929, Annie moved into the Hot Springs Medical Facility. The additional field revenues, along with Eb's and Lon's prize fighting money, helped to pay for her care.

The Fall of 1930, she was sent home. Nothing more could be done at the hospital. To ease her pain, there were basic, aspirin-based drugs. When aspirin lost its effectiveness, basic drugs transitioned to the ultimate pain killer. The ultimate pain medication in 1930 was the same as it is today. Annie was sent home with the promise of mail-delivered morphine every three days, knowing there wouldn't be many deliveries. This was illegal transport of drugs even then, but a quiet exception was made.

"Even morphine couldn't completely cover the pain," my Mom told me. "When it got real bad, they sent us younger kids to the neighbors so we couldn't hear her violent cries of pain."

The postman always delivers, or so the saying goes. Through sleet and rain and wind and snow, the Postman always gets through. But he didn't get through on Christmas Eve, 1930. The drifting snow was deep and the winter winds were merciless. There was no path to the Thompson home.

"We couldn't even get to the neighbors," Mom says, "so we were bundled up and sent outside. We stood in the snow in the front yard and listened to our mother's screams for what seemed like hours, though it probably was not. Then there was silence and we knew her suffering was over. Her death came to our house on Christmas Eve."

Pop was devastated by Annie's passing. Recalling how he cleanly escaped troubling situations in the past, he made a predictable decision. He stayed around for a while after Annie died. But the loneliness of a house without Annie finally overtook him.

He disappeared one night, leaving others to gather up the pieces of their lives and put them back in place without his help. In the past he'd left adult women, forcing them to rebuild fractured lives on their own. This time he left nine children, ages five to twenty-eight. The fact that these were his own kids obviously didn't bother him any more than leaving anyone else, whether the year was 1910 or 1932. True to his history, it was time for Bress Thompson to leave. Call it cowardice, call it unforgivable; call it inevitable. Call it anything you like. Our family calls it fact, and nothing more. It's our get-over-it syndrome, and it's imbedded in our culture.

It's easier for nine people to survive death and desertion than it is for one or two persons. Simply put, grief and the resulting responsibilities spread among many will affect each individual less. The Thompson family had little trouble surviving in a house without parents. Coping without parental guidance had become their way of life. They understood what they had to do to get by.

Without an ailing mother that required tiptoeing and a father that put a stop to anything he didn't initiate, the grown up brothers and sisters had a whole new set of options to draw from. They could pursue new personal priorities outside the home, or they could stick around to support and oversee the upbringing of their orphaned siblings. With no one to tell them what to do or not do, for the first time in their lives they could choose what they wanted to do. And they chose well.

Herb, Mabel, Eb, and Lida were old enough to strike out on their own.

They were free to take flight. Their father had clearly demonstrated how that option worked. But they chose not to go down his winding road of self absorption. They'd also lived under the example set by their matriarch. Annie's grit and dedication to family togetherness through nearly insurmountable hardship had left them with a more lasting legacy than the weaknesses of a fleeing father. And while they were too hard core to speak the classic words of love, they were not so tough that the spirit of family devotion didn't permeate their very being.

"None of us ever considered running away," says Lida. "Herb, and Eb had good jobs at the mill and we got the benefit of most of their earnings. Rightfully so, they kept some for themselves. They earned their right to a few pleasures.

"Because he stopped fighting for pay, Herb worked extra hours at the mill. His extra money went to making himself look good. He bought barbells and other gear to keep in shape. He liked struttin' around and flexin' his biceps for us and the fine ladies he enjoyed courting. Most important to him, though, was that he made enough money to keep himself in a fine car."

Hazel jumps into the conversation. "He kept his car in a stall inside the garage, separate from the tractor and our old beater of a car. We kids would crawl up on a stool and peek over the boards that separated his car from ours. Just to look at his shiny new car was enough to make our day. We didn't dare touch it for fear of what he'd do to us if we did. Though it wasn't likely we'd get anything more than a bawling out, we didn't want even that from Herb. We worshipped our oldest brother's worldly ways."

Lida continues. "Eb was the one most like Pop. He'd get to feeling ornery every now and then and wander off. We never knew for sure when he'd show up. We'd hear about his barroom escapades. He had a way with women, just like Pop, and they'd fight each other over him. Then their men would show up and they'd fight Eb. But we'd also hear that he'd won another bout in the ring and we knew he'd come home and throw some extra money into the family cache. He never came home without something for the family."

Lon and Lida worked the fields. Mabel took over Annie's role as head of the household. The three middle siblings did their share of chores and pretty much raised themselves. The baby, Jack, became Mabel's coddled child. In a large family, older people are busy, younger people are looked after, and middle people just are. If a middle person is going to get any notice or a chance at personal growth, the middle person has to make sure the chances happen through his or her own resourcefulness. Lois was a middle person watching and waiting for her chance to take hold of a better life.

## Promise I'll Stay for Mother's Day

She knew something would come along some day and she prepared for her something by dreaming and scheming. Because she was twelve when her mother died, Lois was denied her moments of mother-daughter conversations that most young girls get to have. She had to think about what she wanted and how she was going to get it on her own.

"It just wasn't right for me to press for things for myself so I could grow like I wanted to, when my Mother lay inside the house suffering," she says. "My dreams were always inside of me, but I couldn't figure a way to make them come out while all that was going on. Then Pop left. But he was always leaving us for days or weeks at a time. We never knew when he'd show up again, acting like he never went away. I didn't want to start something I couldn't finish . . ."

Her voice trails off, I assume, to thoughtfully savor the recollections of her youthful yearnings. Her face goes through a variety of expressions as she retrieves the memory of her struggle to patiently watch for the right moment to bring up her personal aspirations. She lived in a household that was preoccupied with survival. Mere existence requires only the execution of daily habits. Exposing dreams requires an opportunity that comes from perfect timing.

"Pop's absence stretched out to be weeks, then months. We settled in to a routine that seemed to work. Our years of worrying about Annie and the months of wondering when Pop was coming home began to slip into the past. When Pop had been gone a year, I decided to approach Mamie and pour out what I'd been thinking all that time.

"Mamie,' I said, 'I been thinkin'. I know we usually go to school just so far as th eighth grade an' my eighth grade will be over in the spring. So it would be the usual thing for me to quit goin' to school and start doin' more of my share of chores around here. But I want so much to keep on goin' to school. I want to learn so much more. An' it won't cost us nothin' extra if I keep on goin'. I'd keep on doin' my chores an' everything

"Mamie interrupted me. 'I don't see no reason for you to stop goin' to school. It won't hurt us to have you in school. We gotta start catchin' up to other people, if we're to stand a chance of makin' our way in this new world we're livin' in.'

"I was stunned to hear her say that so easy. I was ready to stand there and give her a whole bunch of reasons to make her say yes. But I didn't have to go through all that. Mamie understood.

"You can't imagine what a relief it was to know she understood. I don't know what I'd have done if I had to stop going to school. I couldn't stand to think that my life wouldn't change from the way it was, that I would grow

## Divided by Death and Ambition

up and have to work at home raising a pack of kids. Not that I didn't respect Mamie's choices. I just couldn't imagine the same thing for myself. With her few words of understanding she gave me the gift of a new life, and I can't remember, even now, ever feeling that good or that relieved.

"The school door opened up a whole new life for me. My world expanded, and I cherished every new minute of it.

"Then, near the end of that wonderful eighth grade, my dreams nearly collapsed in on me. I was coming home from school one day near the end of the term, running up the road as fast as I could, nearly bursting with excitement. I'd been invited to go to the eighth grade picnic, and I could hardly wait to tell my brothers and sisters about it.

"Pop was standing in the middle of the road, waiting for me. I froze right in front of him, confused. But I was so excited about the picnic I forgot he'd been gone so long. He was about to become the first person to hear my thrilling news.

*I just couldn't imagine the same thing for myself. With her few words of understanding she gave me the gift of a new life, and I can't remember, even now, ever feeling that good or that relieved.*

"Pop! Guess what?!? The kids want me to come to the picnic after school on Friday. It's the first time they ever invited me to come to a party, and I can't wait to go!'

"I stopped talking, finally realizing the significance of his presence, and I shivered, waiting for his response . . . "

She pauses in her story, seeming to gather strength for what is to come next. "Pop stood there, looking at me. I knew what he was thinking. He was thinking, here I am back home, and she didn't even stop to say 'Hi Pop'. She just burst out with her party news as if I was here yesterday. As if she didn't know I was gone.

"Since when d' ya go runnin' off t' picnics on yer own, without even askin' permission t' go?' Pop asked me in an accusing tone.

"I resisted the obvious reply. *Since you left us, that's when!* I stood there lookin' right back at him, waiting to hear what he'd say next.

"Well, since you seem t' ferget that young 'uns need t' ask their folks' permission t' go traipsin' off t' parties,' he said, 'an' because I'm thinkin' you need a reminder that yer s'posed to do that, I think ya' better ferget about goin' t' that picnic on Friday. You'll stay home. Then we'll see about you goin' to any parties in the future. I'm inclined t' think ya' better stay home a while. You seem a little sassy t' me . . . Fergot to say hello, didn' ya?'

## Promise I'll Stay for Mother's Day

"I couldn't believe what I was hearing. This man who'd walked out on us more than a year before was trying to take charge again, acting as if he'd never been gone. This person I called 'Pop', this person who was supposed to want the best for me was purposely bringing me down. I'd been waiting all day to tell someone my good news. He happened to be the one who got to hear it, and here he was crushing all my excitement into tiny little pieces. It wasn't fair.

*"He's no Pop, I thought. He left us. And he's not going to ruin my life. Not today, not tomorrow, not any day. Not ever! My head was about to explode with indignation.*

"You've been gone too long!' I shouted at him. 'You got no right to come back here as if you never left an' start thinkin' you're goin' to be telling' me what I can an' can't do! I'll do what I want, an' I *am* goin' to that picnic, an' I *am* goin' to be goin' to other parties too, an' you are *not* goin' to stop me!'"

Mom stops to look at me as she tries to explain her feelings at that time. "Young girls just didn't talk to their Pops like that back then. I stopped shouting and stood there in the road, stunned by my outburst, frozen by my fear of what Pop might do. I'd never yelled at an adult before, never imagined I ever would or could. What he did next was so cruel it made me stand up to him. He thought he was breaking me, but his actions only made me more determined.

"Pop slowly bent down and picked up a stick, looking straight at me as he moved. I watched him, scared as hell thinking about what he was about to do with that stick. I stood there for what seemed like a long time, afraid to move. He sauntered around behind me, taking his sweet time, building up tension to see what I'd do. I flinched a little on the inside, anticipating the sting of his stick, but I kept looking straight ahead. Damned if I was going to give him the satisfaction of my cowering or turning around.

"I could hear that stick scratching the dirt behind me. I didn't know what he was doing back there, but I wasn't feeling pain and I wasn't giving in. Finally the scratching stopped and he walked around in front of me again." She winces as she talks, the memory still fresh, forty years later.

"You turn around 'n take a good look at that line I jest drew behind you,' he said. 'Yer on this side a' it right now. If you cross t' the other side of it, you don't come back here.' He paused to make sure I was paying attention. 'Do you understand what it is I'm sayin' to ya?'

"Without waiting for me to reply, he turned and walked away from me, into the house, swinging the stick. As I watched him turn his back on me, I understood what he had done. I've never understood anything in my life more than I understood that line in the road. It stood for a lot more than an eighth grade picnic. That line represented how my life would turn out from that moment on.

"Living with my family was all I'd known, but knowing, even briefly, that I could go to school beyond the eighth grade had taught me it was no longer all I wanted. I wanted so much more. I liked making new friends and learning about a bigger world.

"But most of all, I have to admit that at that particular moment I just wanted to go to the school picnic, and I knew if I didn't cross the line, I wouldn't go to the picnic. Then it hit me that if I didn't get to go to the picnic, I wouldn't get to do all the other things I wanted to do. My dreams would end if I didn't cross the line.

"I never felt so alone as I did on that day, and I've never felt so alone since. It was my defining moment, if there is such a thing, and I had to grab hold of it. Scared and shaking so bad I could hardly make my way, I followed Pop into the house and set about packing my belongings. I put what little I had into my pillow case and a burlap bag I grabbed on my way up the stairs. I looked straight ahead all the way up the stairs and all the way down. I didn't dare look to either side, or lock eyes with anyone, for fear I'd loose my determination. I was especially afraid to look at Hazel. We shared a bedroom and we were very close. But I had to leave. I just couldn't stay and have all my dreams die in that house."

Mom stops talking for a moment and looks at me again. Then she lowers her eyelids, staring at her lap.

"I guess you could say I was acting out the lesson my Pop taught me. If you can't face up to what's happening where you are, you walk away. I left my family behind, just like he did."

CHAPTER 4

## *Middle Child on Her Own*

I PICKED UP MY BAGS and left the house. No one even tried to stop me. Pop was too proud, and my brothers and sisters didn't want any more grief from a Pop who had returned home and taken charge again. They knew if they stepped forward, his wrath against me would turn toward them.

"With all my belongings in my two hands, I walked into town and knocked on the door of my best friend's house.

"I can't stay at home,' I announced. 'My Pop says I can't go to school no more, an' I just have to keep on goin' to school. If I could stay here for a while, I won't cause trouble, and I'll help with the chores. I'll ask the school if they can find me a place to live permanent, so I won't be here long. But I'd sure 'preciate your help right now.

"People in those days didn't fuss over simple matters. I've got no quarrel with child protective agencies, but sometimes miracles can happen just by using common sense. My friend's family accepted my plain, pure explanation and made the decision to let me stay. Hilda's family knew my father had deserted us and they knew I was seeking a way out from under my hopeless poverty. What more did they need to know?

"They took me in and in a short period of time, just a few days as I recall, the school found me the possibility of a new home with a well-to-do couple, named Elwood and Mildred Piper, who lived in the town of Milton, Oregon, later to become Milton-Freewater.

"They were looking for someone who would live in their home to help with the housekeeping and occasionally take care of their two sons, Dick and Don, who were six and eight at the time. They wanted someone who was responsible, and also someone who would stay for a few years. I knew I had to convince them I was the person they were looking for.

"When I entered the house for an interview with Mrs. Piper, I looked around and wished—oh how I wished!—Mrs. Piper would like me. It was the grandest house I'd ever imagined.

## Middle Child on Her Own

"You're pretty young to be looking for employment,' Mrs. Piper said."

Again Mom lapsed into her language of the day. "Well I'm not so young,' I said. "I had plenty a' chores to do at home an' my Mom got sick 'n died, an' my Pop left, an' us kids were left to take care of everything, an' we did. An' I kept goin' to school, an' then Pop came back an' he wanted me t' stop goin' to school an' stay home, so I left. An' I been helpin' out at my friend's house, but they couldn't keep me for long. So I have t' find me some place else to live and help out. Because, you see, I am NOT goin' to quit goin' to school. I just HAVE to find something . . . I am very serious about this.'"

> "So I have t' find me some place else to live and help out. Because, you see, I am NOT goin' to quit goin' to school. I just HAVE to find something . . . I am very serious about this.'"

Mom stops to look at me. "My plea to Mildred Piper was unrehearsed and raw. But it was the most important speech of my life." The plea may have been unrehearsed and raw, as she said, but it worked. It worked because it was from the heart. Ernest pleas from the heart are better said without rehearsals.

"Well, I got the job", she said, "and I spent four wonderful years living with the Pipers while I was going to McLoughlin High School. I was unbelievably lucky to have found them. I've always believed that luck follows preparation and drive. Such beliefs come from good examples. I got to have them as an example at such an important time in my life."

As she suspected, Lois' siblings were not happy with her for leaving their home. Although her share of the household chores didn't amount to much, her leaving made their lives more difficult.

Pop was furious that his own daughter would defy him. He knew she was getting away with her defiance and he knew her brothers and sisters knew it. But he was too proud to go after her so, as expected he took his fury out on those who were still around. He piled more work onto everyone who was left in the household.

"It's her work I'm askin' you t' do," he shouted. "She left it. She up 'n walked out on us. She wasn't thinkin' how her leavin' would affect the rest of us. She was too busy thinkin' a' herself." Never mind that his leaving left others with his work to do. He was not capable of inserting himself into the positions he put others into. Empathy was not exactly his strong suit.

The family could see through his ranting, but Lois was the one who caused it and she'd left them to deal with it. And that was something they hadn't had to do for a long time. It rankled them that she'd done that to them.

## Promise I'll Stay for Mother's Day

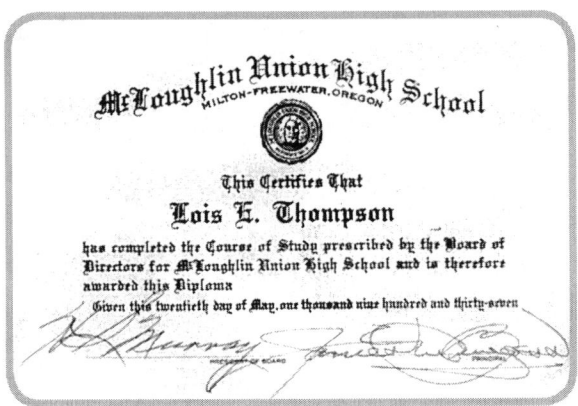

*Lois's Diploma 1937, Milton, Oregon.*

But more than that, they couldn't help but feel she'd rejected them personally. She chose a picnic and a beautiful house over their good, honest work ethic and plain surroundings. None of them had left home, leaving others behind. Maybe Pop was right. Maybe she did think she was too good for them.

When one person in a family makes a change, the lives of the rest of the family change as well. It's obvious to the family, but not so obvious to the person making the changes.

Pop couldn't see the shirking of responsibility in his own behavior, but the picture was clear to him when he observed his daughter's actions. Lois justified her walk out by dismissing her importance to the family, even surmising their lives might be improved by her absence.

"I'm just a middle person," she reasoned while she was struttin' out of the house. "Nobody ever noticed me when I was here, and nobody will notice when I'm gone. They'll be mad for a while 'cause I left. But what difference will it make, 'cept they won't have t' feed me or buy me a pair a' shoes, come fall.

They ought t' be happy 'bout that. B'sides, if I can keep goin' to school, I bet Hazel 'n Dick 'n Jack will get to keep goin' to school too. Pop won't let me get more 'n them. It won't be no big deal, me leavin'.

CHAPTER

## *Romance Turns Deadly*

I was right about Pop not letting me get more than my younger sister and brothers. Hazel, Dick and Jack followed me to high school when they came of age, and they graduated from Mac-Hi, just like I did.

"In fact, Hazel was in high school for one year with me. She was a freshman when I was a senior. I'd seen her a few times since I'd left home. We'd not so accidentally run into each other in town or at the city park. Mamie arranged these meetings. She wanted Hazel to see me as a good example and hopefully become her confidante. My journey away from home seemed to be working. I was learning a lot from meeting new people just like I thought I would. But I didn't have anyone close enough to trust with my feelings and dreams.

"No one really had the kind of background I had and I was too proud to expose my ignorance and vulnerabilities to strangers. Getting to share that last year with Hazel helped me as much as I hope it helped her. Hazel's always been pretty and outgoing and optimistic. People are naturally drawn to her. The fact that she looked up to me added to my self confidence and helped me develop some degree of social competence."

Mom enjoys sharing her life stories with anyone who asks, and she's just as eager to share with those who don't ask. She's justifiably proud of her life and wants people to know how she struggled to overcome her obstacles and how she succeeded in spite of them. Hers is the irresistible tale of the underdog.

We're enchanted by stories of the little person who wins, and quick to cast ourselves into this intoxicating role whenever we can.

But we don't share everything. There are parts of our lives that are not so noble. We tend to leave out passages that don't end well.

In that vein, Lois Thompson is no different from the rest of us. There was a pronounced absence of information about her life and activities immediately following high school. Over the years, as I pieced together the elements of what made her the woman I knew her to be, that void began to peak my interest.

There's a missing chapter in her life story. Where is it and why don't we know more about it?

My inquiries to her about this time in her life were met with shrugs, as if there was nothing worth talking about.

I would have taken her responses for what they appeared to be and let it go, but sometimes my questions produced an abrupt view of her back as she walked away from me. That kind of response led me to believe there was much to talk about. But she wouldn't give it up. I learned the framework of those years on my own, by pestering her siblings. No one knew anything, except for Aunt Mamie.

One summer, my daughters and I were visiting her farm. My girls were outside feeding apples to horses and chasing cats under porches, while Mamie and I were sitting at the kitchen table looking at old photographs. I picked up a picture of my Mom. With her was a man I had never met or heard about.

"Who's that?" I asked.

"That's Samuel," Mamie replied.

"Who's Samuel?"

"Your mother worked for him in Idaho."

"When did she work in Idaho?"

"After high school."

The Thompson folks can get real short of words when the subject of a conversation is not to their liking. With the typical family reticence for divulging private information, Mamie got up from the table and started fussing with the morning dishes. But I'd caught a glimpse of Mom's secret life and I wasn't about to let it go. Over the next few days, Mamie reluctantly began to respond to my persistent prodding about this mysterious person from Mom's unspoken past.

"So, Mamie, was Samuel from Milton?"

"No. He always lived in Idaho."

"If he always lived in Idaho, how'd she meet him?"

"People introduced them."

"Who? And how'd she get to Idaho?"

Aunt Mamie finally told me all she said she knew about Mom's missing year. I felt she knew more, but she was leaving it for someone else to reveal, if I could get her to do it. Here's the gist of what Mamie told me.

My Mom's quest for independence failed to bring her the grand life she'd expected to have from taking tremendous risks and working very hard. She was certain that a high school diploma would open the door to new adventures and eventual glory. What she discovered was, even though her personal world had changed, the world at large had not. In 1937, the opportunity for a young woman with no money to go to college on her own was negligible and the odds of achieving noteworthy employment were equally dim.

Four months after graduation, with help from friends of Elwood and Mildred, Mom secured a secretarial position with a construction firm across the Oregon border, in Boise, Idaho. They also funded her move to the new city.

Once there, Mom began writing to Mamie. Enthusiastic words about the person she worked for far outweighed the news of her position, or anything else about her life away from home. Mamie shared some of the letters with me.

"I met a wonderful fellow today. His name is Samuel. He's my boss and he's really good looking . . ."

"Sam asked me to dinner tonight . . ." she wrote. . . . "Sam promoted me to be his private secretary . . ." said one letter. . . . "Sam is taking me to meet his parents . . ." said another. Lois was obviously captivated by her relationship with her boss.

Then the letters abruptly stopped and Mamie knew nothing more about Idaho, or Samuel. All she knew was that one day Mom returned to Milton, looking for a new job.

Mamie figured Sam had dumped Mom and she was too proud to talk about it. I had a feeling there was more to it than that. Being dumped would have been a blow to her ego, but if that were all there was to it, she'd have made up a cover story—we call it spin these days—and I could have wormed it out of her.

A few weeks after my conversation with Aunt Mamie, I decided to risk telling Mom what I knew, and ask her what happened after she met Sam's parents.

I used a direct approach, figuring the surprise factor was the only way I'd get a straight answer. "Mom, I was looking at some old pictures at Aunt Mamie's house when the girls and I were there last month. There was a picture of you and a man named Samuel. Mamie said you worked for him in Idaho. Was he your boyfriend?"

Just as I'd hoped, I caught her off guard. She looks at me and says nothing for a while. I can tell she's considering if, or how she's going to answer my question. Waiting for her response, I think about what she might say.

She could shrug and say, *"No."* Or she could say, *"I don't care to talk about it,"* and walk away as she's always done when I poked into this part of her past.

I decide that either response will be all right with me. I'm ready to accept

## Promise I'll Stay for Mother's Day

whatever she chooses to say, and let it go, if she declines to answer. On this day, for whatever reason, she chooses to talk.

"Yes, Sam was my boy friend. In fact, we talked about getting married." That's all she says. Rats. Is that all I'm going to get? Sorry, Mom. One answer begets the need for another. Now I know too much to let it go. We're going to finish this conversation.

"But you didn't get married," I press. "Why not?"

She frowns. She thought we were done with this.

"There were problems with his parents," she says.

"What kind of problems?"

Now she scowls at me. "They were Jewish and I was not."

"And that was a problem?" I pretend ignorance to prompt more discussion.

"I didn't see it as a problem," she says. "I didn't know what being Jewish meant." Two sentences this time. Progress.

"What did it mean?"

"It meant they were different from me and I was different from them, and they didn't want different people in their family. I couldn't see the difference, so I couldn't see the problem." I feel a floodgate about to open. She continues.

"There was only one kind of church and one kind of people in Milton, Oregon. My experience, such as it was, led me to believe that all churches in America were pretty much the same, which meant they taught some version of how to be a good Christian.

"I knew there were different kinds of Christian churches, like Baptist or Presbyterian—or whatever—and there were bigger differences in other places that caused problems, like being Catholic or . . . you know . . . having a different skin color. And I knew they worship a little different than we do. I wasn't totally ignorant about the rest of the world. But where I came from, all the people were white and Presbyterian."

This conversation is taking a turn I didn't anticipate. I'm fascinated.

"I'd heard of Jews," she says, "but I thought they lived in another country, a long time ago, like in Bible days. Sam was white.

"When he said he was Jewish, I thought he meant it was like we're Scots-Irish. Our ancestors came from Scotland and Ireland and I assumed his family came from wherever Jewish people come from. And when people come to America, they become Americans. They go to the same churches and schools, and all that, just like everyone else."

> "It meant they were different from me and I was different from them, and they didn't want different people in their family. I couldn't see the difference, so I couldn't see the problem."

She looks at me, more than a little embarrassed. "Pretty naïve, wasn't I?"

"Mom, it was a different time, and you lived in a very small part of the universe.

You hadn't the experience to be anything but naïve."

"Well, anyway, Sam was right. There were problems. I never got to meet his family."

"Why?" I ask.

"They refused to see me. They told their son if he wanted to have a gentile-woman as a secretary that was fine, but there was no need for them to meet his hired help. They wouldn't entertain a discussion that I might mean more to him than my office skills. They said they'd wait to meet a nice Jewish girl who might become his prospective wife some day." Her eyes look down, her tone is bitter.

Then she looks up at me and grins. "Since I'd never met another Jew living in Idaho, I wondered out loud where the hell they thought he'd meet such a prospect."

"And he said . . . ?"

"Sam said he thought they would change their minds if we were patient and gave them time to get used to the idea that he loved a gentile. He talked me into continuing to see him.

"We went together for about a year. Then family pressure came down hard on Sam to get on with his life, and seriously look for a Jewish girl."

"And did he?"

"No. He told me he didn't want to look for another girl. He said he wanted to be with me, and I believed him. I don't know what he told them. I suspect he said nothing. After a certain amount of time it became clear, at least to me, that Sam's family wasn't going to give in.

"Unless Sam asserted himself, which he was unlikely to do on his own, our relationship was going nowhere. He seemed content with that. I wasn't. I started to push him. I told him he needed to stand up to them, tell them he loved me; tell them he wanted me to be his wife."

"What was his response to that?"

"His response was it was more complicated than that. He said he ran the family business; it was his livelihood. 'If I go against their wishes,' he said, 'I could be out of work, and then what would we do? What kind of future will we have if I don't have a job?'

"What kind of future will we have if you don't stand up to them?" I asked.

"They'll come around," he said.

## Promise I'll Stay for Mother's Day

"When?"

"They'll come around."

"You could get another job," I said. It seemed simple enough to me.

"It's not that simple,' he said, reading my mind. 'I'm a Jew, and this is Idaho.' That fell on ignorant ears.

"I'd managed to find work and live on my own since I was a child. It was preposterous to me that a grown man needed to cling to his Mommy and Daddy to earn a living. Was being a Jew harder than being a girl on her own?"

She shakes her head in disbelief. "He seemed so weak," she says.

"So, what did you do?" I ask, having a pretty good idea what her answer will be.

"Well you know I don't have a lot of patience with waiting around. I can't stand an impasse. I have to get on with what needs to be done, and it seemed so obvious to me what needed to be done. I didn't have the knowledge or maturity to consider the bigger picture and see the tight spot I'd put him in. I just knew I couldn't wait any longer for him to take a stand.

"Sam had to choose between his family and me. I was sure when it came right down to it, he would choose me. He said he loved me, didn't he? Love means sacrifice." She looks away again.

I press on. "He didn't choose you, did he?"

"No, he didn't. He chose *them*."

"What did you choose?"

"I chose to leave him and move back to Milton."

"Did you ever see him again?"

"No."

"How could you leave it like that—never seeing him again?"

"He made one more choice. It proved his cowardice."

"And what was that choice?"

"He chose to kill himself."

"How?" I'm stunned by her disclosure and her dismissive tone.

"Doesn't matter."

She leaves the room. Our conversation is over.

I hope her revealing this closely held part of her life has given Mom some measure of peace for what had to have been a horrific experience, in spite of her superficial, well-practiced shrug. But I don't know.

We never spoke of it again.

CHAPTER 6

## *Husband to the Rescue*

I DON'T KNOW THE EXACT DATE of Mom's return to Milton, and I don't know when or how she received the news of Sam's death. So I don't know her state of mind when she returned to her home town. It had to have been a tremendous blow to her pride as well as her heart to return home knowing that her first venture on her own was a defeat of epic proportions.

"I do know that it was November, 1938, when she met the man she would marry, the man who was to become my father. This story is a splendid tale with a happy ending. It has proven to be worthy of many conversations with my Mom.

"Hazel had a boyfriend named Joe," she says. "He helped me get a job at the State Line Diner on the Oregon-Washington border.

"It was a good job, and just what I needed. It was easy work. I didn't have to think. All I had to do was flirt and laugh while I handed out plates of food and collected plates of garbage. Good pay too. The more I flirted, the better the tips.

"I was living with the Pipers again, and once again they offered shelter to this confused but determined child. I don't know what I'd have done without them. My life could have turned out very different without their safe haven.

"One Friday night, Hazel and Joe walked into the diner with Joe's best friend, a fellow named Tom Wilson. He wasn't particularly good looking, except when he smiled. He had a great smile. It took over his whole face and made his eyes sparkle. And he had a slow, easy gift of gab.

'How come a pretty gal like you is working in a place like this?' he asked. 'How come you can't find yourself a husband to take care of you?'

'It's not that I *can't* find one,' I answered pretending to be a little put off. 'It's that I don't *want* to find one.'

"Well, I think you found one anyway. I'm going to marry you," he said to me.

"I looked at him and smiled. There was something about his manner, and the way he looked at me and grinned, that made me feel warm and safe. There

## Promise I'll Stay for Mother's Day

wasn't any fancy talk or flowery promises. Five minutes after we met, he simply said he was going to marry me. He took charge so easy. I guess I needed that.

"I don't remember an official proposal, and I don't remember saying yes if there was one. I just know that we went on a few dates with Joe and Hazel and a few dates by ourselves and then, six weeks after we met, we got married.

"It was December 11, 1938, the day after Tom's birthday. He said I was his birthday present. Hazel and Joe stood up with us.

"I invited my two families, both the Thompsons and the Pipers. The Pipers came and Mamie came . . . and Hazel, of course. I wanted all my brothers and sisters to come, but they were still mad at the Pipers for taking me in. They didn't want to be in the same room with them. But I couldn't exclude the people who stood by me for five years, from sharing my happiness . . . and I was very happy to be marrying your Dad.

"Tom loved me for who I was, stubborn, rebellious, the whole damn package. He could appreciate the proud and determined woman I'd become. He could also perceive and protect my vulnerabilities.

"He understood the choices I had made because he left home early, just like I did."

Tom Wilson was born in Black Oak, Arkansas, in 1906. His upbringing was even more ragged than Lois Thompson's was.

When he was six, his dad was shot by his own brother in what was called a hunting accident. There was a bit of bad blood there, so the accident part was questionable. Soon after the tragedy, his mother took to drinking and pursuing male companionship. Tom hung around home with his older brother, Oties, and younger half sister, VC, and their mother's various male friends and occasional husbands.

Then in 1920, at age thirteen he decided to leave home for parts unknown. It wasn't as dramatic a leave taking as Lois' was, but it just as final.

He told me about it. "One day I walked out of the house, through my back yard and across the gully that led to the railroad depot. I hopped the first boxcar rolling away from the station. I didn't know where it was going, and I didn't care.

"Boxcars became my home base for eighteen years. I didn't expect it to last that long, but it was easy, so I just stayed with it. It was my version of a mobile home." He shot me that teasing, irresistible smile Mom fell for. "I met some interesting people; never felt the danger some people like to talk about.

"I hopped off the trains when they stopped near a farm ripe for picking, and hopped back on when the crops were done. Sometimes the work lasted a few days, sometimes weeks, sometimes even months. And sometimes I elected to stay a while longer, if a town felt friendly. That usually happened during the winter months, when crops were scarce. I could always get odd jobs to put a roof over my head. Nothing fancy, of course, but I never knew fancy, so it didn't matter.

"It might sound like a strange kind of life to you, Shirleyanne, drifting for almost twenty years, but it was easier than living the way I was under my mother's roof.

"In the six years after my Dad died she had two men she called husbands, and several who were introduced as special friends. Eventually I would have taken issue with one of her men friends, and who knows what kind of mess I'd have put us all in.

"Instead, I got to travel through thirty-eight states by boxcar," he proudly tells me. "I saw a lot of this great country of ours. 'America the Beautiful' we call it, and it surely is.

> "I was working there when I met your Ma. I planned to move on, come spring but after I met the woman of my dreams, my travelin' days were over. Meeting her was the luckiest day of my life. I won me the jackpot that day."

"In 1938, my eighteenth year on the road, I stopped off in Walla Walla to pick peas and onions—those famous Walla Walla sweets. I worked in the fields all spring and summer. That's where I met my friend Joe. His folks owned the biggest farm. It was one of the friendly towns. I decided to see if I could stay around Walla Walla even after the farm work was done.

"I found work at Headquarters Cigar Store in town. It had a back room for cards. I'd dealt some cards along my travels, so I knew the deal. Made some pretty good money—you know the house always wins."

His voice moves from a tone of rote recollection to one of striking enthusiasm. "I was working there when I met your Ma. I planned to move on, come spring but after I met the woman of my dreams, my travelin' days were over. How could I ever leave such a woman? Meeting her was the luckiest day of my life. I won me the jackpot that day."

In Lois Thompson, Tom could see the possibility of sharing a home with one very special person after nearly twenty years on the road living alone or in the company of drifters like himself.

In Tom Wilson, Lois felt she could have both independence and the security of a supportive, safe harbor. He adored her enough to let her do whatever she wanted to do, and to protect her if she needed shelter from her self-driven storms. No conflicts were foreseen in this fateful pairing.

Their meeting was the perfect set up for a couple of souls adrift, meeting at a roadside diner, finding true happiness in a tale that would end with the words, "and they lived happily ever after." Theirs is a true American love story. No playwright could have set it up any better.

Mom's choice of husbands significantly helped with the Thompsons' attitude adjustment toward her.

She'd obviously put together a decent life without their consent and support, and there was a certain amount of begrudging admiration for her having done that. But more important, Dad's simple, easy-going disposition with his reasonable expectations about what brings happiness put to rest some of the resentment they'd felt when she left them to pursue material pleasures. With Tom at her side, she showed them she still held some sense of down-home values. Tom Wilson had no material wealth, but he was a good man, and she chose to marry him for that reason.

"We found a little place to live in Walla Walla," she said. "We got moved in and settled before Christmas. It was nice, just the two of us, at least for a while.

"Then Hazel moved in with us so she could go to a beauty school nearby in Walla Walla. Pop contributed fire wood for the stove, and venison and vegetables for the table. The rest of the family stopped by now and then, to see how we were all doing.

"It was good to have them back in my life, even if it was Hazel that brought them back. They always brought something for the house and table when they came.

"And of course they brought music. You know there's always music at a Thompson gathering. Your Dad learned to play the banjo somewhere in his travels and he picked one up along the way, so he joined in. Family, food and music go a long way to hedge the cravings for more."

The marriage didn't put an end to Lois' quest for nice belongings, but it did alter her approach and timing. Security had moved to the top of her list of needs, with her quest for independence moving into second place, a close second to be sure, but second nonetheless.

She wasn't about to let go of her dreams, but neither was she going to leave this man and their small home for a fancier life in town.

CHAPTER 7

## *The Matriarch Steps Forward*

I WAS BORN TEN MONTHS after the wedding. Twelve months and two weeks later, the arrival of a second child was imminent. Two kids, too soon.

"I believed, with all my heart that Annie lived in poverty and died young because she had too many kids, not that I wished any one of them hadn't been born. I know there was the problem of catering to that ne'er-do-well husband of hers, but it was all us kids that kept her bound to him. Because I'd lived with the reality of a nine-kid household, I expected my life would be different. I knew I had the will to change the direction of my life. I'd already done it. Yet here I was, married less than two years, with my child number two about to enter the world. This had to stop.

"I looked at the nurse wheeling me into the delivery room and said, 'It better be a boy. I have my girl. I want one of each and I'm not coming back.'

My brother Gene arrived that evening, and she never went back "I got my one each," she said with a measure of accomplishment in her voice.

"Even with only two kids it was tough, Shirleyanne. I had to quit work when you came along, so we were living on one income.

"Tom was paid a salary for working at the store and a percentage of the house for dealing cards in the back room. The back room money came under the table. The arrangement was a little shabby and probably illegal, but we needed the money, so we took it. With Pop's contributions we managed to get by. It wasn't a bad existence, and I tried to be content living with my little family. But I couldn't help wishing that something would come along to move us past just getting by."

Something did come along. Another wish granted. It was the quintessential, be-careful-what-you-wish-for conundrum.

The something that came along was our country's official entrance into World War II. On December 7, 1941, the country of Japan launched an unprovoked attack on a Territory of the United States of America. Their planes dropped tons of bombs on our navy ships docked in Pearl Harbor, on the island of Oahu, in Hawaii.

## Promise I'll Stay for Mother's Day

President Franklin Delano Roosevelt asked for and received congressional permission to declare war on Japan. Soon thereafter our country was drawn into the war against Nazi Germany, being fought by our allies on the European continent. World War II was truly global. It brought about enormous changes to our home, and to nearly all the homes across our great land.

The Boeing Company in Seattle, Washington, was recruiting able-bodied men ineligible for active war duty, to build the aircraft our country needed to win the wars overseas. Dad was our family's lone bread winner and too old to be drafted. But he was young enough to develop new skills and as Mom pointed out, the recruitment ads promised good wages. She saw to it that he received an application to work for Boeing.

"We should take advantage of this chance to move to a bigger place," she said as she handed him the application, "where there's room to grow and build a better future for our kids."

Always ready to please Mom and eager to provide opportunities for his cherished family, Dad filled out the application and scheduled an interview in Seattle. Boeing tested his mechanical skills and his intellect. He passed on both counts. He was hired and Mom was thrilled.

"At last, my life was taking the turn I imagined when I left home to get my high school diploma. I thought then that I could earn it all on my own, but I learned by experience the practicality of doing it through marriage. Not that marriage wasn't wonderful on its own," she adds quickly.

"If Tom could get on with Boeing, I knew we'd have a fresh start on our own, and I knew good things would happen for us in Seattle.

"I was so excited when he told me he got the job . . .

"We were going to have a house of our own in the city, and I knew exactly what it would look like. I'd seen pictures of little houses built in port cities for the people moving to new war-time jobs. The house wouldn't be fancy, but it would be clean and neat on a big city block with other young families. I was beside myself with excitement!

"Tom went to Seattle ahead of us to begin his new job and look for our new home. Only a few days passed when he called me to say he'd found a nice little place for us to live.

"I packed our belongings and with high expectations, we moved to Seattle . . . almost. Almost was a two-room shack on the outskirts of town. I couldn't believe what I saw! This little shack in front of me was not the house I had in my head. I was struck dumb. I didn't know what to say. My face must have registered some of what I was thinking.

## The Matriarch Steps Forward

"Look Ma,' your Dad said, 'it's sitting on two hundred acres. We'll have all that property and we can fix up the house any way we want. This could be a great investment for us.'

"Over the next few months I got so sick of hearing him talk about his damn investment, I thought I'd die of frustration. I wanted the house in my head, and I didn't want to wait for it. I told him the day we got there I wasn't living in that little shack for long and he better start looking for something else."

Dad understood the directive and immediately began to make improvements to the house, thinking if it were nice enough, she'd agree to stay with their good investment. He chiseled, sawed and hammered every weekday night and every weekend day.

Gene and I, sensing the urgency in the air, got caught up in watching the house grow and we wanted to help him make it get bigger, fast. We followed Dad around, bringing him his tools and begging to "do that too." He was very, very patient with us, allowing us to do as much as three- and four-year-old kids can do. He made us feel that handing him tools was a big deal. Once in a while he would let us swing a hammer, with him holding the nail. And once in a while we actually hit the nail.

Gene is particularly fascinated with Dad's toolbox. He loves touching and carrying and banging those tools. Being told over and over that he is not to touch the tools unless Dad is with him doesn't stop him from sneaking a tool out of the chest on his own now and then. Three-year-old boys are impatient and industrious little people, not easily put off from exploring attractive no-no's.

It's Saturday afternoon and Dad is working on a project outdoors. In his haste to get started, he left the toolbox open. Have you ever watched a little boy pick up his daddy's tools? It's got to be one of those unspoken male-bonding experiences that escape the female sense of something really cool happening. My little brother simply can't resist these unattended treasures.

Gene looks around and, seeing no one besides me watching him, toddles over to the open toolbox. I watch him as he takes each tool in his hands. I can almost see his mind imagining the workings of each one.

Finally he settles on the big chisel Dad used to hollow out part of the door frame leading into the new addition. He picks it up with a big smile on his face as he rolls up onto his feet. He carries the chisel with him to the place where we saw Dad using it just a couple of hours ago. It doesn't take long for something very bad to happen.

## Promise I'll Stay for Mother's Day

As he tries to dig the sharp end of the chisel into the frame I see the chisel slip on the hard wood and slam into Gene's eye. I see the look of shock and pain cover Gene's face, and I gasp in horror. Gene is too stunned to cry. His face is turning bright red; he throws me a frightened look that pleads with me to help him. Mom's in the kitchen and Dad is outside. No one else has seen what just happened. I run over to Gene and put my arms around him.

"Don't tell," he whimpers. "Don't tell."

"We have to tell," I whisper in panic. "Gene, you poked your eye!"

"No! NO!" he pleads with me in a desperate whispered response.

My little brother's face is contorted with pain, but this stubborn little toddler somehow makes his pain take second place to his fear of getting caught. To this day I don't know how he did that.

> We sneak outside and hide in the car. Gene finally gives in to the pain and he cries and screams, and screams and cries. I keep saying to him over and over, "We have to go tell . . . we have to tell."

His injured eye is squeezed shut. Tears are spilling out of both his eyes and rolling down his cheeks. But no noise. No shrieks. No cries of pain. I can't believe it! It's got to be what they call frozen in fear silence, with the shock thick enough to absorb his excruciating pain.

We sneak outside and hide in the car. Gene finally gives in to the pain and he cries and screams, and screams and cries. I have to do something but I don't know what. I keep saying to him over and over, "We have to go tell . . . we have to tell . . . we have to tell Mom and Dad!"

At last he gives in. Pain has outgrown the safety of our togetherness. We go to Mom first.

She's standing at the kitchen counter with her back to us. Gene stands behind me with his head down, whimpering. He isn't about to volunteer that he'd been into Dad's toolbox. It's clearly going to be up to me to do the confessing. Mom, feeling our presence, turns around.

"Gene hurt his eye!" I blurt out.

Mom scowls. "How'd he hurt it?"

I take her to the toolbox. "With this . . ." I pick up the chisel and show it to her.

She looks at it for a moment. She doesn't panic or show any sign of fear.

"It's dirty," she says. "He's probably got dirt in his eye."

She calmly picks Gene up and carries him to her bed. She lays him down and forces his eye open. Sure enough, there's a lump of something on his eyeball.

## The Matriarch Steps Forward

Gene is shrieking and kicking wildly out of control. He doesn't have to hold back his rage any more. We're no longer hiding. We've been discovered.

Deliberately, Mom leaves him there on the bed and goes to the sink to get a damp cloth. She brings it back to the bed and begins probing into his eye, trying to get the lump out.

Gene's shrieks turn into full blown, shattering screams. He's screaming his head off ... bloody screaming his head off ... and she keeps right on calmly probing, probing, probing. But the lump refuses to dislodge. Dad finally comes in to see what the ruckus is about.

"What's going on in here!" he demands.

"He took your damn chisel and poked it in his eye. I'm trying to get the dirt out, so it won't get infected," Mom shot back at him, without looking up.

Dad hurries to the phone and dials for an operator. "My son has hurt his eye. We need a doctor, fast."

The operator quickly finds an eye specialist and calls back to say we'll be hearing from a doctor, soon. Dr. Shannon calls us within a few minutes.

"What's happened to your son's eye?"

"He poked a chisel in it. I'm fixin' up the house and I left the toolbox open. There seems to be some dirt stuck on his eyeball. My wife's trying to remove it ... "

"Please! Don't touch the eye again," Dr. Shannon says. "Put a clean cold pack over the eye and bring him to me, immediately."

The doctor's urgent tone gets us moving. The four of us pile into our 1937 Dodge Terraplane and we make a fearful trip into downtown Seattle, getting there as fast as we can.

The floating bridge that crosses Lake Washington today has not yet been built. In 1943 we have to sit in the car and wait for a ferryboat. It takes nearly an hour and a half to go fifteen miles. Gene is beyond pain, reduced to quiet, mournful whimpering. Mom is fuming. "If we lived in Seattle instead of way out here ... "

Dr. Shannon meets us at the door and takes the three of them into another room, closing the door, leaving me in the waiting room by myself. It's Saturday and no one else is here.

The office is in a building at Fourth and Pike, in the middle of the city. The doors have crinkly, translucent glass above the doorknobs. It looks like the detective offices you see in old black and white Sam Spade movies. Nothing seems real.

Through the door I can see adult shadows huddled around a small mound of flailing arms and legs, and I can hear my little brother screaming. For what seems like an eternity, I hear his screams. Then suddenly it's quiet and for a long minute, I wish I could hear the screams. There's something about the silence that follows screams in a doctor's office that feels coldly ominous, even to a little girl who has never been in a doctor's office. I'm alone in the waiting room, and they're in there. I don't know what's happening and they do. It's the first time I've ever felt alone, and I don't like it.

The three of them come out together with Dr. Shannon. Dad is carrying Gene in his arms. Both my parents' faces are red and pale at the same time, and there are signs of wetness on their cheeks. Gene's injured eye has a big gauze bandage over it, secured with adhesive tape. It's hard for me to describe the rest of his face. Except for his beet-red cheeks, it's chalky white. The gaze in his unbandaged eye is steady and dull. It's a peculiar look. I've never seen a drug-induced stare before.

Mom looks at me and says, "Thank God I couldn't get the lump out of his eye. It wasn't dirt. It was his pupil, punctured by the chisel . . . spilling out . . ." her voice fades.

Dr. Shannon says he thinks he's saved Gene's eye. He turns toward me with an explanation.

"There's a new drug called penicillin," he announces. "I had a sample of it in my office. It's supposed to fight infection. Infection is what causes trouble in wounds of this kind. I gave him a shot of penicillin," he says to me, significantly.

I don't know why these adults feel they need to explain what went on in that inside room to a frightened little girl. I'm only four and a half years old. Until today I didn't know eyeballs could spill out and be put back in, and I'd never heard of something called penicillin that could fight infection. I never even heard of infection until Mom said the word while she was working over Gene on the bed at home. I'm still not sure what it is, but their tone tells me it's bad.

I listen to them, and promise myself I'll remember everything they're saying. I'll remember the sounds of their voices and the looks on their faces. I'll remember everything about this day, because I know, even though I am very young, all that I've ever known is going to change. I'm scared for the first time in my short life. I'm alone and scared. And I'm four years old.

The trip back to our house is quiet, except for the sound of the car's engine under the hood and the tires turning 'round on the country roads. Gene has spent his energies fighting the fright and the pain. He's asleep.

Mom and Dad are silent too, but it's a noisy silence. I can tell Mom's mind is in a furious state of action.

## The Matriarch Steps Forward

Something about the atmosphere swirling around her place in the front seat is sending out messages that she's thinking real hard. I'm getting a strong feeling that whenever she chooses to tell us what's going on in her head during this ride home, there will be major adjustments to life as we know it. There's nothing concrete, like the road we're traveling on, to make me think these things. It's only a feeling.

It's nighttime and I'm supposed to be asleep, but my eyes are open and my ears are straining to hear what Mom and Dad are saying across the room.

I've been keeping myself awake at night, hoping to overhear the secret, adult conversations that parents have when kids are supposed to be asleep. It's not right to snoop, but I have to find out what's going to happen to us. I know something's going to happen. I hear Mom's voice.

> I suspect this new divorce word will make our lives a whole lot worse. Unless Dad moves us to Seattle, where the doctor is, we're going to move back to Oregon.

"Tom, either you take us into town to live, or I will divorce you and take the kids back to my family in Milton. It won't be an easy thing for me to do, but they'll take us in and I'll find a way to pay them for it.

"Gene's going to have a lot of doctor visits and I'm not going to sit in a car for hours at a time getting him into town. I'm not going to stay in this place. If you want to keep your family together, you better get looking for another place for us to live."

Divorce is another new word for me. I'm not any surer about what that word means than when I heard the penicillin word for the first time. But I understand now that the penicillin word made Gene a whole lot better. I suspect this new divorce word will make our lives a whole lot worse. Unless Dad moves us to Seattle, where the doctor is, we're going to move back to Oregon. And if that happens, Dad won't be moving with us.

I have my head under the covers so they won't know I'm awake, so I can't see Dad's reaction to what she's saying. If Mom's words bring a talking response from Dad, it's a quiet one, because I can't hear it. And I'm listening as hard as I can.

I'm listening to hear him say, "Okay Ma, I'll find us a house in Seattle."

Please say that, Dad. I can't imagine living someplace without you. Please say you'll find us a house in Seattle. But he doesn't say it. I don't hear any words at all coming from Dad's side of the bed.

This time it's Lois Wilson drawing the line, and she's prepared to walk on either side of it, so long as it leads her away from the two-room shack located almost to Seattle.

## Promise I'll Stay for Mother's Day

She is taking control of her life again, willing to make another huge sacrifice to get what she wants. She's unable to stop herself from reaching for the life she imagined when she was a thirteen-year-old girl, dreaming of new worlds far from the mountain home she grew up in near Promise, Oregon.

Although he didn't seem to react when Mom gave him the ultimatum, Dad must have understood her resolve and loved her very much, because soon after I overheard Mom laying out the choices to him, we moved.

In fact we moved three times, until Mom finally found the house in her head. It's a typical World War II bungalow, thrown up quickly to accommodate the people moving into manufacturing and port cities to carry out the civilian work of war. It's small, but it's new and clean and finished, and it's located in a family neighborhood where there are kids for Gene and me to play with. I like it. But more than that, I'm relieved, because I can tell that Mom likes it too. I don't think we'll have to move again.

As I approach the ripe old age of five and a half years, I join my Dad in understanding exactly how our lives are going to work.

It's pretty simple. If we're to stay together as a family, we will do whatever we have to do to see that Mom gets whatever it is she wants.

CHAPTER 8

## *It's a Fun War*

THE YEAR IS 1944, still wartime. In addition to building airplanes, Seattle is a port city and a center for the housing and training of military troops.

Fort Lewis Army Base and McCord Air Force Base are located a few miles south of Seattle. The Bremerton Naval Base is west of the city, across Puget Sound. Every day there are soldiers, sailors and Army Air Corps personnel awaiting deployment and returning from action aboard the ships that dock in our harbor.

Mom's sister, Hazel, joins the service after her fiancé from Walla Walla is declared M.I.A.—Missing in Action—in the war with Germany. She's a WAC—Women's Army Corps. Four of their brothers are also members of the armed forces. Herb, Lon and Jack joined the Navy; Dick is a Marine.

Hazel gets stateside duty in California. Her assignment is to greet and offer encouragement to the seriously wounded servicemen sent home from the front lines for treatment and recovery. It's a very difficult but rewarding assignment. Her pretty looks and sunny disposition attract attention. The story of Hazel's service is chronicled in Look Magazine.

The brothers' war assignments are to fight the Japanese forces in the South Pacific. The Navy Men are on ships defending the seas and providing back up for the United States armed forces that go ashore to recapture American Territories. Lon is a signalman on a battleship, waving colorful flags in code to communicate with other U.S. ships sailing the oceans and with our planes flying overhead.

He told us years later that one day his best buddy was standing next to him on the deck of the ship, when he was literally blown away by enemy fire to be forever stationed in the everlasting sea. The only trace of his buddy's existence was a few drops of blood on the deck of the ship.

Dick's duty as a Marine is to leave the ship and wade ashore under heavy enemy attack to secure landing sites for our troupes. His specific task is to

## Promise I'll Stay for Mother's Day

take out the Japanese machine gunners positioned to defend the islands. It is a tremendously dangerous assignment.

We heard about Dick's experiences many, many years after the war was over. During the real time of war Gene and I don't hear of these dangers. As we live through the war, we have only an inkling of a larger world and our places in it.

Our real experiences are nothing but joyful. Our extended family has shared our phone number with friends who are passing through Seattle so they'll have a place of contact as they matriculate to and from their war-time assignments. These energetic young people bring us treats and trinkets, and share stories of their travels. What they tell us sounds like they're on vacations to places they've never seen before, meeting people of different colors and customs they've never experienced before. We hear nothing about injuries or death, or facing the fire of machine guns. There seems to be a military code of honor that keeps our fighting forces from talking about their personal hardships. Or perhaps the horror of combat is simply unspeakable.

Mom's war temperament helps to further our disassociated attitude toward the distant world struggles. She's delighted to have her house full of relatives and their friends. She happily fixes food and makes up beds. She's thrilled that her home has become War Central. She's reveling in her role as international hostess. She leads the celebrations as we hear how our GIs are kickin' ass all over the world.

We hear Edward R. Murrow on the radio with news from the war, telling us the Allies are advancing, the Germans are retreating, and our Marines have landed in the Philippines. Our president, Mr. Roosevelt, says we have nothing to fear but fear itself. He is our leader and he knows best, so we put on our confident faces to show the world we are fearless.

We hear music. Glenn Miller and the Modern Aires are "In the Mood." Bing Crosby croons in his signature easygoing style. Bob Hope travels overseas with Jerry Colonna and an assemblage of pretty girls to entertain our troops. We sing "Don't sit under the apple tree" and "Drinkin' rum and Coca Cola", with the Andrews Sisters. It's easy to be brave when we're having so much fun.

There are sights and sounds that allude to the darker side of war, but since this is our first memorable expanded life experience, Gene and I accept the heavy draperies that hang from our windows, and the whistles' that blow to tell us to close the drapes and cover signs of life to the outside world. We accept it because our questions are answered simply, without dread from our adult protectors.

It's a Fun War

*(Left) Gene and me with Mom and Dad.*
*(Right) Gene and me with Grandpa Bress 1943, Milton, Oregon.*

"Why do we close the curtains when the whistles blow, Mom?"

"We have to make it dark outside in case bombers fly over our house to drop bombs on us. If they don't see lights, they won't know we're here and they won't know where to drop 'em."

"What are bombers?"

"They're airplanes that carry things called bombs. Bombs are like giant fire crackers. When they hit the ground, they explode and blow everything up."

"Somebody's going to drop giant firecrackers on us?" we ask anxiously.

"They won't get this far because we have ships and bomber planes ourselves that will stop them.

"But we practice making it dark, just in case one of 'em gets through."

"Where do they come from?"

"They come from a country far away that doesn't like us. They dropped bombs on our ships in Pearl Harbor."

"What's a Pearl Harbor?"

## Promise I'll Stay for Mother's Day

"That's a place in Hawaii where some of our ships were, until those bastards bombed 'em."

"Will they bomb our ships in Seattle?"

"That's not what they'd be looking for here.

"They'll be coming after the airplanes we're building. That's what they'll want to bomb if they come here."

"Dad makes airplanes, doesn't he?" we ask with a measure of concern.

"Yes. At the Boeing Airplane Company."

"Does Boeing have curtains?"

Mom laughs. "No, but they keep the airplanes inside buildings that are painted on top to look like trees. So when the bombers fly over, they'll see what looks like a forest below, and they'll fly right on by. They won't even see the buildings where your Dad works and where our airplanes are."

"Then they won't get him?"

"No, they won't get him."

To help us understand, Dad secures clearance to take us on the Beacon Hill road overlooking the Boeing plant.

We drive up there and look down on the buildings and we see what looks like trees and houses on the roofs. But they still look kind of like roof tops. We frown. We're worried, and Dad senses our hesitation.

"It looks kind of fakey from here. But high in the sky where the planes are, it'll look like quiet, regular neighborhoods down here," he assures us, "and that's not what they're interested in bombing."

His words reinforce what Mom said. Dad is safe because he works in a building that looks like neighborhoods, from up where the bombers fly. We know Mom is always right, but it's nice to hear it from Dad too. Dad is safe, and so are we.

Even having to use ration stamps that keep grown ups from getting everything they want when they want it, doesn't trouble us. Mom can't get nylons and Dad can't get new tires, so she wears cotton anklets and goes bare legged, and we patch our tires when they go flat. We stay home a lot because it's a happy place to be, and because it helps us save our gas stamps so we can make trips home to Milton, whenever Mom gets her irrepressible urges to go there. She loves her new home in Seattle, but Oregon is still her heartland.

We kids have our ration stamps, too, but they're not quite so utile as tires and nylons. Our rations have to do with bananas and bubble gum. Bananas and gum are scarce because they come from lands in the South Pacific and that's where we're fighting the Japs—they're the people that fly the bombers.

## It's a Fun War

The scarcity of bananas and gum makes them prized goods, so we're constantly on high alert for rumors of new shipments.

"Heard anything about when new bananas are coming?" we ask our friends.

"Next week, we think."

"How about bubble gum—that coming too?"

"Don't know—maybe."

When word arrives that these coveted items have actually arrived, we run out the door and race to the store to get our rations of bananas and bubble gum before they're all gone. The gum of course, lasts longer than the bananas. Bananas don't stick to bed posts. Happy times, happy war. Incredibly small sacrifices.

> ... we run out the door and race to the store to get our rations of bananas and bubble gum before they're all gone. The gum of course, lasts longer than the bananas. Bananas don't stick to bed posts.

It wasn't until I made a trip to France a few years ago and visited the American Cemetery in Normandy, when I looked down on bunkers left over from the D Day invasion of June 1944, and saw thousands of tiny white crosses standing in a beautiful field of green marking the graves of those who didn't come home to the real America, that the reality of war finally hit me. I completely fell apart, sobbing as I remembered how secure and carefree we were in our little home in Seattle, protected by a Mom and Dad showing only their fearless facades, telling us that everything was going to be just fine. We never counted the corpses left on the beaches and forests of continents and islands far away, or felt the suffering of thousands of families whose loved ones are still there.

Standing in a field of crosses, pounded into the ground over the bodies of a generation of young men, brought me face to face with the reality that crosses are real, and so is a grown up life. The importance of bananas and bubble gum has given way to the urgency of making money and keeping a semblance of family order in the midst of competition, chaos, and questionable priorities.

Once upon a time, war was fun and life was perfect. But once upon a time isn't real. It's only a phrase at the beginning of a fairy tale. The real tale is murky. Will there be a happily ever after at the end of our story? I don't know. I can't see that far ahead.

*Mom, 1970.*

CHAPTER 9

## *Lois Goes to Work*

THE WAR IS SUDDENLY OVER. People run outside, yelling and banging on pots and pans, hugging each other with unbridled joy.

The men and women of war can come home and restart their lives. Many did not return, but our men and women did, and we are celebrating along with other families who are as fortunate as we are. Family and friends in uniform are going through Fort Lewis to muster out of the service.

This is their last trip through Seattle, and one last hurrah for our home as the center of our personal war effort. The people in uniform are leaving us for good. Mom's family returns to Milton, and Mom, Dad and Gene and I are left to be by ourselves in Seattle. It seems kind of quiet. The atmosphere is changing. Not quite so happy. Not quite so carefree. Not quite awful, but more than a little tense.

During the war Mom had moved herself into the center of family attention by playing hostess to the wartime travelers. She got to show off how well we are living in the big city. Her move away from home has been an unqualified success, and she is very proud of what she's accomplished. But she can't show off without people around to notice, and the people are gone. Routine is settling in. It's time for Mom to stir the pot again.

Dad works all day and Gene and I are in school most of the day, Monday through Friday. That leaves Mom alone and bored five days a week. She needs to find something to fill up her time and bring new people into her life.

The economic necessities of war sent women into the work place in numbers never seen before, to fill positions never held before. "Rosie the Riveter" worked alongside male colleagues, sharing equal responsibilities to support the war effort.

The doors to the work place for women have been open for a few years now, and while she wasn't a part of the wartime work force, Mom has noticed this new world of choices. Working outside the home seems to offer the perfect situation to appease her restless energy.

She begins to explore the want ads for work opportunities. Even though we are managing quite well on the income he provides, Dad doesn't mind if she works. He offers no opposition to her job search or to any of her needs and desires. Dad is pleased if Mom is pleased, and Mom is never pleased with the status quo. Life is better for us if she is busy. Mom needs to go to work. We need Mom to go to work

She is hired by Sears Roebuck and Company to be a sales clerk. She promptly throws all her energies and considerable charm into her new job. Her efforts, enthusiasm, and abilities do not go unnoticed.

Less than a year after Sears hired her, she is rewarded with placement in their management training program, followed by a department head assignment. Mom has been named manager of the combined departments of photographic equipment and office furnishings, both of them the kind of big-ticket merchandise departments usually assigned to men. This is 1947, and this is a major position for a woman. She even has a man working for her. The attention she receives for these accomplishments is both conspicuous and consistent. She's in a heady position and absolutely glowing in the importance of it all.

The best way for Dad, Gene, and me to adjust to her added responsibilities is to stay out of her way. I say added responsibilities because, not surprisingly, she has relinquished nothing at home. She attacks her domestic days with the same fervor as her work days, and we let her. To question her is out of the question.

She works Monday through Wednesday, is off Thursday, works Friday night until nine, and until six pm on Saturday. Sunday she's off work again. On her days off she scrubs the floors, washes clothes in the bathtub, and fixes big, traditional down-home meals such as turkey, pot roast, meat loaf, and chicken 'n dumplings. The Sunday meal provides leftovers for Monday; the Thursday meal is served again on Saturday.

On Tuesday and Wednesday Dad and I fix dinner. Tuesday its pork chops with pork gravy poured over boiled mashed potatoes, and lettuce and tomato salad tossed with large globs of mayonnaise. Wednesday its chicken fried steak, same accompaniments. Friday night Mom works late so Dad, Gene and I go out for greasy hamburgers at Brownie's Burgers.

There isn't a lot of variety in our nutritional intake, and it isn't particularly healthy, but it fills us up and that's all that's expected of food during these years. Nutritional examination is for later generations. We're not at the table to eat, anyway. The evening meal serves as a stage for Mom's monologues about her important work and the important people she works with.

"I told Mr. Wandell we'd do $45,000 in December and he said we couldn't do it. I told him I thought we could. I called my camera and film reps today and placed the orders. They're going to have to help me push 'em over the counter with new displays and packaging, but I think I can get 'em to do that. Sears is going to have to give us some ad space in their next newspaper layout. And we're going to have to make our reps get into this thing. I think I'll invite the Relles over for dinner next Saturday . . . " and on and on and on . . .

Her important people will become our important people. Family support is near the top of the check-off list for people looking to advance in the business world, and we do want advancement, don't we?

But before the parade of guests begins, we have to buy new furniture, dishes and carpets. The furniture and dishes we already have aren't quite good enough for these new important guests. We don't have carpets yet, so that'll be a whole new look.

Dad, Gene and I have to look good too. We're as much on display as the new chairs, carpets, and China plates.

Mom always looks great.

Her hair is perfectly coiffed in the hairdo-of-the-day, featuring a smooth crown and a halo of pin curls all around her nicely-shaped head. Her nails are a national treasure. She spends two hours every Sunday night meticulously manicuring her fingernails. They are long and oval and slightly curved down at the end. She has absolutely magnificent nails. Her clothes are the latest Dior fashion knock offs of the late 1940s, featuring boxy shoulders, nipped in waists, and because fabric is no longer rationed to make military uniforms, calf-length skirts.

Dad and Gene have it easy. Being of the male gender, they don't have to contend with the Mom comparison. All they have to do is put on their best clean clothes and smile and be polite.

My presentation isn't quite that simple.

Standing next to Lois Wilson and maintaining a measure of confidence in one's appearance is a formidable assignment for any female, let alone the nine-year-old daughter of this Super Woman. I never feel quite pulled together. My posture is atrocious. I know that. My body stands kind of sideways and pigeon toed, with my hands held together loosely behind my back to keep them from doing anything unexpected. This pose my body elects to fall into makes my dresses hang funny, hiking up a ways left of center front, and down a ways, back right. The head on top of my body tilts down in front, requiring me to look up at people from under slightly lowered eyelids. The face on the front of my head manufactures a slow, shy smile attempting to phony up a bit of confidence in this otherwise unsightly presentation. I manage to be the only goofy looking person in the room.

"Shirleyanne," Mom says with an eye for improvement, "Hold up your head and pull in your chin . . . no, not like that. Pull it in and lift it up. Now open your eyelids and look straight at me. There, that's better. Oh Shirleyanne, you're so pigeon toed. Turn your feet out. Stand up straight, and let go of your hands. Clasp them in front of you. No not like that. Loosen up. Relax; look natural."

Okay Mom. I know this is important stuff, but I can't loosen up and look natural. This is not natural. I feel like I'm going to fall over trying to remember all your tips on how I'm supposed to stand. I'm sorry.

You're clearly disappointed in me. I wish I could be more like you. I wish for you that I liked all this dressing up, but I don't. I wish I liked meeting your business friends, but I don't. I want to run outside and ride my bike. I want to put on my baseball glove and play catch with my brother. I want to pick up a bat and smack something, preferably a baseball, clean over the back fence. This goofy looking girl in an ill-fitting dress is not happy. But I'll try harder. A happy Mom makes this a happy home.

We're as ready as we'll ever be to welcome the important people into our home. Mom loves being around these sophisticated business men, with their charming manners, twinkling eyes, and ingratiating smiles. How they flirt with her! How she loves the attention!

Looking back from a more worldly perspective, I realize that most of these men were of the Jewish culture. I didn't know about Sam or her experience with faith-based prejudice when we were hosting these men. But now that I know about these things, I understand her needing their approval as much as their business. She brought these charismatic men home to meet her husband and kids in order to take charge of the relationships and then rebuff their seductive advances. Clearly they wouldn't have minded testing the sheets, but giving in to them would have meant giving in to Sam all over again, and she wasn't going there.

I also understand and applaud her insatiable need to have everything beautiful and in perfect order. We were not wealthy by a stretch of anyone's measurement, but what we have in our small home reeks with class. It's amazing how well she's able to put things together in a stylish and comfortable presentation having relatively little money to work with. But she is an amazing woman. So I guess it's not so amazing.

With a lovely home, a happy family, and a successful career, Lois Wilson, nee Thompson, has come a long way from the back hills of Promise.

CHAPTER 10

## *Dad Fills In*

IT'S A GOOD THING most of our efforts were directed toward Mom's career. Peace time at factories whose output is geared for war brings production shut downs and personnel lay offs when the war is over, and Boeing is no exception. Dad is not one of the lay offs, but he's been asked to take a lesser job at reduced pay. Rather than accept the demotion, Dad, with Mom's full support and encouragement, is looking for a position with another company.

The company that hires him is Sears and Roebuck. He will work at the warehouse a few miles south of the retail store where Mom works. She arranged for the interview and Dad got the job. This is a pattern of work application that works very well for our family.

Dad proves to be a surprising leader. In a short time he is named manager of the appliance maintenance department. The fact that he has a quiet demeanor hasn't lessened his ability to lead in his own way. People like following this quietly self-assured man.

Since his work hours are shorter and more standard than Mom's retail position, Dad is our more available parent. He takes us to our music lessons, takes charge of our practicing, and plans our Saturdays.

He was raised with the same interest in traditional American music and literature as Mom's family. Appalachia traditions are not that far removed from the Ozarks. He contributes a frailing banjo style to our family music sessions, and sings a pretty fine bass in our bluegrass and spiritual quartets. I never learned to play an instrument of traditional American music like Gene eventually did, but I can sing mournful train songs and yodel to the Jimmy Rogers and Carter Family tunes of the 1930s.

"I had a friend named Ramblin' Bob, used to steal, gamble 'n rob . . . yodel-a-ee-hee-hee . . . "

But Dad isn't satisfied that we know only this music. He signed us up for classical violin lessons soon after Mom went to work.

Our lessons are Saturday mornings; our practices are daily. Immediately

## Promise I'll Stay for Mother's Day

after school we stay with Mrs. Johnson who lives across the street. Dad picks us up at 4:00 and takes us home to practice our music lessons for at least a full hour every day. He stands over us, counting time as we slog our way through the scales and notes on our sheet music, demanding do-overs for every mistake. It's like each day is a recital, mandating flawless performances. We silently watch the clock and count the minutes, sometimes with tears running down our cheeks onto our violins, as he drives us to perfect our exercises. He is so proud that his kids are learning sonatas and symphonies he pounds on us to practice, practice, practice.

By the time we're nine and ten years old, we hold first and second chairs in the Seattle Youth Symphony, where we practice even more and play in performances nearly every Saturday afternoon. It's grueling. We long for the simpler tunes of our relatives' living rooms and back yard chaise lounges. "Oh I'm dreaming tonight of my blue eyes, who is sailing far over the sea . . . " Yeah, dreaming. Dreaming we could lay off the classical music grind.

About this time, we move fifteen miles south of Seattle to a larger house with fruit trees and a bit of acreage. It's time for Gene and me to have separate bedrooms. We need more room for our personal closets and beds and toys. Gene likes to build model airplanes and I like to spread paper dolls all over the place. They're the only dolls I remember having, and about the only girly activity I spent any time on.

There are no girls in our new neighborhood for me to play with, so girly hours are scarce. The absence of girlfriends, coupled with hanging out with my Dad and brother, and having Mom only at a distance steers me more toward traditional boy activities rather than the usual girly stuff. But that's okay. I'll turn girly soon enough.

Every once in a while, Mom says something about staying home and taking care of her kids "like other mothers do," as she puts it. The thought of it, frankly, petrifies us. Whenever Mom starts with her "I should stay home with you kids" ramblings, Gene and I upgrade our behavior to prove that her working has no effect on our ability to grow up as happy and obedient children. And Dad and I fix a meal other than pork chops just to prove we can.

It isn't that we don't want her around. We just don't want her around all the time. She has so much energy to burn we know she'd be a daily internal buzz saw, disrupting what we consider to be a pretty easy way to pass each day.

Where we live now is farther from where Dad works so he gets home about an hour later than he used to. The move has given Gene and me freedom from baby sitters and nightly violin practices with Dad. We still take music lessons

## Dad Fills In

*Shirleyanne and Gene with violins 1948, Seattle, WA.*

and practice, and go in to town Saturday mornings to work with the symphony, but the daily practice pressure is lessening and a more relaxed leisure time with Dad is emerging.

Saturday afternoons after the symphony practices the three of us stay in town to browse through book stores, or go to movie matinees, or sit in the left field bleachers at Triple A baseball games. The three of us enjoy each other's company on the weekends and Gene and I enjoy our time alone during the week. It's better for the personality of our particular family to have Mom at work.

My brother and I haven't learned that we are supposed to be lonely, unhappy, maladjusted kids on the verge of delinquency because we're at home a lot without parental supervision. We're latch key kids without the label. And we're content.

There aren't enough people living like we are to make it worthwhile for psychologists and social researchers to study us and write articles and books that tell us how dangerous it is for us to be living like this. They don't know about us, and we don't know about them. All we know is that certain things are expected of us, and our parents aren't afraid to set us straight if we forget what these things are.

## Promise I'll Stay for Mother's Day

Our Mom and Dad are grown ups who know how to provide standards and guidelines. They're adults secure enough to allow themselves and their offspring a few hours of freedom each day to develop our own thoughts and activities. We're certain that we'll hang with Dad every Saturday, and Mom will wash our clothes and fix wonderful dinners on Thursday and Sunday. There's enough predictability in our lives to give us the security it takes to be home alone and fill our vacant hours without complaint.

Lest I get too carried away painting a picture of angelic obedient children, I need to add that sometimes the halos go missing. Gene and I are no angels. We create our share of mischief, sometimes pulling stunts so stupid neither we nor our parents can explain why they occur. I have a three-cornered scar on my forehead as a result of a neighborhood rock fight.

> We look for certain size rocks and pile them up behind our fabricated walls of combat. When both sides declare ourselves to be fully stocked, we throw rocks at each other. It's a simple, mindless activity that fills hours of time.

For some reason, we love rock fights in our neck of the woods. Our home south of town has a big, unstructured back forty where we choose up sides and build opposing fortresses by rounding up junk, like old tires and stacks of wooden boxes to protect ourselves from direct hits. We look for certain size rocks and pile them up behind our fabricated walls of combat. When both sides declare ourselves to be fully stocked, we throw rocks at each other. It's a simple, mindless activity that fills hours of time. We've learned to bob and weave and turn our backsides to the flying ammo so we won't get hurt.

Ow! I forgot to duck. A rock hits my forehead. Down I go; my hands cover my face and my blood covers my hands. But the blood soon stops flowing and we wash the wound and cover it with a big band aid. This brings a halt to today's rock contest. Hurting people is no fun.

"What the heck did you do to your forehead, Shirleyanne?" Dad asks when he gets home and sees the purple bump protruding from under the bandage.

"Tripped and fell."

"You gotta be more careful."

"Okay." I wonder what he thinks the forts and rock piles are for.

Gene and I also manage to conger up our share of mischief without neighborly assistance. For several years, breaking windows seemed to be our favorite form of idle time activity. Our own windows, of course.

I'm looking out the kitchen window watching Gene pick up apples and

## Dad Fills In

I make a face at him. He sees me and acts like he's going to throw one of the apples at me. I can't let him get away with that, so I challenge him with an obscene gesture. An apple comes sailing through the window. This time I duck. There's no damage done to me, but we have a broken window to explain. "It slipped" doesn't quite make it, since it was an uphill toss of about fifteen yards. We are banished to our rooms without dinner.

That was a piddling break. Another afternoon we're playing baseball with a few friends. After they go home, Gene and I start gathering the equipment to put in the garage. I'm dallying and he wants to finish the job.

"Hurry up," he grumbles, as he walks into the garage with a load of gear.

Okay Gene, you want me to hurry, catch this. I hurl a baseball straight at him through one of the small-paned windows in the garage door. CRASH!

Unfortunately, there are three garage doors, each one with eight windows. Gene laughs and tosses the baseball back at me through another window. You guessed it. We toss the baseball back and forth to each other through every one of the twenty-four windows. What in the world were we thinking?!? We sweep up the glass and go inside the house to await our moment of reckoning.

"How'd the windows get broken?" Dad's home.

"We, uh . . . We threw a baseball through 'em," I said. I'm always the one to give up the explanations. It started with the chisel incident, when Gene was too scared to speak.

"You did what?!?" Dad's tone was understandably incredulous.

"We, uh . . . We broke 'em."

"On purpose?!?"

"Well, not really. We accidentally started and we couldn't seem to stop."

"So you broke ALL of 'em . . ."

"Uh . . . Yeah." Our rear ends stung for a week.

But the mischief had nothing to do with Mom's working outside the home. We would have found time to break a few windows with or without her presence. The only explanation I can think of as to why kids break windows is they need to know that someone will stop them. There's more than a little security in understanding that a safe life requires boundaries. We need to know how to live in the world we grow up to. It will demand far more accountability from us than the familiar realm of parental love. I'm grateful Gene and I had parents who cared enough about us to limit our misbehavior to a few acts of mindless mischief.

I'm not going to claim our way of living was the best and only way to live. It would have been nice, perhaps, if Dad had spoken up to Mom a little

## Promise I'll Stay for Mother's Day

more and shown some occasional assertiveness. And it would have been cool if Mom had taken more time to listen to us talk, rather than so much of the other way around. And a parent serving up milk and cookies at the end of each school day would have been pretty swell, I suppose. But I don't know. All I know is what our home provided.

So what if Gene and I came home from school to an empty house every day. The problem with working parents is not that they both work outside the home. The problem is they feel guilty for doing so. They pamper and spoil their precious little offspring to cover their useless feelings of guilt. Life is not nirvana. It's not meant to be.

Life is supposed to have its passions and imperfections so we can all be a little bit different and a lot more interesting. There are people who may dispute that, but I believe we are real people created to make mistakes, lose our tempers and dish out and receive our share of injustices.

Anyone who expects perfection on this earth is not grasping our reason for being here. Life is not the perfect ending. It's the process we go through to get to the perfect ending. I hear tell there are green pastures awaiting us at the end of our trials and errors. If that's true, it means we'll have plenty of time to lay down our labors and roll around in those green pastures when this day is done.

CHAPTER 11

## *We Yield to Tradition*

ALTHOUGH OUR HOUSEHOLD has successfully evolved into a new, modern lifestyle, we are not entirely emancipated from a traditional point of view. The most prosperous and socially accepted households still have men bringing home the paychecks and women bringing up the children.

Up until now our family has existed very well on the fringe of polite society, but it is fringe nevertheless. Mom and Dad stepped forward into a new frontier for themselves, and they're quite content with their chosen lifestyle. But like most parents, they want their kids to travel an easier road than the one they chose. There will be no hopping onto a freight train or stomping into town with nothing but a pillowcase and burlap bag full of personal belongings, for their son and daughter.

Gene is second in line, but decisions about his future come before mine. He's the male child, you see. His gender dictates first choice. And the choice he is offered is an Aeronautical Engineering Degree from the University of Washington, located in Seattle. This is the natural course of study for the son of a man who helped build airplanes at the Boeing Company.

This life direction was determined by our parents when Gene entered high school. Then, at the beginning of his senior year of high school in the fall of 1957, the shocking launch of the Russian space capsule, Sputnik, made the pursuit of engineering degrees a national mandate. Our family was right on target in choosing their son's career.

There is no doubt that Gene will be accepted into the school of engineering. He is certifiably brilliant. His IQ test scores are off the charts. If people were accepted into universities and/or paid for scoring high on IQ tests, Gene would never have to attend school or go to work.

One month into the first grade, school officials wanted to jump him to the fourth grade. "We feel it would be a waste of our time and his to leave him in the first grade. He is capable of at least fourth-grade work," the educators say to Gene's mother.

Promise I'll Stay for Mother's Day

*Senior photos: Shirleyanne 1957, Gene 1958.*

"It's a waste of time to teach a six-year-old child how to read and write in his own grade level? That's ridiculous!" says our Mom. "No, you may not skip my son to the fourth grade. You will find a way to teach him with students his own age."

We never figured out why she was so adamant about holding him back. It seemed to fly in the face of her penchant for bragging about our family's achievements. Perhaps she thought Gene would get better grades by staying with his age group, and high grades would produce their own bragging rights. Whatever her rationale, it was not a good decision. Gene stayed in the first grade as she dictated, and progressed through the rest of the twelve grades in order, whiling away his school years unchallenged and bored. He graduated with better than average grades, but well below his potential for learning.

School isn't particularly difficult for me either, but higher education isn't the primary component of my mother's agenda for me. The only reason I get to consider college at all is because kids are supposed to surpass their parents' accomplishments.

Since my mother finished high school, I get to go to college . . . for a while . . . if I want to. But going so far as to graduate from college probably won't be necessary. Surely it won't take me four years to get my M-R-S degree. I actually began working toward my M-R-S when I was fourteen, not by personal choice, but as with my brother, by parental dictate.

## We Yield to Tradition

I asked for a new baseball glove for my birthday present. What I received was eight weeks of personal growth at Kathleen Peck Modeling Agency and Charm School. I learned to set my hair, put on a colorful face, and walk with a book on my head. All three of these sparkling new skills were designed to draw me away from my tom boy tendencies. The goal was to fashion me into becoming an alluring young woman who would learn to catch boys rather than baseballs. A pair of white cotton gloves replaced my preferred gift choice of a southpaw's mitt.

Never should we underestimate the feminine power of white cotton gloves and a cosmetically colored face. I just passed my seventeenth birthday and Lloyd Anderson, a family acquaintance, has taken a romantic interest in me. He now sees me as more than the young cousin of his best friend, Tommy, who is my Uncle Eb's son. Lloyd is five years older than I am, with two years of college and three years of work experience behind him. It's my senior year of high school, and what appears to be an accomplished young man is asking me to go out with him. Lois Wilson's plan for her daughter is taking shape.

A week after my high school graduation, Lloyd is picking me up in his new light blue Ford Fairlane 500, to take me to a movie. As soon as we're seated in his impressive new car, still parked in front of my house, he drops a small box in my lap.

"We might as well get married," he said.

I open the box and put the ring on the third finger of my left hand. It is not accompanied by the words, "I love you," or "I want to spend the rest of my life with you or anything close to that. But the result is the same as if he did say those words. I'm engaged to be married, and it's a very pretty ring.

My brand new fiancé turns the key in the ignition of his brand new car and we're off to a drive-in to see a first-run movie, "Bridge on the River Kwai." The chosen site does have its romantic moments. Hey! That's what drive-in movies are for. The back seat of the new car is duly christened with heavy necking under a dark, clear, starlit June night in Seattle. All in all, it's not a bad evening to become engaged.

Movie over, Lloyd drops me off at the curb in front of my house. I let myself out of the car and walk up the porch stairs by myself. I enter the house and Lloyd drives away. Dad's bedroom is downstairs, Mom has a room upstairs. Because Dad has had two back surgeries in the past two years, he needs his own special bed. I don't want to wake him.

I climb the stairs to Mom's bedroom, wake her up and show her the ring. "Lloyd and I are engaged."

## Promise I'll Stay for Mother's Day

"When are you getting married?" she asks.

"We talked about next summer."

"Sounds good."

No need to get all excited about this. Charm School didn't teach me how to do girly giggles. It's hard to giggle when you're walking with a book on your head. And besides, I'm just following the plan. My M-R-S. degree is assured; my college degree is unnecessary.

A letter from Colorado Women's College arrives in the mail a few days after the engagement. I had applied to a number of schools. This is the top choice; this is the one we were hoping for. I open the envelope in front of Dad.

"I've been accepted at CWC," I say to him, "but I guess I won't be going."

"Why?" he asks in an astonished tone. A look of shock and disappointment spreads across his face. "Why wouldn't you go to such a school?"

"Well, I'm engaged," I reply. "We probably should save the money for the wedding."

Dad doesn't say anything for a few minutes. His head bows a little. Then, in a quiet voice, "Don't you want to go to college?"

"Well yes, but . . ."

"Then don't think about the money. We've saved so you can go."

I can't bear the crestfallen look on my dear Dad's face or the soft, subdued voice coming from it. I've just shot down a dream. "Okay then. I'll go."

Dad has the most glorious smile when he's happy. And it just flashed my way.

I'm engaged to be married *and* I'm going to college. I've accomplished quite a bit for my tender age. It says something about my maturity that an older man would choose me to be his wife. And as we all know, men want to marry an attractive woman. Score that point for the mother who successfully prepared me to do what it takes to secure myself a safe and traditional future.

So thank you, Mom, for pushing my agenda, and thank you, Dad, for getting me that year of college.

Appealing options are still limited for a woman after high school. Unmarried young women don't live by themselves, even now. I'd have had to continue to live at home with the two of you for who knows how long, if my future were not so clearly defined. The life you've laid out for me will liberate us all from the dread of uncertainty. Glad I could follow the path.

Colorado Women's College offers a curriculum of theater arts. In addition to the violin lessons, I took drama classes throughout my high school years and I had several years of voice lessons as well. I sang in the choir and jazz ensemble, and successfully auditioned for all the drama events West Seattle High School produced during my three years there. I love being on stage, especially in roles that are contrary to my quiet demeanor.

The senior play was an old fashioned melodrama. My role was that of a goofy old woman named Mrs. Yoder, who sang off key in a very loud voice, to calm her nerves. I also played the role of Gladys Hotchkiss who sang "Steam Heat" and "Hernando's Hideaway"—on key—in our "Pajama Game" Broadway show presentation. I was never the ingénue leading lady; always the character actress, which was a lot more fun. Mom went to see every performance of every concert and every play. I could count on her attendance. She got a kick out of seeing me project my out-of-character confidence in front of a crowd.

> I elect to forgo the drama at school to avoid the drama at home. It would have been a fun year, but there's no need to kick up a maelstrom for something that's going to last only a year. Home Economics it will be.

What if I were to choose my college electives from the theater arts courses? One last year of playing make believe before I settle into the real role of a real housewife would at least provide me with additional happy memories while I push that future dust mop for the thousandth time.

Well, that idea is nixed.

"Don't you think it makes more sense for you to learn the skills you will actually be using?" Mom asks, with Lloyd nodding right along. They make for a formidable duo.

I elect to forgo the drama at school to avoid the drama at home. It would have been a fun year, but there's no need to kick up a maelstrom for something that's going to last only a year. Home Economics it will be. If I had a middle name is would be Gutless. Shirleyanne Gutless Wilson. Do I still need Mom's approval that much? As long as she's paying the bills, I do. Bottom line reigns over aesthetic whims.

Lloyd checks in with the draft board lottery listing, a monthly requirement for men of draft age in 1957. His service number is about to be called. He decides to enlist so he can exercise some control over the location and assignment for his tour of duty. The United States Army has a small unit in the state of Alaska put there to protect our world-wide communications systems. They have a vehicle maintenance team there, along with the trained decoders. Since he worked in the fishing industry in Alaska during his summer school breaks, and since his civilian work is as a diesel mechanic, Lloyd joins the army and puts in his request for vehicle maintenance in Alaska.

This done my fiancé is off to boot camp at Fort Ord, California. I don't know when I'll see him again.

The end of August, Dad and Gene help me pack the car to drive me to Colorado. We'll detour through Yellowstone National Park for a bit of vacation along the way. Mom's decided to stay home for now and come see me during Parent's Weekend in October.

When it's time to go, I look for Mom and find her squatting in the back yard pulling weeds out of her vegetable garden. She doesn't get up; she nods to acknowledge my presence and keeps on pulling. She obviously doesn't want to talk. I turn to leave. Bye Mom.

When I think about it, she never really got on board with this college thing. There were a couple of summer meetings with other Seattle girls going to CWC, and their mothers. She accompanied me, but took a background role. We never planned or shopped together for a college wardrobe or school supplies.

Through work connections she opened a Sears charge account at the Cherry Creek Mall near Denver so I can get what I need when I get there. In addition, we agreed to a monthly cash stipend of $125, which she would deposit in my bank account in Seattle. I can get checks cashed from it at the school bank. While these things are nice, it would have been nicer to hear her say something like, "Yippee—my daughter's going to a prestigious college, and I'm happy for her!"

What's the deal here? I'm a little put off by her missing in action on this important part of my life.

So the enduring trio, Dad, Gene, and I, head off on a wonderful trip to Colorado. Dad is showing a very proud face when we arrive at CWC and take our first look around the beautiful campus. Fewer than a thousand students attend this seventy-year-old institution. Getting accepted here is no small accomplishment. Dad gets it.

We go to the mall to get what I need for the room—bedding, throw pillows, etc. I've corresponded over the summer with my roommate, Louise Rundlett, from El Cajon, California. We agreed I'll contribute the bedroom stuff, and she'll bring an area rug and buy the bath linens. The color scheme has been determined by the area rug, which she already has. It's a start.

It's time for Dad and Gene to leave me and finish their vacation. Gene gets to go to Arkansas with Dad to see where he was born and raised. And they're going to stop along the way to see baseball games in major league ball parks. Watching a Major League Baseball game in person is another fantasy of mine. They travel on and I stay behind. The trio becomes a duet. I stand alone.

Louise arrives the day after they leave, as do our suitemates, Cathy Turner from San Mateo, and Judy Aitken who, like me, went to West Seattle High School. I didn't know her there, but I met her at the summer meetings. I think we make a good foursome. We're smilers, not gigglers. We're pretty smart, too. Can I say that? Conversations have a little substance. Louise is in political science, Cathy is liberal arts, Judy is our journalist, and I'm Miss Home Economics. There are two careers in there I never thought of, but a career was not part of my plan so that's not surprising. Cathy is engaged to a boy back home who's attending San Jose State. I put Lloyd's picture on the small table next to my bed and settle in.

October comes quickly. My birthday coincides with Parent's Weekend. Mom has arrived. When the round of scheduled activities is over, we decide to spend an afternoon at the Denver City Park. It's a beautiful, sunny October day.

We sit down to eat our lunch in a picnic area where we can watch swans glide gracefully across the lake. Suddenly one swan leaps out of the lake and comes running toward me, squawking and flapping its wings. It's a scary looking thing and it's coming after me. Without thinking, I throw part of my sandwich at it. Fortunately it was the right thing to do, at least for our safety's sake. The swan grabs it in his beak and heads back to the water. Swans are lovely and serene in the water, but awkward and not so even tempered out of their accustomed arena. There's a bit of the swan in all of us, I think.

Mom and I are struggling a little, to find a conversation.

I don't remember spending a quiet afternoon in a park with her while I was growing up. I'm wondering if she's not remembering too. Today I am eighteen years old and grown up, living in Denver Colorado, twelve hundred miles away from her. This time next year I'll be married and living away from her in Alaska. Did her daughter grow up too soon? Does my Mom wonder where the time went, and is she wishing we'd spent more time together? She's awfully quiet today. Like I said, I don't remember ever having quiet times with my Mom. It's different and puzzling, but it's kind of nice.

CHAPTER 12

## *The Arranged Marriage Begins*

How is it that I am sashaying my way into marriage without having experienced any kind of life on my own, and without so much as one serious thought as to what I'm getting myself into?

The most obvious answer to this sensible question is that young women don't burden themselves with serious thought in 1958. The brainless 1950s isn't exactly a decade of personal growth in our country. We're still living off the prosperity of waging and winning a war and feeling that nothing in our lives will ever change or challenge us again. It's intellectual down time, and marriage is the biggest no-brainer of all. No one questions the wisdom of teenage brides in 1958.

The only person who seems to be thinking at all is Mom, and she's thinking that my getting married is the right thing to do. In her mind, eighteen is not too young for a young woman to get married, especially a young woman who has spent a full year away from home, living on her own. What she's not thinking is that I was not living on my own. I was living under the protection of a dorm mother and campus rules.

At a traditional women's college in 1957 we are told what to wear to dinner every night—no jeans, no pedal pushers, and no skirts and sweaters unless they match in color and design. We're dressed like that because we are served sit-down meals on white table cloths with cloth napkins set up by college hired help. There are no jeans in the classroom either, and no leaving the campus unless we are properly attired in feminine formality. We sign out at the front office in the presence of the Dorm Mother just to walk to the corner drug store ... in a skirt ... with hair properly combed and face made up to greet the public at large. I may have roomed away from home, but I have not lived one full day on my own without adult care and supervision. My age eighteen is a far cry from Mom's age eighteen. I am *not* ready for marriage. How do I stop this parade down the aisle? I don't. It's too late.

There is an upside to this trudge toward the altar. It has brought about

## The Arranged Marriage Begins

*Tom, Lois, Shirleyanne wedding August 1958.*

a time of change in my relationship with my Mom. Leading up to this trek, we're spending the summer laughing and teasing each other, behaving like I've always imagined girl friends interact. It's something I never actually experienced first hand until now. We dress up and eat lunch together away from home a couple of times a week during our shopping forays, sampling the life of quiches and freshly tossed salads.

Like meowing cats we look around while we eat and compare ourselves favorably to the appearances of other women . . . "I can't believe she's wearing *that!*" And like alley cats on the prowl we flirt outrageously with cute young men who wait on us and react with giddy self-satisfied smugness at their smiling responses. We look G-o-o-d!

I didn't have close girl friends in high school, and I really got to know only my suitemates at college. And since we were not a silly foursome, this girly, giggly thing is new to me and definitely new to my relationship with Mom. No more the critical eye directed toward me or comments as to my posture or

## Promise I'll Stay for Mother's Day

personality. This is not the Mom I grew up with. And I am absolutely delighted with my new Mom.

To add to the fun, we have that wedding thing coming up. We're addressing invitations, selecting flowers, looking for a photographer, and ordering the cake. I acquiesced to her favorite color for the flowers and the bride's maids' dresses. Pink it is. There'll be two attendants for me; Cathy, my CWC Suitemate, and Connie, my cousin, Tommy's wife. They will wear pink.

Mom makes sure the gift registry is complete. "Don't forget to put down a waffle iron, Shirleyanne, and a bed spread. You'll need a new bedspread."

We've also been going to church together every Sunday, just the two of us. It's been at least a decade since that last happened. The pastor, Reverend Holmes, is an excellent speaker who offers his parishioners a thoughtful and calming harbor from the world outside. Mom is as relaxed as I've ever seen her.

She seems eager to be with me, and with Dad and Gene too. She hurries home from work to fix dinner so the four of us can sit down to the table together. And we all get to talk. Gone is the overbearing career woman. We get to experience the smiling soft 1woman I always imagined Dad fell in love with, and I get to have the mother and daughter experiences I'd missed before this lovely, warm summer came along.

I can't help but wonder what brought about this difference, but I can't just walk up to her and say, "Hey Mom, how come you like to be with us now? What makes you so relaxed and content this summer?"

Is it because she sees the end of the road to my upbringing? Is it because she's satisfied with the result? Very soon I'll be marrying the man she chose for me. From her point of view my happily-ever-after life is about to begin. After protecting and controlling my environment for eighteen and a half years she can relax now and watch me enjoy the fruits of her labors. As recently as a year ago, she didn't know if the ring would be enough to keep me on the course she'd laid out for me. What if I'd decided to take those drama classes? What if I had met a young man she didn't know and what if he lived far away? Or worse, what if he had rejected me and broken my heart, and I missed my chance to marry the good man she's chosen for me? Maybe she was worried about the choices I might have made on my own.

If all my conjecture is true, there was no need for her to worry. I never questioned my obedient return home from college, and very soon I'll be marrying a man who will take care of me in her place. After a period of uncertainty, my Mom is in control again.

## The Arranged Marriage Begins

Now I'm on the verge of being unfair. I need to embrace what's happening between us right now. And besides, what if she really does enjoy my company? Maybe I'm the one who's changed. Maybe I *have* grown up, and maybe she really *is* proud of me.

"Here comes the bride . . . dum, dum de dum . . . "

I'm walking down the aisle on my father's arm toward the person standing in front of the altar. That person is about to become my husband. He arrived from Alaska two days ago. Today is August 9th, and I haven't seen my fiancé since Christmas break. We've spoken on the phone maybe three or four times since then. Not a lot of contact with the person who, in ten minutes will be my husband. Is the man standing at the end of the aisle going to be a husband like my Dad? If he is, and if I *have* grown up, this could be a good day.

> In two days this man and I will be leaving for Alaska to set up housekeeping in a small cabin in the woods that has no electricity or running water. What the hell am I doing?

We're nearing Mom sitting in the first pew on our left. She's wearing the light green dress I made for her from the brocade Hazel sent us from Okinawa, where she lives with her husband, Don. I made my dress too, in Colorado. It was my home economics elective sewing project. Made of ivory brocade, it features a sweetheart neckline, short cap sleeves, and bubble skirt with the front gathered at my knees by a large flat bow pulling it all together. Wearing it, I was the star of the sewing class fashion show at the end of the semester. Someone told me its bad luck to make one's own wedding dress.

Well that's just too bad. I'm wearing the dress I made and I'm the star of the family wedding pageant at the end of the summer of 1958.

"Dum-dum-de-dum-dum . . . "

Mom smiles at me. It was within the security of marriage that she got to chase her rainbows. Her husband loves watching her soar in pursuit of her dreams. I think my husband-to-be will prefer to have his wife live a little closer to the ground. Well, we'll see, won't we?

The aisle is getting shorter. I'm almost there. Husband-to-be is about to become husband-for-real. The vows begin.

"Do you, Shirleyanne, take this man . . . " Oh, I guess so.

In two days this man and I will be leaving for Alaska to set up housekeeping in a small cabin in the woods that has no electricity or running water. I'm moving from a luxurious dorm at an exclusive women's college in Denver, Colorado, to a small cabin without modern conveniences in Tok Junction, Alaska. What the hell am I doing?

## Promise I'll Stay for Mother's Day

"I now pronounce you man and wife . . ."

So here we are at Mile 1313 on the Alcan Highway in Tok Junction, site of the U.S. customs office you pass through to enter the Territory of Alaska. Traveling the Alcan on our honeymoon to get here was a special treat.

Yes, we walked around Lake Louise in Banff, British Columbia, and it was beautiful. We also spent one night in a broom closet—not kidding—in White Horse, B.C. No other rooms were available, and there was no way we could travel safely at night on the long dirt road the Canadians like to call a highway.

Compared to our accommodations in White Horse, the cabin we will call home for the next year is quite nice. Even *not* compared to the broom closet, it's nice. It sits in a lovely spot surrounded by large, beautiful trees. It has a good-sized living room with a floor furnace, dining ell, kitchen, and one bedroom. Of course, one room and a couple of utilities are missing.

No bathroom, no water, no electricity, and no problem. I'm not unprepared for this pioneering gig. No one spared me the gritty details about the physical demands I would be facing in the frozen tundra. My fiancé and both sets of parents fully preached this truth into my head. They were certain the absence of 20th century conveniences would be a major adjustment for their sheltered little bride-to-be.

They misjudged the effects of my early years. I lived in a two-room shack long enough to remember it. I saw my Mom use a wash board in the bath tub rather than a washing machine, and I recall the use of kerosene lamps instead of light bulbs. A cabin in the woods is not going to be a problem for me. I expected this and I am prepared to use the honey bucket.

As it turns out, what I'm not prepared for is marriage. Living with a husband is not the same as living with a father. Fathers give their daughters smiles and twinkling eyes and nods of approval. Fathers raise their sons to become men and their daughters to be cared for by their men. At least that was what the father did in my home. Neither my Mom nor my Dad expected me to follow in my Mom's footsteps. They raised me to be cared for. I've learned how to cook and sew and manage household routines. I can do women's work. But because Mom worked outside our home, the home caring part came from Dad. He noticed my moods. He offered his ears for conversation and his arms for comfort. I didn't expect to lose what Dad gave me. I'm not prepared for this shift from daughter to wife.

Rather than being here when I need him, my husband is here when he needs me. My wifely role is to make my husband's life wonderful, even if my husband is not around to experience the wonderfulness. Sometimes my

## The Arranged Marriage Begins

husband is here to eat and sleep and drive me to the General Store. And sometimes occurs sometime between work at work, work at home, and play time with his male friends. This wife is lucky if she finds herself in third or fourth position on her husband's list of priorities.

And speaking of positions, another fact not fully explained prior to the taking of the vows, is that sex changes too. Not that I'd had sexual experience before marriage; a little petting, but no going all the way. The Pill was a few years away, and Lloyd's sister had a "hurry up" wedding. My new mother-in-law told me she nearly took a gun to herself because of that marriage. I learned later from other sources it was because the groom was Catholic, not because of the shotgun wedding. But still, their hasty wedding made it even more imperative that Lloyd and I have no slip ups on our way to virginal wedded bliss.

But I've heard about sexy romps and lingering in bed in the morning for a turn in the sheets. In fact, we had a few of those moments at first, but alas. A few months after a trip to the altar, when the newness of lawful sex wears off, this eager and hungry animal I imagined I fell in love with and married with wanton anticipation will now get naked only in the bedroom, and under the covers. A kitchen encounter all of a sudden becomes an embarrassment. What a disappointment!

Whatever happened to the man who once faced a policeman's flash light in the back seat of a Ford Fairlane 500 at a drive in movie? Gone forever, it seems, to the stigma of the marriage bed. It's been said that women turn away from sex after marriage. Not from my experience. And not from the experience of most of the women I know. I checked out my disappointment, to make sure I'm not alone in the lust lost department. The results of my little survey indicate that many men leave their fiery lust and sexual imagination at the altar. Sanctioned sex is just not that exciting to them.

After a time, the routine of marital intercourse leaves their wives sexually bored and frustrated as well. That's when garden clubs begin to replace garden sex, and ice maiden house flowers cease to bloom. I ask my husband what's changed.

He looks puzzled. "You're my wife now," he says.

There are other changes. Before marriage we enjoyed doing things together. We went for rides just to be alone in a car together, we went to see movies and we occasionally got dressed up and went out to dinner. My sweetheart seemed to like being with me. It wasn't the most exciting courtship that ever occurred, still I was his most frequent companion while we were courting. The new wife and the husband don't do fun things together. My husband ignores me. I ask my husband what's changed.

## Promise I'll Stay for Mother's Day

He looks puzzled. "You're my wife now," he says.

"What is that supposed to mean?" I roar after about the hundredth time I hear that lame response. Miss nice-nice is tiring of his one-sentence, uninformative responses to what I believe are legitimate questions.

"Well, when it comes time to take a wife, men do the things we have to do, to get a wife. Then, when we get married, we go back to doing the things we want to do."

My husband explains this to me as if it were a genetic given that I should have known. Husbands and wives behave differently from single men and women. Everyone knows that. From his frame of reference, "You're my wife now", explains everything.

So now we get down to what we should have noticed before we got married, but didn't. His responses to the questions I ask reflect his upbringing, not mine. The answer to the question in my mind as I walked down the aisle— "Will my husband be like my Dad?"—is no, he won't. Would I have married him anyway? Probably. The dye had been cast.

Our backgrounds may have appeared to be the same, family and all, but they were not. Inside the home of my upbringing, the woman was the center piece. Her marriage was the catalyst for a more satisfying life. The man was an active participant in the running of the house and the raising of the kids. This is what I expected to have. This is what Mom expected me to have. Even in her attempt to recapture tradition, it seems our home stood about forty years ahead of its time.

In Lloyd's boyhood home, women disappeared from the living room as soon as they married. They retreated to the kitchen, to the garden and to the do-gooder clubs with other women. Conversations with men ceased forever after the "I do's." It was I do this and you do that, and we'll catch up with each other at the dinner table should you choose to come home from work in time for dinner.

Neither Lloyd nor I are happy, and neither of us understands why. We blame it on living in the wilds of Alaska. We rationalize our marital disappointment as being due to an unfortunately tough beginning to a marriage that will work itself out as soon as we return to the civilized world. I hope we're right. I don't know what we'll do if we're not. Marriage is for life. No family differences there.

After a year of living the experience of Alaska, I leave before Lloyd finishes his army obligation, to stay with my family and go to secretarial school. There are three months left on his tour. I'll finish school about the same time his tour

## The Arranged Marriage Begins

of duty is over. I'll be busy and he'll be home before we have time to consider this a separation. Lloyd and I both want to have a home and be financially well situated before we start a family. The kind of start we have in mind will require a two-person household income. My husband is not so traditional that he doesn't want his wife to bring in a paycheck.

Lloyd is hired back at Marine Power & Equipment Co., the same firm he was with when he enlisted. I've done well in my secretarial classes and the school is sending me out on their best job leads. I'm hired by a radio station, owned by Gene Autry, the singing cowboy. Together Lloyd and I are making enough money to buy a new, three-bedroom house. New, three-bedroom houses in 1960, cost $11,700. Our house payments are $78.50 a month. Between the two of us we are making $1,298.55 a month. Take home pay is about $900.00. Economically, our marriage is off to a great second year!

> I am rewarded with lunches at nice restaurants, presents, and "You're wonderful" ... and ... "Great job!" compliments, none of which occur at home. I definitely prefer life as the Traffic Manager in the radio station to life as the wife at home.

Personally, I'm off to a favorable career position. Mr. Autry's Golden West Broadcast Company is putting up enough money to make KVI/AM a well-run, highly visible radio property. The format is called "personality radio", which means a mixture of music, news, and disc jockeys that people like to talk about. It's top of mind in the city of Seattle. People are excited about working at this radio station, and I'm having a great time being part of the growth of this new company.

Being a secretary is all right for a start, but it's becoming kind of boring. I'm not crazy about sharpening pencils and pouring coffee for the male employees, or changing typewriter ribbons, or getting my hands blackened on carbon paper. My boss prefers a Dictaphone to actual dictation so the hours I spent learning Gregg's Shorthand were a waste. But I'll survive the absence of that pseudo alphabet. It's the "yes sir" mentality that kind of bugs me. I don't know why.

As soon as there is an opening in the Traffic Department, I apply for it and get it. When I do my new job well, the salesmen make more money, so I do my best to find room for all the commercials they sell. And for doing that, I am rewarded with lunches at nice restaurants, presents, and "You're wonderful" ... and ... "Great job!" compliments, none of which occur at home. I definitely prefer life as the Traffic Manager in the radio station to life as the wife at home.

## Promise I'll Stay for Mother's Day

Uh-oh! A bit of Déjà vu is hovering. Have I already lived this life, or did I watch someone else living this life in the house where I grew up? I never wanted to be like her... no, no, NO!

I thought I would prefer the haven of a warm home wearing pedal pushers, driving suburban roads to garden clubs and PTAs to the daily strife of getting myself out of bed, dressing for success and driving to work maneuvering the urban highways. But I'm beginning to understand my Mom's enthusiasm for professional challenges. The emotional rewards of a mind-bending job well done are more easily measured than the mundane chores of washing clothes, cooking dinner, and cleaning floors. I'm sorry folks, but getting to put down the dish cloth at the end of the day to watch night time TV can't compete with having lunch in the mink booth at the El Gaucho. It's not even close.

This situation is not what I expected, and certainly not what I thought I wanted, but the marriage and career thing might work out. Like Mom's husband, my husband is glad I'm working. Unlike Mom's husband my husband does not vacuum or fix dinner—ever. But I'm getting enough satisfaction outside the marriage to want to keep the marriage going.

Lloyd is freed from my probing questions about the meaning of life and whining about wanting us to spend more time together. And I'm freed from having to ask the big life questions and resenting the insulting little answers. There's nothing wrong with accepting this dearth of conversational exchanges. There's a certain satisfaction in finally understanding how our version of marriage is going to work.

We're adults. Our take on this thing we call marriage will survive emotional distance.

CHAPTER 13

## *We Lose Dad*

WHY IS IT IMPOSSIBLE TO KEEP our contentment tucked away in a comfortable, safe place, forever sheltering us from the cruel realities of the outside world? I have no answer for that. It's a stupid question.

Dad is sick. He's in the hospital undergoing a series of tests and I'm scared. I had a dream a few weeks ago that put me in front of a casket. When I walked up to the casket and looked inside I saw my Dad lying there, stone cold still, his eyes closed. There were no glasses on his nose. He didn't need them. He couldn't see.

I kept the dream to myself. I'm more frightened now than I was when I heard nothing but his silence following Mom's threat of divorce. Threats are temporary and they can be worked out. Caskets are forever. There's no negotiating with death.

Dad hasn't felt good for a long time. The doctors are having a difficult time finding out what's wrong. They think his arteries are clogged. Or it could be an aneurysm, they say. That's a weakening in the arterial walls that forms a sort of bubble. That kind of thing can burst, and life is over in an instant. They're going to squirt dye into his arteries to find out if he has an aneurysm. I don't want to hear your eternal silence, Dad. Please get well.

A few days later I'm sitting in my office at work trying to focus, but it's hard. Mom's at the hospital and I'm waiting to hear from her. Whatever would we do without our sweet, quiet Dad to balance the noise of the rest of our world? The dream just can't happen. I'm lost in dread when the phone rings. It's Mom.

"Well, they found what they were looking for, Shirleyanne. The tests show a blockage in his main artery, the aorta, but they can fix it. It shouldn't be a problem, they say. Surgery is scheduled for next Tuesday to clear it up. It's called open heart surgery. I'm going to see if I can watch it."

I put down the receiver and breathe a sigh of relief. The doctors say they can fix what's wrong with our Dad. He's going to be fine. The dream can go

## Promise I'll Stay for Mother's Day

*Left, Gene in Air Force 1961; Dad before he left us.*

away now. It was just a night-time mirror of my day-time concern for his health. The fact that Mom said she wanted to watch the surgery just whizzed right by my stream of consciousness. Who in God's name wants to watch heart surgery performed on her husband? Who else?

We're calling Gene home from the Far East. After one year at the University of Washington, he dropped out and enlisted in the Air Force. His first choice was to get into the Air Force Academy, and even though he scored high on their tests and applied with signature backing from the two Washington State Senators, Warren G. Magnuson and Henry "Scoop" Jackson, his splattered pupil made the appointment impossible. Air Force cadets have to have perfect vision, so there will be no Academy for Gene. But he loves air planes, and he was determined to make them a part of his life work.

When Gene spoke with the Air Force enlistment officers he asked about their Special Forces Division. He was interested in their language training programs, hoping to be sent to Germany where he could buy a Porsche and have it shipped home when his tour of duty ended. Second to airplanes, Gene likes fast cars. He took their language aptitude tests and again scored high. But he didn't get Germany. The Air Force sent him to Yale University to learn Chinese. He was one of five recruits selected for the Chinese program.

## We Lose Dad

Following the language training at Yale, all five were sent to survival training in the mountains of Nevada, and then to the Far East.

We don't know where Gene is or what he's doing. We suspect he's in an airplane somewhere, listening to the Chinese talk and translating what they say. The Red Cross will have to find him for us.

Not only will Mom watch Dad's surgery, a whole crew of doctors will watch it as well. It's a new procedure they call a by-pass. A camera crew will be there too. They're making an instructional film for the University of Washington Medical School. It's quite a production. Did we really think Lois Wilson would allow her husband to undergo a new experimental surgery without fanfare?

The surgery is supposed to last about six hours. Mom's in there watching it. Gene arrived home yesterday. He and I are in the family waiting room. I ask him where he's been and what he's been doing. He's noncommittal. Mom enters the room and walks up to us after only three hours.

"It's all over," she says. "It went well. You might as well go back to work, Shirleyanne. He'll be asleep for a long time."

I'm not buying it. Something's up. The dream is lurking. But I go back to work because there is nothing else I can do.

A few days later, Dad is still in the hospital and seems to be all right. My concerns apparently were unfounded. I'm at work, not even thinking about him when the phone rings. It's Dad.

"I know what's wrong with me," he says. "I have cancer." That's all he said.

"I'll be right there," I hear myself say. I wonder what happened to "It went well."

I walk into his hospital room, sit down beside his bed, and wait for him to speak.

"Orderly told me," he says.

"An orderly told you?" I ask. "Why would an orderly tell you something like that?"

"He thought I already knew."

"How do you know he's right?"

"I called Doc Jacobs. He said he was just coming over to tell me himself."

I feel motion across the room and look up. Mom has been standing near the door. She nods. Dr. Jacobs is right behind her.

"Don't worry, Tom," he says. "You'll outlive me. We'll start cobalt treatments in a couple of weeks, after you've had a chance to rest up from the surgery."

They found the cancer when they opened him up. That's why it was over so quick. They planned to tell him later today. Then I assume they'd have

## Promise I'll Stay for Mother's Day

told Gene and me. It's April 7, 1961. Dad is fifty-four years old. I'm twenty-one. That's too young for him to leave me and too young for me to lose him. But they said they'd treat him. They wouldn't be treating him if he were already lost.

Gene is sent back to Okinawa. At least we found out where he's stationed. There was no need for him to stay here. Nothing is going to happen soon. That's the good news. The other good news is that Dad gets to go home from the hospital.

The not so good news is that the cobalt treatments are making Dad sick. He's losing a lot of weight, weight he can't afford to lose. He's always been slight of build. He hasn't got as much to lose as most people. Mom and I take turns driving him to the hospital for his three-times-a-week treatments. We take him to the hospital so they can fill him with poison, then we take him home so he can rest and puke, so we can take him back to the hospital so he can go home again and puke some more. It seems insane.

He finally gets so sick he has to go back to the hospital for blood transfusions to get his strength back. One Friday night, mid July, I walk into his room and see him reading the newspaper upside down. I realize he's putting up a front, faking his daily routine. I don't know if the façade is for me or for him.

He puts the newspaper down and looks at me. "I'll be bug dust soon," he says.

I make no reply. We've chosen not to discuss the possible finality of his illness. Mom walks in. She doesn't look her usual dressed-for-success self. Dad looks at her with a frown.

"You spending so much time up here looking after me you forgot to look at yourself?" he asks.

"Oh, I'm a little tired today. Work is busy. I'll dress up tomorrow," she says.

"Don't come up here if you're tired. Don't be letting yourself go to take care of me. I'll be okay," he says.

Dad doesn't tell her he'll be bug dust. I realize for the first time how much he protects her, how much he loves and worships her. I also realize that I have a special place with him too. She's his fantasy; I'm his reality.

The last week of July, Dr. Jacobs tells us he will be ordering morphine soon, to cover Dad's pain. "You might want to begin the procedures to get Gene home," he says.

Oh God. It's happening too fast.

Gene arrives August 2. August 4, the four of us are together in Dad's room. Dad is lying down, his head is on the pillow, his eyes are closed. He feels our

## We Lose Dad

movement and he opens his eyes and smiles. He takes us on a little journey.

"Let's stop at this motel, Ma, and see what it looks like inside." His eyelids flutter shut. We wait for him to continue.

A few moments later, he opens his eyes again, looks at Mom, and smiles again. "Look Ma, it has a pink room. Let's stay here."

We're smiling with him now. Pink is Mom's favorite color. Her houses always have at least one pink room. When we took our summer road trips in real life, Dad would walk up to the motel registration desk and say, "Got a pink room? Ma likes to sleep in a pink room."

I don't remember there ever being a roadside pink room, but he'd always ask, and we'd always laugh. It doesn't take much for us to laugh. We're guffawing at our latest pink room encounter when a nurse walks in and dusts us off with a cool, disapproving look. Laughing out loud in the room of a dying man is not considered acceptable behavior. But for us, a little reminiscent trip to California looking for Ma's pink room seems a better way to remember Dad's final days than standing around, wringing our hands in somber silence. We're not hanging any crepe in here.

> Pink is Mom's favorite color. Her houses always have at least one pink room. When we took our summer road trips in real life, Dad would walk up to the motel registration desk and say, "Got a pink room? Ma likes to sleep in a pink room."

It's Saturday morning, August 5. We've just been told that Dr. Jacobs died last night from a massive heart attack. He's kept his promise to Dad. Dad is on his own now.

I see a new determination in Dad's face. Not a determination to live, but a resolve to end living, in a semblance of dignity. How many days on morphine?

When visiting hours are over, the three of us leave the room together, leaving Dad behind. Mom stops at the nurse's station. She asks the nurse to see that she is called when the new shift comes on tomorrow. This done, she turns to me.

"I'll call you at 8:30 tomorrow morning," she says.

I get my 8:30 wake up call. "He's gone, Shirleyanne." That's all she says.

She knew when we left him last night he would be gone this morning. I'm numb. He died alone. Is that okay?

Lloyd drops me off at Mom's house and goes to work in the pits of the hydroplane races on Lake Washington. Today is race day and he's part of the crew. He's a busy man.

Mom and I have been going to church on a fairly regular basis for the past few years. It started the summer I got married. It's not a family thing, and I'm not sure it's even a religious thing. The truth is I don't know what kind of thing it is. Mom has studied religions all her life, and she's read the Bible several times. But we've never discussed God or religion. We go to church, we listen to the sermon, we go home, and we go about our business.

"We should call Reverend Holmes and ask him if he will do the service," she says.

"That's a good idea," I say.

I'm struck by how few words we are exchanging, and have exchanged since this chapter of our lives began. I guess that's good. Our family has never been what we call "loquacious." That's our word for too many words. In fact, we kind of smile at each other when we're in the presence of others who go on and on about matters we leave unsaid. We know what we're thinking and we move forward with what we know. It doesn't work for everyone, but it works for us.

Mom and I attend the Presbyterian Church where Reverend Holmes is the pastor. We continue to go there because we like him and his sermons. No Hell, Fire and Brimstone, just quiet, thoughtful messages that we can take home with us and consider in our life choices. He'll do well by Dad, even though Dad doesn't—or didn't—go to church. I wonder if that matters.

"Where is Dad?" I ask. This is all so strange.

"Oh," she says. "I told the nurse last night to call Howden and Kennedy Funeral Home. He's there now. They're fixing him up. We can go see him later."

She picks up the phone and dials. "Reverend Holmes, this is Mrs. Wilson . . . well, actually he passed away this morning. My daughter and I would like for you to conduct the service . . . 3:00 today? Yes, that would be fine . . . our address is . . . " She hangs up. "He's coming to the house at 3:00 . . . after lunch . . . after the church services. We probably should go to church, but I don't feel like leaving the house . . . "

"It's okay Mom. Where's Gene?"

"Upstairs."

We haven't cried yet. Or at least I haven't. Mom's face shows no trace of having cried either. Is that odd? I don't know how we're supposed to act. I'm glad Dad's not sick any more. And we were prepared for this. We knew when Dr. Jacobs said it was time for Gene to come home. We knew when Dr. Jacobs died. We knew it was close. We're ready to take care of this. We're ready to accept this.

"What about after the funeral, Mom?"

"We both have plots," she says. They're next to each other at Forest Lawn. I've ordered a marble urn to be put between us, one that will hold fresh flowers.

## We Lose Dad

And I've arranged for a head stone that has a carving of Mt. Rainier on it. He loved to see that mountain. You can see it from the site where he'll be."

Wow! I guess she really *is* prepared for this. I had no idea.

"I don't remember meeting Mr. Wilson," Reverend Holmes says. "Did he go to church?"

"No," Mom answers. "But he supported our going to church. He was just a home body, especially the last few years. He's not been well."

"Was he a good man?" asks the Reverend.

"Oh yes, a very good man . . . a wonderful husband and father," Mom says quietly.

"I'd be happy to conduct the service, if I can," he says. Have you scheduled it?"

"Tuesday afternoon, 2:00. We need to give our relatives time to get here from Oregon."

"Is there anything you'd like for me to say . . . any scripture you particularly like?"

"The 23rd Psalm and the Lord's prayer. Here's his biography. Mention the kids. Then do whatever you think is appropriate."

"Is there anything I can do for you, Mrs. Wilson, before Tuesday?"

"No, I'll be fine. Thank you."

Of course she'll be fine. She's always fine. Reverend Holmes leaves.

"Shall we go see him now?" Mom asks.

"Okay. What about Gene. Is he coming with us?"

"No, I asked him. He said we can handle it."

What a strange day we're having.

Dad doesn't look natural. Too much make up. I ask Mom to ask them to wipe some of it off. His face shows no pain and there is no more need for pretense. Dad was very sick and he died. I guess that's why you go see dead people; to experience their peace. And to know they are really gone.

This is my first experience with death, so I have nothing to compare it to. The body I'm looking at is not breathing. The body is absolutely still. I call it the body because there is nothing of my Dad in this room. He's gone from us.

Even so, I don't believe you, Dad. You're not bug dust. You're not here, but you're somewhere. I just don't know where.

*Lois, Shirleyanne and Rebecca, Mother's Day, 1963.*

CHAPTER 14

## *A New Generation Arrives*

LLOYD AND I HAD NOT PLANNED to have children for several years. My secret plan is to not have any at all. Working at the radio station is way too much fun. But, what's the phrase? Even the best laid plans... Damn!

Mom has no immediate comment when I tell her she is to be a grandmother. It takes her several weeks to get used to the idea. She has the ability to hold off judgment until she figures out what she can change or fix, and what she can't. She decides she cannot change or fix her becoming a grandmother, so hang on to the reins all ye who know us, the arrival of the first baby since Jesus is less than nine months away!

"I'll be called Ol' Granny," she says, and the word is spread all over the land.

My pregnancy is healthy and uneventful, filled with an emotional mixture of curiosity and dread. I work into the ninth month then leave the workplace to prepare for the birth of our child. I know absolutely nothing about babies and it's nothing I care to know about. But there are no options. I'll have the baby and stay home to take care of it. That's it. Work is over; family life begins.

I'm a week past my due date, not feeling so good. Mom's on the phone from SeaTac Airport. She's been in Hawaii with some gal pals for the past ten days. She told me to wait until she gets back to Seattle before I give birth to her grand child. I did what I was told, and she's back now. Can we get on with welcoming our new life?

"It's time for me to be a granny", she says. "How're you feeling?"

"Nothing's happening," I respond. "I've been having some lower back cramping since I woke up. It's uncomfortable, but no pains or anything."

"Shirleyanne, you're in pre-labor. Call Lloyd."

"It's 10:15. He doesn't like to be disturbed at work. I'll call him during his lunch hour."

"I'm coming to get you. Call your doctor," says granny-to-be.

My Doctor tells me to go to the hospital. Mom is on her way to take me there; Lloyd will stop by on his way home from work. No need for any silly

## Promise I'll Stay for Mother's Day

cartoon scene with the expectant dad rushing around acting like an idiot because his baby's on its way. This dad-to-be knows that the labor thing takes a while. It's another one of those no-need-to-get-all-excited-about-life routines. Kind of like dropping a diamond ring in my lap in the front seat of a car.

This is taking more than a while. It's Friday night and I've been here in the hospital since yesterday about noon. I'm still having contractions but they're not awful. I can't seem to get them to come any harder or move them closer than five minutes apart. Lloyd's been stopping by on his way to and from work. He's getting irritated that the baby's arrival seems to have stalled.

"This is costing me money," he says. "Can't you wait it out at home?"

Now it's Saturday morning. A few minutes ago Dr. Siverling noticed a break in the baby's heart rhythm at the mid point of each one-minute contraction. He's frowning and he's ordering a placenta-gram to see what's caused this change.

In the placenta-gram room, everyone is frowning. Something's up, and it's not good.

"The baby's umbilical cord is restricting the delivery," Dr. Siverling explains. "It's wrapped around the baby's neck and pulling back when the baby pushes down. That's why there's been no progress. The baby is constrained and could be in peril. It's time to bring this baby into the world. We're going to do a Section."

A section means Caesarean delivery. But where's the baby's father? The hospital doesn't want to do a C Section without his permission. Mom's here, but Lloyd is not. She's getting anxious, meaning cranky. I'm oblivious to what's happening. Tired, I guess, or I'm dropping my convenient mind veil to forestall panic.

"Where is he, Shirleyanne?"

"I don't know. I thought he'd be here by now." It's noon.

"Can't you call him? Why doesn't someone call him?"

"We've tried, several times," the nurse says. "No answer."

Finally, it's determined the baby's life depends on an immediate C Section. The hospital gives permission to proceed and I am prepped for surgery.

At 2:30 PM, as I'm being wheeled out of my room into the delivery room across the hall, the baby's father walks up. He's been browsing through junk yards, looking for parts for the large diesel engine for a boat that's housed in the extra bedroom of our three-bedroom home. He's repairing it for a friend. We don't have a garage, just a carport, so it's not safe to leave the engine outside. Since we have the extra bedroom, we might as well use it for something useful. I say that facetiously, of course.

## A New Generation Arrives

Lloyd is briefed on the situation and he nods. Lord Lloyd has nodded and I'm wheeled into the room where our baby will be born.

I thought I'd be asleep by now. I am *so* ready to embrace the escape of sleep, but I'm not even drowsy. The sleep doctor gave me what he called "a saddle" anesthetic. I hope it will take effect soon. The delivery doctors are chatting as they approach my delivery table, or whatever they call this hard as a rock thing I'm lying on.

"What side do you like to work from, Bob?"

"Left side's fine. I had a great golf outing yesterday." They move to their surgery positions, one on each side of the table.

*Excuse me. Hello! I'm having a baby. I'm having surgery. When do I get to fall asleep?*

Turn's out, my sleeping is not on the agenda, so I wait and listen, unable to move from the waist down. The saddle is working. There's no feeling down there where the baby is.

"You have a baby girl."

They rush her to a table against the wall. She's not crying. I thought babies cry when they are born. Uh-oh.

"WAAAA!" There she goes. Whew! I fall asleep.

When I wake up, Mom is by my bedside, grinning from ear to ear.

"Have you seen her, Mom? What does she look like?

"Prettiest one in there," she says. "She's got curly red hair. I bet Millard (Lloyd's Dad) ten bucks I'd get me a little red-headed girl."

Lloyd's not here. He had to get back to the diesel engine.

It's time to feed the baby, so Mom has to leave the room. In 1963 they only bring babies to the room when the baby's mother is by herself. Fear of germs. The nurse places Rebecca—that's what we pre-named her—in my arms, expecting me to begin my mothering. I look at the baby in my arms, then at the nurse standing beside my bed expecting me to do something.

"What do I do with her?" I ask. "I've never held a baby before."

The nurse frowns, pinches the baby's cheeks, jams a bottle into her mouth and struts out of the room, leaving this new mother to figure out the rest on her own. Mothers are supposed to know what to do with their new bundles of joy. It must be one of those genetic things we're supposed to have. I must be missing the Mother gene. I better get this figured out.

"Come on little one, I need your help. Suck." She opens her eyes, squints at me and does exactly what her mother tells her to do. We're going to get along just fine.

## Promise I'll Stay for Mother's Day

When Rebecca finishes her nourishment the nurse takes her back into the nursery and Mom comes into my room. "I can't wait to get my hands on her!"

Lloyd stops by Sunday morning about eleven.

"Have you seen her?" I ask.

"Yeah. If she'd been a boy, I'd have brought you flowers."

I can't comment on that. What can I possibly say that would do justice to such a stupid remark?

CHAPTER 15

## *The Arranged Marriage Ends*

STAYING AT HOME with a new baby is a bigger adjustment than I anticipated. When Lloyd and I were both working away from home I didn't mind his long hours at work or his weekends doing men things like hunting and car racing. It left me with time for doing women things, like shopping and vacuuming. We didn't need companionship from each other when we both had professions in the outside world.

A man doesn't change his busy life when a baby arrives. A woman does. A woman changes from putting on beautiful clothes to swishing dirty diapers. A woman changes from adult dialogue to seven days a week of baby babbling. Delightful as it is, it's not enough. When a baby arrives, a woman needs her husband more than ever. But my husband doesn't feel a need to change his preferred routines. And I've not yet learned the art of cajoling to get what I want. With no husband around to fill the void in my adult world, life becomes, shall we say, less than challenging. I decide it is I who must change.

I join a Garden Club and a Federated Women's Club. I earn blue ribbons for flower arranging and work on community do-gooder projects for a feeling of personal accomplishment. With Rebecca straddled onto my left hip and later, toddling along beside me, I am a very busy woman. Shannon, our second little package from heaven, arrives three years after Rebecca. She is included in our busy female schedule. We're three babes in the woods, learning as we go.

Lloyd works and plays wherever it is he works and plays, while I take care of the girls and raise funds for libraries and state schools for the handicapped. I set up children story hours at the new library in Renton and help to procure a piano for the state school in Buckley. Even kids with severe disabilities respond to music. It's essential to our well-being. Life with my girls and the community is becoming quite rewarding.

Life with my husband is rare. We seldom see each other. We're together at family holiday meals, which we share with relatives. Lloyd is too busy to have

## Promise I'll Stay for Mother's Day

even Sunday breakfast at home. But there's no complaining from my side of the table. I understand that our relationship is not a lot different from other spouses. My husband hunts with the men in the family and races cars with the men in the family and the neighborhood. Neighbor John with his Austin Healy and Uncle Jack with his TR3, accompany Lloyd with his Sunbeam Alpine to Pacific Raceways two or three weekends a month all summer long. My complaining about the frequency of their sport would upset the balance of serenity in more than one household and who wants to be the town spoil sport?

> My husband and I finally have a project we can share. Life has changed and life is good. We settle into our separate three-generation households under one big roof.

The girls are growing and we need a bigger home. Together Lloyd and I find and purchase hillside property with a beautiful view of a cozy water inlet in the foreground and Mt. Rainier in the background. On it we build a large, beautiful home designed by me and built by us. The planning and construction of our new house is invigorating and fills many hours with conjugal cooperation. My husband and I finally have a project we can share. Life has changed and life is good. We're proud of our new home.

Our new home includes Mom. I don't know exactly how this came about, but she and Lloyd worked out a mother-in-law apartment agreement. Her apartment is located on the lower floor of our hillside home, separate from our upstairs residence. It's a very nice home with a fireplace, a view, and a pink bedroom. Mom finally has her pink room. We won't have to be concerned with her living by herself as she ages. She still works at Sears, but life evolves and we'll be ready when her life changes begin. And for now the girls get to have their young Granny nearby. Since her apartment is fully contained, there won't be two grown females sharing the running of a household. She and I each get our own turf. We settle into our separate three-generation households under one big roof.

We're really quite lucky that things have worked out so well for all of us.

Today is Valentine's Day. Lloyd has taken Rebecca and Shannon to his parents so we can have Valentine's Day dinner to ourselves. Is my husband getting tender, maybe even romantic? Maybe he wants another child. Maybe it's try-for-a-boy time.

I'm standing at the kitchen counter, tearing lettuce for a salad. Lloyd is sitting on a stool at the end of the counter.

"We might as well get a divorce," he says, nonchalantly.

## The Arranged Marriage Ends

*Lois and granddaughters, 1967.*

"Can it wait until I finish tossing the salad?" is my clever response. What he just said makes no sense. I put steaks on the indoor barbecue.

Lloyd chuckles. "Yeah, why not."

My mind is chewing this over. My southern-bred relatives would say, "Think I'll chew on this a while." So I'm chewing. Divorce? Is he serious, or will he change his mind? Hope not. *Hope not?* That's an odd thought. He's not home a lot, keeps awfully late hours at work. Maybe it's not so odd. The salad's tossed. The steaks are done.

"Dinner's ready, Lloyd."

We sit down to eat. I suppose I should remember what we talked about, but I don't. All I remember is my husband asked me for a divorce on Valentine's

## Promise I'll Stay for Mother's Day

Day, and it turns out he meant it. A month after Valentine's Day, the girls are playing in their bedrooms.

"Have you seen an attorney?" Lloyd asks. I ignore him. Why would I see an attorney?

"Have you seen an attorney?" he asks again.

Why would I see an attorney? Divorce? Nah, that Valentine's Day conversation was a month ago. It went nowhere.

"No, no I haven't," I reply.

"Don't you think you better?"

"I guess so."

I guess so. Is that all I can say? That's what I remember thinking at the altar when the pastor asked if I took him to be my husband. Now Lloyd is pushing me to take steps to end our thirteen-year marriage. No yelling, no conflict. I guess so, once again is the appropriate response . . . I guess.

Apparently he's serious about this. Okay smart boy, I'll call your bluff. I'll see an attorney. A friend of mine works for an attorney. I'll ask her to arrange an appointment.

The attorney asks me a bunch of questions which I answer the best I can. "Why are you here?" he begins.

"My husband asked me to see an attorney. He wants a divorce."

"Do you want a divorce?"

"I have no objection to a divorce." I almost said *"I guess so!"*

My complacency is apparent. It appears there's not much hope for saving this marriage. He ends the interview by saying. "I believe the marriage will end. I'll begin the paperwork."

"What'll I tell my husband? He'll want to know what we've discussed."

"Is he still living in the house?" he asks with astonishment.

"Yes."

"Tell him he'll have to move out."

I bring the news to Lloyd. "I saw an attorney today."

"What'd he say?" he asks.

"He says you have to move out."

A look of dismay crosses Lloyd's face. What'd he think the attorney would say, that he could keep living here? I won't force it. I'll give him time.

A week later I decide it's time, "Lloyd, you have to move out."

"I got my own attorney," he says.

"You still have to move out. People don't continue to live together when they get divorced."

## The Arranged Marriage Ends

"We have to work out a financial deal."

"Put it in writing," I say. Is this my voice I'm hearing? Do I detect a bit of backbone?

I continue. "I'll prepare the girls. How about the end of the month? That's a couple of weeks away. The girls and I will go away for the weekend, and you can move while we're gone. I'll tell Mom too."

Oh yes. I'll tell Mom. Oh God! What is she going to say?

"I just can't understand why you would divorce somebody who has given you all this," were the first words out of her mouth, as she waved her arms in the air indicating the expanse of our home.

"I'm not divorcing him, Mom. He's divorcing me."

"Can't you fix it?"

"I don't want to fix it. He's seldom home anyway. What's the point?"

*All this* refers to the sweet deal she worked out with Lloyd. She gave him money to build the apartment downstairs and she pays $100 a month for her share of the utilities. Not a bad retirement deal for her, when she's ready.

"The point is he is supporting us . . . you."

"Well then Mom, if you're worried about his support, why don't we just have him move downstairs with you?"

"Don't be ridiculous."

"Our lives are going to change, Mom. Get used to it."

"What'll you tell the girls?"

"I don't know. I'll think of something."

"What will you tell everyone else? It's not going to be easy, telling everyone how you could divorce someone who's given you all this."

There's the "all this" sneer again. It's probably not the last time I'll hear it. "I earned some of this," I say, "and I'll find a way to keep *all this* for you, Mom."

*All this* refers to the sweet deal she worked out with Lloyd. She gave him money to build the apartment downstairs and she pays $100 a month for her share of the utilities. Not a bad retirement deal for her, when she's ready. She and Lloyd are very close pals. With him gone, she might have to ante up a bit more to stay here.

Rebecca is eight and Shannon is five. It's time to talk to them about what's going to happen to our home life. Their dad may not be around a lot, but he is here sometimes on weekends. And he does come home every night, eventually, to sleep in our bed.

"Girls, we're going away this weekend, you and me. When we come back

## Promise I'll Stay for Mother's Day

home, your Dad will be gone. He won't be living here any more. He's going to move to a place of his own.

"Why?" asks Shannon.

"He doesn't want to live here any more."

"I don't believe you," she says evenly, challenging me with a direct stare.

"You're right. It's not that he doesn't want to live here. He doesn't want to live here with me."

"Why not?"

"Well, I'm not sure. I don't know how to explain this. It's just that people need to be with people they lo . . . people they love, and he's not so much in love with me any more."

"Does he love us?"

"Oh yes."

"Then why doesn't he stay here and love us?"

Great. Just great. Why did I think I could explain this to my five-year-old daughter, when I can hardly explain it to my fifty-five-year-old mother? You see, that's a problem for me. I've never had to explain things. I just do what I'm told. No explanations. No emotions. Move along, Shirleyanne. Just move along. Shit.

I don't remember the rest of my feeble attempts to explain the situation to Shannon. A lot of "I don't remember" going on in my life these days. Do I not remember because I didn't think the words were important, or because my mind was too full to hold everything? I must have stumbled along throwing out a bunch of irrelevant nonsense until Rebecca, the fixer, Becca the sensible eight year old, finally spoke up.

"Does this mean we can have a puppy?"

That I can answer. "Yes, we can have a puppy." A puppy will be here for dinner every night. A puppy will be here on weekends, too. Can a puppy replace a dad?

Mom is not done with me. "Well, what *am* I going to tell people?"

"Why do you have to tell people anything?"

"People will want to know how you could give up all he's provided for us. We have a perfectly good man to provide . . . "

"*We* have a perfectly good man?"

"Yes, WE," she says triumphantly.

"Well guess what, Mom. WE do not have a perfectly good man. We HAD a not-so perfectly good man. And now he's gone, and he's going to STAY gone. Lloyd does not live here any more. If you'd rather live with him than stay here

## The Arranged Marriage Ends

with us, go right ahead. Ask him to take you in. But you may have to talk to his secretary too. I think Judy may have something to say about where Lloyd is going to live and with whom . . . "

There. I said it. And may I also say a grateful thank you to the lovely young trollop who has given me the opportunity to get out of a dreadful marriage. For a long time I chose to ignore the late hours. Then I chose to look into it. Denial was useful for a while. Knowledge will prove to be even more useful as we move forward with the financial arrangements.

"And I trust you, Mom, to not mention her name to the girls . . . ever. That's for him to explain."

As for us, we'll manage just fine. Due to the circumstances of the divorce, there will be a handsome financial settlement. We'll keep the house and everything in it, and we'll have child support. I don't want alimony. Lloyd will fully support us for three months while I look for work. I've kept my hand in the radio business, filling in for vacations and special projects when they came up, so I still have industry connections. They'll help me find a job. Don't you worry, Mom, about how we're going to keep all this. "This" will survive the loss of the man who, as you like to say, provided it.

I heard Mom say the divorce word twenty-seven years ago, but Mom and Dad found a way to stay married, and Gene and I grew up in a two-parent household. My girls are not going to be so fortunate. But we'll survive. My name may not be Lois Wilson, but I'm sprung from her body, and if she can manage a household and a career, I can too. Let's get on with it.

CHAPTER 16

## *A New Family Order*

It's said that when two or more persons live or work together, a leader must come forward or anarchy will take the leadership position, and the group will fail to survive. So here we are a group of females living under the same roof. There is no man to take charge or allow his chosen woman to take charge. We're literally living in a no-man's land. Who's in charge here?

I can feel Mom taking stock of the situation. Her attempts to keep a man and primary wage-earner in the house failed because I failed to keep him here. There'll be no cow-towing to a daughter who can't even stay married.

But there's that wage-earner quandary. She who controls the finances will control the household, and right now my Mom is the only one in the household with a paying job. However, she's made it clear she's not about to fork over more money to live here. Unless she chooses to change her position, her paying job won't buy her control of the group. She's got more to think about than I do.

My position is more easily defined. Simply put, I've got two daughters who need a home and three months to get a job before the full support agreement comes to an end. Fortunately, newspapers print divorce filings, and fortunately some people actually read them. A former colleague in the radio business read the Anderson divorce notice and she called me. An industry connection has arrived on its own.

"I just read about your divorce," Dorothy says. "I can't believe it. Gol, Shirl, what are you going to do?"

"Hopefully I'll find a job."

"Do you need one right away?"

"I'll need one by the end of summer. So I'm looking now."

"Well, I think you're in luck," she says. "The traffic manager at KOMO radio has given notice. She's leaving at the end of summer to have a baby. Call them and use my name as a reference. They know me."

Some things are just meant to be, and isn't it my turn for a bit of luck? I interview for the position Dorothy recommended and I'm hired to be the

## A New Family Order

*Rebecca, Shirleyanne, and Shannon, 1972.*

traffic manager for a very good radio station. When summer is over, I'll begin my trek into the super woman world of full-time bread winner, part-time Campfire leader, and some-time cookie baker. Like many other single working mothers, I carry the false illusion that I'll be able to continue to do everything a Mom is supposed to do, even though Mom time is cut in half.

My own Mom's contribution turns out to be the giving of sage advice, rather than hard-core participation. She's acquiesced to the household situation. I'm in charge of upstairs and she gets to live downstairs. But fix a meal now and then? A thing of the past. Pay a little more? Only under protest. Watch the kids when I need a time out? Hell no.

"So you want to go out Friday night. Why? Looking for Mr. Goodbar?"

She actually said that. Do I care? I don't have time to care. But time is our friend. It has a way of righting listing ships.

Mom finally settles in, backing off on some of her fabulous advice. She's done a 180. I don't know why, but I'll take it. The girls have taken on their new responsibilities with an air of confidence and a sense of contribution. In fact, Becca and Shannon are feeling pretty good about all the things they've learned to do for themselves. Our three-generation, four-woman family is getting along very well.

But I have concerns about our ability to survive over the long haul unless we're on a more solid financial base within the next couple of years. My car has a few thousand more miles left in it, but it won't last forever. Both girls will need braces on their teeth, and I'd like to offer them at least the option of participating in extracurricular activities, maybe even music lessons. A vacation would be nice, too, and Lord help us if anyone gets sick. Our budget is just too tight for my feeling any sense of security.

Short term is fairly easy. I have a couple of skills that'll bring in a few extra dollars. The first comes from the dreaded home economics courses that Mom and Lloyd insisted I take at Colorado Women's College. I wanted drama classes; they wanted sewing lessons. They won, and now we'll all win. KOMO, owned by Fisher Broadcasting, has a television station as well as a radio station. They'll pay me to make costumes for their locally-produced children's programs. Puppets need clothes too. I can do that at home part time and make an extra couple hundred dollars a month to give us a small cushion for emergencies.

The other skill comes from my sports interests and a routine Dad and I used to have. We'd call each other every Tuesday night during football season to go over the previous weekend's game statistics and use them to pick winners of the upcoming weekend's games. No money on the table, just family bragging rights.

There was also a sub routine I still laugh about. Tuesday night the phone rings. It's Dad.

"Are you there?" he asks.

"Nope," I answer. He hangs up the phone.

A few minutes later I call him. "Hello?" he says.

"Are you there?" I ask.

"Yeah, what do you want?"

"Are you pickin' the Dawgs or the Ducks?"

We don't suffer fools well, and we don't answer stupid questions. Every time he'd hang up on me I'd crack up laughing and call him back. We averaged better than eighty percent on our predictions each week, but I had the most wins because I had a feel for upsets.

Let's see what happens if there *is* money on the table. There are plenty of football pools that offer cash prizes and I still have the touch. Netting an average of seventy-five dollars a week from September through January, football pools underwrite my evening college classes to bring us longer-term financial rewards. Money grubbing they call it, using my wits and a couple of learned skills to bring in extra dollars.

It doesn't leave me time for developing personal relationships with members of the opposite sex. It's not that I don't meet male prospects. My interest in sports does generate conversations, but guys are uneasy talking sports with a gal who knows more than they do. A male friend gives me some advice. "Flirt more, compete less."

Okay, I'll try to curb my sports acumen. But on the larger playing field—oops, there I go again—few men are willing to be sandwiched into a schedule that includes three jobs, two kids, lurking matriarch and evening college classes. Frankly, I don't care. I have other priorities.

"Can I have piano lessons, Mom?" It's Shannon, asking a reasonable question.

"Sure. I think we can afford piano lessons."

"But, Mom; we don't have a piano."

That's a problem. Buying a piano will require a big cash outlay, with no cash to lay out. What to do?

Incremental salary increases each year are not going to buy us a piano. Selling advertising on a commission basis will bring in more money, if I can learn how to do it. Using my current work experience as a Traffic Manager, I begin to think about how I might increase the station's ad sales. Then I begin to practice sales speak with local and national salesmen, negotiating my control of their inventory to grow their incomes. As their confidence in me grows, my confidence in myself grows even more.

> Then I begin to practice sales speak with local and national salesmen, ... As their confidence in me grows, my confidence in myself grows even more.

A year after Shannon asked me if she could take piano lessons I'm ready with my plan to move into the radio sales arena. With a plan in hand, I make an appointment to see Fred Kaufman, KOMO Radio's Sales Manager.

"Fred, I would like to talk to you about a move into sales," I boldly say. Across the country there are a hand-full of women working in media sales. In Seattle, I can think of only one.

Fred smiles and says, "I was wondering when you were going to do this."

He's noticed my change of focus over the past year. Together we draw up a job description that includes sales training starting with a few of what we call small-to-medium size direct accounts. No advertising agencies or large accounts with big money on the line.

"If this should come about, Fred says, "We're not interested in your going out and trying to force sales to put money on the books. This radio station has its heritage for good reason. We're in business for the long haul."

It's the perfect setting for a sales novice.

"A little quiet for sales, aren't you?" says Fred's boss, the General Manager of the radio station.

"I'm not quiet," I respond, "I'm observant. I think if you really listen, people will tell you what they want. Assuming we have what they want, the next step is to establish how much they're willing to pay for it. I won't be afraid to ask for money when the time is right.

"I've been here four years now, and I think the time is right to ask you for the opportunity to make more money. My daughter wants to take piano lessons and for her to do that, I need to buy a piano. I can't do that without changing my career focus."

He nods. "If this works out for you", he says, "You could make more money than you've ever dreamed of."

I smile on the outside as I say to myself, "Why does he think my dreams are less than his?"

Mom is cautiously supportive of my professional move. "Is your pay going to be commission only?"

"Yes, Mom, but there is a six-month guarantee, and six months from now I will have enough accounts to cover it. I'm confident of that. They won't let their first sales woman fail. And I won't let them—or you—down."

The new family order is in place and there is no threat of anarchy. The nine-year-old girl with the bad posture and shy, phony smile has grown up. She's hunched her shoulders, lifted her chin and stared down the uncertainties. No more "I guess so." Born from necessity, a new leader has emerged.

CHAPTER 17

## *Messing With the Order*

THE HOUSEHOLD SYSTEMS and responsibilities are in place and my professional expansion has eliminated the need for part time projects. Our years of sacrifice, preparation and hard work are literally paying off. No question, laughter and growth are easier to come by with a surplus of time and money. The four of us are sharing and growing. No need to mess with a good thing; no need to bring in a man to screw things up. For eight years we women have had each other, and it's enough.

Then along comes Barry, and the systems dissolve. No, let me adjust that. The systems aren't dissolving, they're exploding. My passions may have been buried, but they were far from dead. The handsome prince has arrived and kissed away the systems.

Barry, affectionately known as "The Express" is a good-looking, charming man with an infectious, child-like exuberance. He's a lot of fun to be around. People who know Barry laugh, shake their heads, and say, "He's kind of crazy, but he's soooo much fun!"

Women especially like Barry, and he is more than receptive to their pursuit of his company. He's a top contender for playboy of the year in our part of the world. He could have just about any woman, and for some reason that still puzzles me, he's decided he likes me enough to forsake all his pursuers and take himself out of circulation. Four days after our first date, Barry asks me to marry him. That's right. Four days! Go figure.

I figure I must have been sending signals that I am ready for Barry's brand of adventure. Playboys don't take personal risk when it comes to their relationships with the fair sex. Barry is not about to risk feminine rejection. The Express is a not turn-around train. He knows I can be had.

"I want to marry you," he says, after a poetic trip to Snoqualmie Falls and a sumptuous breakfast in the inn at the summit.

"Why me?" At least I didn't melt in his arms and blubber out a mushy, "Yes, my darling Barry."

## Promise I'll Stay for Mother's Day

"Because you're strong, you're supportive, you're decent, and you f–

"Stop!" No further explanations necessary."

After eight years of emotional caution and sensible decisions, why not? The leader of the well-oiled domestic machine is ready to marry a man like this. Barry knows what I do for a living and what kind of income it brings in, and he's not intimidated.

With this handsome, confident man, I can lift my hard-working sacrificial lid and openly enjoy what I've earned. I can leave Daddy's little girl behind at last, and become a complete, fulfilled, grown-up woman. My sleeping passions can express themselves and nice will become a part of the total presentation, not the whole picture. I can become less predictable and make surprising choices. It will be okay to laugh out loud. My answer to Barry's proposal comes easy. I am more than ready for this explosive leap forward.

"Yes, Barry, I'll marry you."

The rest of our world is not so ready. Shock waves rock our circle of family and friends. Barry and Shirley? No way! She's much too serious for him, they say. He's much too out there for her, they declare. It won't work.

Public opinion will not get in the way of this new woman. Six weeks after our first date, Barry and I are married in a restaurant called "Sundays", located in a restored church building. Following the wedding ceremony we move from the restaurant to the downstairs disco, to dance the night away. Three hundred curious people celebrate with us, placing their bets as to how long the marriage will last.

Barry and I are confident we'll have a good marriage. He's run through all the women he can in the greater Seattle area, and he's ready to settle down. I've led a moderately boring, nose to the grindstone existence, and I'm ready to jump on board his wild ride. We honeymoon in Hawaii. We're engulfed in our heady romantic world.

Funny thing about weddings and honeymoons. As soon as they're over, two people find themselves in a marriage, where existent daily habits override the excitement of hurried, passionate courtship days.

The weekend following our Hawaiian honeymoon, Barry and I have our first marital confrontation when I toss by bathrobe onto the bed after my morning shower.

"Are you going to leave that there?" Barry asks.

"Until after breakfast," I reply.

"Why don't you hang it up now?"

"I'll hang it up after breakfast."

## Messing With the Order

"Why is it important for you to wait until after breakfast?" he asks.

"It's not important at all," I say. "Why are you making an issue of something so unimportant?"

"If it's not important, why don't you just hang it up?"

"Why don't you just open that door and take a flying f--- off the deck?"

Now that's a rational statement. I heard myself say it and I'm a rational person, so it has to be rational.

"That's a stupid thing to say, over something so unimportant," my new husband says. Just hang up your f------ robe!"

Hanging up my robe before or after breakfast seems to have become an extremely important issue. So important it requires a half hour of shouting and a full weekend of hurt feelings to get over it. In my years of single blessedness I'd forgotten how important such issues are in the pursuit of shared happiness. But this incident ruined only a weekend. Other issues are not so easily overcome.

The Express is not only used to a neat and tidy house, he's also accustomed to giving advice and having a controlling hand in the running of the household. Our new family is now blessed with two advice givers, Mom, who has abandoned her wait and see station downstairs, and Barry, who is establishing his upstairs rank. Then there's that former head of household, Shirleyanne, who's trying to determine if she has any position left at all. And let's not forget the two teenagers who are observing and testing all of us, to find out whose advice will be followed and whose decisions will prevail.

Did I forget to mention that every other weekend Barry's seven year old daughter, Natalie, and twelve year old son, Rob, come to our home to throw their needs and desires into this roiling pot of household stew?

Everyone's place in this new contest of wills is being redefined on a daily basis. I am becoming a referee in this absurd new game of life as the advice-givers turn to me to make the, whose in control decisions. I look at our kids and wonder what's going on in their heads as they try to figure out how to spot their loyalties in this new arena, where the adults they're supposed to count on for security and guidance are behaving like a pack of emotionally disturbed children. For their sake, something has to be done.

My marrying Barry has produced a shift in the balance of power. Mom has reasserted herself; she has a position to protect. Barry has a position to establish. They're not sworn enemies. Eliminate my presence and they'd probably get along very well. But we're not going to eliminate me, so "me" will have to figure out how to deal with two stubborn people who are accustomed to

## Promise I'll Stay for Mother's Day

having their way with me. I can't allow their conflict to bring about a second divorce. I've put my family through that hell already.

After more than two years of trying to balance the scales of impossibilities, the only way I see to avoid a marital split is to split the household. Mom and Barry can't live in the same house with me, and my home is going to be with Barry. This decision offers a dilemma in the truest definition of the word. There are no good choices.

Mom thought she'd be living in the family home for the rest of her life. She was counting on me to take care of her. She fought the good fight and it was her time to rest. I was supposed to carry on the fight and allow her to retire in peace. And here I am about to drop a big boulder right in the middle of her trip down retirement lane. She's going to have to bear the brunt of my misadventures. I don't know what I'm going to say to her.

I'll have to tell it to her straight. I've got to wade into this turgid pool of trouble and see what emerges from this mess I've put us into. I dropped my first big life boulder onto our family nearly a decade ago and we managed to climb our way out of it. The second one is about to drop. How many chances do we get under my questionable leadership?

"Mom, this living arrangement is not working out. There are too many ties to my marriage with Lloyd in this house, as well as the remnants from my years as a single person. If my second marriage is going to work, Barry and I are going to have to set up our own household."

I watch her closely as I speak. She takes a moment to gather her thoughts.

"What are you going to do?"

"We're going to call a real estate company and put this house up for sale. Then Barry and I will look for another place to live, with the girls."

Is this blunt enough? I'm dying inside.

"I guess I better start looking for a place to live," she says thoughtfully.

"The price of real estate has increased considerably since we built this house. There'll be plenty of money for you to move into another place."

The price of real estate is not the point. I sound like a fool.

"Okay, I'll get working on it," she says.

Mom knew this day would come when I told her Lloyd and I would be getting a divorce. I felt her distress then and I am experiencing her resolve now. There's no need for me to worry about her ability to understand and survive. Mom will never be a problem for me. I'm an eternal problem for her.

This situation didn't suddenly spring up out of nowhere. I've been internally fussing about what needs to happen without discussion, without giving

## Messing With the Order

us a chance to make the multiple households work together. I've been hoping this hopeless state of affairs would resolve itself. I abdicated the leadership position leaving others to jockey for their parts in this swirling eddy of emotions. This catastrophe is the result of teeth-grinding passiveness on my part.

The four-woman household worked itself out without my really having to stop and take care of others' wants and needs. I wasn't a leader, I simply provided the setting, wherein four people—four very strong people—determined their own roles and moved forward with me. In spite of the so-called need for women to talk about everything ad nauseum, we didn't talk about it. We four, even though two were very young, understood our roles and lived in peace. It never occurred to me that bringing a man into our nifty little organization would upset the workings of this family order. How stupid is that?

> Mom trusted me to take care of her. It was her time to be cared for. But I took care of myself, and she's on her own again. She's not fourteen years old with time for recovery from misadventures.

I wanted this to work, but wanting doesn't get it done. Planned, overt action is required. I ought to know that by now. Will I ever get over my reluctant reserve and follow the example in front of me? It's right here, for God's sake. She's living right here with me taking one blow after another administered by my mealy mouth assumption of wants being magically delivered. And when they aren't, I don't take the fall. I just keep moving forward in my own time and way, expecting others to pick up their lives and move with me or cast their lot and move toward their own directions.

Mom trusted me to take care of her. It was her time to be cared for. But I took care of myself, and she's on her own again. She's not fourteen years old with time for recovery from misadventures. She's sixty-one, wondering again where she will live.

Now I must talk to the girls. This won't be so easy. They don't have their Granny's experience with change. They surely won't want to move. This has been their home for all the years they can remember. They've been going to the same school with the same friends since kindergarten. Becca has one more year of high school, Shannon has four.

I wish Barry were more patient. I'm taking the crap, but he precipitated this turn of events. He's the one who wanted to move and I became the façade to get it done. A few more years at the same address would make such a difference in my daughter's lives and so little difference in ours. There I go again

## Promise I'll Stay for Mother's Day

with my silent wanting. God forbid I should speak up to the person who could make a difference here.

"Barry and I are trying hard to make our marriage work, but it's very difficult for us in this house. To stand a chance as a couple, we have to find ourselves a home without the family history this house carries. Barry feels like he's living in someone else's home, and he is. We're going to put this house up for sale and look for another place to live."

Becca asks. "Do all of us have to move?"

"I think so. Why?"

"I want to finish high school with my friends, Mom. It's only one more year, and I can't start over for just one year."

Becca is a cheer leader, a class leader, a Girl of the Month kind of high school student. I understand. She can't move. "I think you'll be able to finish high school here with no problem, Becca. It takes time to sell a house."

Shannon asks the elephant in the room question. "What about Granny? I don't think Barry likes her."

"It's not a case of like or not like. It's unusual for a mother-in-law to live in a married couple's home. It's unusual because it doesn't usually work."

"So she's not moving with us, right?"

Leave it to Shannon to cut to the quick again. There's no sweet talking her perceptions. It's kind of like when I was trying to explain her father moving out. "He doesn't want to live here any more," I said.

"I don't believe you," she said then, and she's not buying what I'm trying to say now. Its bull shit and she knows it.

"No, Granny's not moving with us. But we'll have time to get used to all this."

Less time than I thought. Barry is anxious to move. It doesn't take long for him to find a new house for us. It's lovely, it's perfect, and it's in another school district. Of course it is.

Luckily, a friend of mine is looking for someone to rent her basement apartment and it's in our current school district. Becca is young to be on her own, but she's mature for her age. She wants to stay and finish school where she started. It'll be all right. I hope it'll be all right. It has to be all right.

Mom has found herself a new place to live, as well. She's chosen a mobile home in a retirement community, and she appears to be pleased with her decision. Barry, Shannon and I, and Becca and Mom have new places to live, and we are moving forward. We make an offer on the lovely house in Bellevue.

Messing With the Order

But what about Shannon? Shannon doesn't know how to communicate her feelings to others. I wonder where she gets that maladjustment. She doesn't address problems directly. But her avoidance is different from mine.

Shannon has developed a package of useful guises to register her level of acceptance to new ideas, plans, or situations. If she's going to go along with a plan, she doesn't say, "Okay, I'll do it." She just goes along and her behavior remains positive. If she's not going to go along with the plan, she appears to accept it, but her behavior changes in other ways. She skips school, or comes home late on school nights, or she tosses disrespectful sass in my direction for no apparent reason. We know something is bothering her, but we have to dig to find the underlying reasons for her behavior.

Becca is more like Barry and Mom in her forthrightness. Shannon's more like me, which makes Shannon much more difficult to deal with. No one knows where she's coming from.

"Shannon, I know we'll miss having Becca live with us, but she's not home very much anyway. With her cheerleading and Pep Club activities, and all the senior class events she's participating in, plus her job at Sport Mart, we hardly see her. And come next fall, she'll be off to college. There'll only be three of us living together next year, even if we don't move."

It all sounds so reasonable in my mind. I think I've convinced Shannon, but we'll see.

During the summer, we move into our new home. Shannon is enrolled in her new school and she's trying to make the adjustment, but it's difficult for her. I can feel her growing gloom. It's hard to make new friends in the ninth grade. The kids looking for new friends at this age are either new themselves or already living on the fringe of peer acceptance. They're either nerds or trouble makers. We know Shannon's not going to join the nerds. We're hoping she can avoid the trouble makers.

Hoping hopelessly. Resentment and defiance are creeping into her posture and Barry's chosen to fight her behavior rather than ride it out. He and Shannon are getting pissy with each other, sparring at every twitch of the eyebrow signifying an imagined slur. Barry's not familiar with the changing moods of teenagers and he's not about to deal with any of it. Shannon feels she's entitled to her moods and she doesn't see any reason to hold back for Barry's sake. If it weren't for Barry, she's thinking, none of this would be happening.

"I don't know why you can't exercise more control over her behavior. She's openly defying us," Barry says.

"I don't like the way Barry treats you, Momma, but he's your husband, so

## Promise I'll Stay for Mother's Day

you must like it. But he's not my Dad, and I'm not going to let him tell me what do," Shannon says.

Barry thinks I favor Shannon, and he may be right. Shannon, after all, is my daughter. We've been together since her birth, giving us fourteen years to learn how to fulfill each other's emotional needs. She's only fourteen, Barry. Her age deserves a little consideration and understanding from the two adults who've completely changed her life without her permission. Bend a little, Barry. Give it a chance.

> She knows how to turn the screw just far enough to avoid retribution. Dealing with her is a daily battle of testing boundaries and personal wills.

I struggle with Shannon's unhappiness for two years. She is petulant and disrespectful. She skips school often enough to cause consternation, but not often enough to be suspended from school. She knows how to turn the screw just far enough to avoid retribution. Dealing with her is a daily battle of testing boundaries and personal wills. One of us is going to have to make a significant move toward center.

I move first. Unfortunately it's not toward center. It's inflamed and without warning. Her snotty behavior finally snapped my emotional reserve.

On her way out the door to go to school, she turned and hurled one more parting insult my way. Without thinking, I grab her arm as she twirls away from me, and I slam her against the dining room wall.

I hear a rip and see a piece of her blouse in the hand that just slammed her . . . my hand.

"MOM!" She screams. She throws me a look of horror as she jerks away from my frightening grasp and runs downstairs to her bedroom slamming the door behind her, sobbing alone.

I sit down, stunned. I couldn't have just thrown my daughter against a wall. The scene I just witnessed took place outside my body. I must have been watching another mother and daughter. It was too emotional, too out of control, too childish for it to have been me and my Shannon. Not possible. We're civilized. I'm civilized.

A half hour later, Shannon left for school in a different blouse and I left for work not knowing what new kind of havoc I'd provoked. With dread, I return home after work and fall into the family room sofa. I don't know how I got through the day. Shannon enters the room and plops onto my lap.

"I couldn't stop myself, Momma. I get so mad sometimes. It's not easy, you know, with you changing things all the time."

As parents we're supposed to set guidelines and help our children to mature and accept responsibility. We're not supposed to let them live as two-year-olds their entire lives, fighting everything that gets in the way of instant gratification. It's our job to help them rise above their primitive instincts.

Even wild beasts look to their parents for guidance. The lions in the jungles and the fish in the ocean teach their offspring to grow and meet challenges. But not us. We're afraid of our offspring. We want them to be "happy." Let me tell you, they are not happy. They are lost and confused. Shannon has a right to be angry. I stopped parenting. And she still needs a parent.

Although our parents chose to be together and raise Gene and me different from other people of our era, they were consistent in their ways. Different, but consistent. It's the consistency that counts. Kids need to count on something.

One of the toughest things to oversee is our children's choice of friends. Peer selection often is a reflection of self esteem, and right on target Shannon has fallen in with less than desirable companions. They reflect her current anger and uncertainty. They drink, they're promiscuous, and they consider school attendance to be optional. It is becoming more and more difficult to keep Shannon in line. I don't know what to do. I can't slam her against the wall again. Shock value works only if it's used sparingly, and I've already used my allotment.

We get a break the summer after her sophomore year. Shannon's done so well in her Russian language class she's been invited to spend six weeks in Russia with her teacher and a group of older, more advanced students. She's receiving encouragement from her school and her family to go, and getting nothing but harassment and threats from her envious friends. Her boyfriend says he will break up with her if she's going to be gone that long. He refuses to see her off.

Our ride to the airport is uneventful, but when it's time to board the airplane, it's Shannon's turn to lose control.

"Please don't make me go, Momma," she sobs. "I don't know these people. Denny will break up with me. I won't have any friends when I get back." She throws her arms around my neck and begs me not to make her get on the plane.

Nothing is more important to a teen age life than friends, even questionable friends. Belonging to any group of human beings is better than being alone to a fifteen-year-old person, and for many persons well beyond the age of puberty. But this young person needs to move beyond her limited frustrations.

I firmly take her arms from around my neck, turn her around and force her to walk toward the boarding gate. Fortunately, her traveling companions are stronger and more caring than the friends who chose not to see her off. Having witnessed the scene of her fear of leaving, without fuss, Shannon's new acquaintances take her from me, and gently walk her onto the plane. Please, let these people help her to help herself.

Years of turmoil and uncertainty are not wiped out in a six-week trip, but it can help to bring a new perspective of what's available to most of us in this country and not available to people in other lands. Dealing with a new stepfather and having to change schools pales when compared to having to cope with the minimal food, shelter, and clothing standards deemed adequate in other countries. In the Russia of 1982, Shannon begins to understand the scale of her problems. On the plane home, she writes me a letter that opens the door for a new approach to solving our domestic difficulties.

"... I've seen what it's like to really have no freedom to come and go, and no choice in clothes and friends and school subjects. I've eaten what looks like bird seed, and had tongue in aspic, and a bowl of borscht nearly every day. The buildings are dirty and gray, and people walk with their heads down so they don't see their poverty. But they don't complain. If people are having trouble with their kids, they should send them to Russia. I was not lost, but I was in a deep forest headed in the wrong direction..."

These words were written by a fretful, scared teenager, fighting against nearly everything in her life. Why is it that when we are the most scared, we seem to have our most lucid and poetic thoughts. Are creative thoughts tied to the increased output of survival adrenalin? Is it chemically impossible to make major decisions in the absence of fear? Fear of repression, fear of change, fear of the unknown ... is fear the necessary ingredient for moving forward? Fear drives prejudice and violence. Perhaps it also drives progress.

When Shannon returns from Russia, we talk about what she wants out of the next few years of her life.

"I got to know the kids on the trip pretty well," she says. "I hope I can be friends with them at school too. They're a lot of fun and they don't act stupid and hurt each other."

She begins her junior year trying to be with her new friends, but her old friends are jealous. They tease, taunt and follow her around before, during and after school. They harass her to the point where she's afraid to go to school. But they stop short of breaking civil laws or school rules, so nothing can be done about their tormenting her. Their bullying forces us to make another difficult decision.

"Shannon, Granny lives in your old school district. What if you lived with her during the week and go back to school with Kristen and Rikke, and all the other kids you've known since kindergarten? You can be with me on the weekends.

"Do you think Granny will let me live with her?"

"Of course she will."

The four-woman household that had survived and thrived so well is now completely extinct. It lasted for more than eight years and dissolved in less than three. My family is gone and I am living with this strange, impatient man. What have I done?

> The four-woman household lasted for more than eight years and dissolved in less than three. I am living with this strange, impatient man. What have I done?

Does love change in an instant, or is it a process? When do you stop saying "please" and "thank you" and "I love you"? Do you drop from five "I love you's" a day to four, three, two, and then none? Why does it go away? Do people stop caring, or do they just get too busy? Let's slow down for a while, Barry. Let's have breakfast together, if not every day, then on Sundays. Can we set aside Sunday to have breakfast together? Sunday breakfast is important to me.

Sunday was the sure thing day when I was growing up. Mom didn't have time for breakfast Monday through Saturday, so it was Sunday. It carried over with my young family too. The electric griddle was always on the counter on Sundays. Pancakes and bacon were the staples. Then Lloyd got too busy for Sunday breakfast. I think that's when the marriage started falling apart. The girls and I had Sunday breakfast together, and we continued with Sunday breakfasts as long as we were together. The girls are gone now, and so is Sunday breakfast.

This is not how I imagined life would be at this piece of the road. I thought life would be simpler when I moved into autumn. I thought if I worked hard and kept positive thoughts I'd have more rewards by now. I imagined my girls' needs would diminish and I envisioned quiet times with my husband at the end of fulfilling work days.

I imagined many things without the benefit of real life experience to set me straight. Life is different from innocent young dreams. It's so much harder. But it'll get better. I need to be more patient. Barry will help me.

Where is Barry, anyway? I could use a little spousal support from him right now. Aren't husbands supposed to offer emotional assistance? Why else would I have remarried? The first time was a child's mistake. What's my excuse for this fiasco? Marriage is supposed to offer at least a few benefits. What are they and where are they?

Oh grow up, Shirleyanne. There's no Prince Charming to replace your father. Your Daddy's long gone. Let go of the little girl. Life requires more than pleasing your Dad and following your Mother's directives. Your divorce should have buried the little girl and the prince. You don't need a husband to have a happy home.

But I do have a husband. I need to give him and myself a break. The little girl I keep remembering never really existed. Wonder Woman was there all along, waiting to break loose. Accept her presence and say goodbye to the childish fantasies. Take what Barry offers. Count all the blessings we have that add up to a good life, and leave the rest alone.

CHAPTER 18

## *Summer Celebrations Turn Cold*

Two years have gone by. Shannon has just graduated from High School. Yes, she made it. The move to her Granny's house and the return to her life-long friends brought the results we'd hoped for. She has been accepted at Western Washington University, located in Bellingham, ninety miles north of Seattle. Becca is now a junior at the University of Washington. My girls have managed to overcome their mother's poor choices. We've weathered the storm of a dysfunctional family. I don't know how, but I'll take it.

Along the way I've become the General Sales Manager at KOMO Radio. Whatever happened to the timid home maker? Gone forever, it seems to opportunity and personal evolution. My Mother's genes overcame my Mother's wishes, and we're accepting our good fortune.

Barry's store opens in two weeks. After working fifteen years in the retail clothing business, we decided it was time for him to take this inevitable professional step forward. On the day of the store opening, we will celebrate our fifth wedding anniversary. Wedding day bets be damned. To all the nay sayers, we offer our most benevolent smiles. We've worked very hard to be where we are today and we deserve the satisfaction we're feeling. Life is good all around.

The phone is ringing. It's Mark, Becca's boyfriend. This could be serious.

"'lo. I'd like to make an appointment to come speak with you, please."

"Sure Mark. When would you like to come?"

"How 'bout next Tuesday, 7:00 PM."

"Sounds good to me."

He thinks this is going to be easy. Maybe it will; maybe it won't.

7:00 PM, Tuesday, a knock at the door. Mark is dressed in slacks, sport coat, dress shirt, and tie.

"Hello Mark. Come in."

We sit down in the living room. After a few cordial words, Mark gets right to the point. "I've come to request permission to marry your daughter."

"Why?" I ask.

## Promise I'll Stay for Mother's Day

"I love Rebecca very much, and I like her as my friend. I want to spend the rest of my life with her."

We spend the next hour discussing expectations and responsibilities. He gives solid answers to some tough questions... "What about your diabetes ... will you take care of that? ... What about your religion ... do you know that Rebecca doesn't attend church?" I want everything on the table now. Then I'll shut up forever.

"There's one final thing, Mark. Do you understand that even the most independent woman needs to be held sometimes, and maybe even pampered?" Might as well get for her what I can't seem to get for myself.

"Yes, I understand that," he replies. I can see that he does. This is a no-nonsense man of few words, but good words, solid words.

"And did Rebecca warn you that sometimes tender moments bring a tear or two ... and this could be one of those moments?"

"Yes, she did," says Mark, "and I came prepared."

He reaches into his pocket, I'm thinking, to get me a handkerchief. Instead, he pulls out a Snickers candy bar and tosses it to me.

"Your daughter told me this would take care of any emotional outbursts I might encounter."

"You have my permission, Mark, to marry my daughter."

My permission? What about her father's permission? He's not an active father right now. He still pays child support; give him credit for that. But seeing his girls and taking a part in their lives? Not so much. Life decisions are made in this household, and I just made another excellent decision, thanks wholly to the good sense and acumen of a daughter who chose to fall in love with an exemplary young man. Way to go, Becca!

The engagement party guest list includes our family's typical gathering of people from different backgrounds and lifestyles. In addition to our family cast of characters, we welcome a variety of folks, from homemakers to disc jockeys, from bluegrass musicians to retail merchants, from artists to sales people.

Mom is the biggest character of all, commanding center stage every moment she can. She is ecstatic about this engagement; she has high hopes that my daughter can succeed where I haven't. She wants a homemaker in the family; she wants great grandchildren. Oh Lordy, here it comes. Don't pay any attention to her, Becca. That would make me a grandmother, and I sure as hell am not ready for that step. No, no, no, no, no.

While my secretary, Donna, is belting out her operatic versions of "Ave

Maria" and "O Holy Night" to the startled neighbors, as she auditions for the part of Wedding Singer, Mom is passing her pickup key to all the men so they can take a look at the latest Penthouse Magazine with the pictures of our most recent Miss America posing lasciviously with another woman. Perfect. This is us. This is who we are—varied personalities sharing center stage in a singular cause. This is my family and these are our friends . . . our version of perfect harmony. Finally!

When the party is over, I'm very tired and very happy. We needed this day and this long, warm summer to heal our emotions and bring a new contentment into our lives. My head hits the pillow and I begin to dream.

*A number of people are boarding a large boat, the size of a ferry boat. The boat is docked inside a dark shed that looks like a covered wooden bridge. Colored Christmas lights are hung around the dock and outside the ferry boat. They are the only illumination. I board the boat carrying a baby.*

*Accompanying me are my daughters, my brother, and our cousin, Texie. The boat is facing toward shore. We're not ticketed, so we have to keep moving, to keep from being discovered. Our mood is somber. Texie is softy crying, the rest of us are silent. It takes the boat a long time to get out of the shed and turned around, but we are finally under way. The water is black and dense. It's dark outside, but we can see sunlight and bright sky in the distance. We pass each other during the voyage, walking inside and outside the boat, nodding, but not touching.*

*I remain outside most of the time, carrying the baby. Occasionally, Rebecca carries the baby for me while I go inside the boat's cabin to check our progress. When the pilot says we're on course, I walk back outside and take the baby again, and pace the deck, wondering what's beyond the sunshine, wanting to know how long the journey will last.*

*We finally reach our destination, beyond the dark seas, into the sunlight. The boat docks alongside a long, narrow building. We disembark and walk along the pier beside the wooden structure until we reach shore, still in a group and still not speaking or touching. The dark side is behind us, but we know the journey is not over. We must return to our original port of embarkation, without the baby. She must stay in the sunshine. I look at her before I let go. She smiles for the first time since the journey began.*

My eyes fly open and I lie in bed, trying not to move, feeling my heartbeat accelerate as if it is preparing to run away from an unknown, frightening enemy. I'm afraid to move, but I can't lie here hyper-ventilating the rest of the night. I have to do something to slow down my runaway heart.

## Promise I'll Stay for Mother's Day

Quietly, so as not to disturb Barry, I leave our bed to put distance between this strange dream and my conscious mind. For some reason, I feel the dream will become reality if I go back to sleep. I can't let that happen. I have no idea what the dream is about, but I do know I don't want it to happen.

Foolish thoughts for a practical mind. Enough of that nonsense.

Mark's sister Brenda is getting married this weekend. There's wedding news all over the place. Our family is invited, since we are now officially betrothed. We'll all be there, except Barry, who is busy with the new store. I want him to be at this wedding. The next wedding will be Becca's. I'd like to hold my husband's hand and think about Becca's wedding with him. Quitcher bitchin', Shirleyanne. Enjoy the summer.

It's a beautiful wedding and a bountiful reception, and I'm sitting here staring at my piece of cake ready to snap at somebody. I don't know what's wrong with me. Life is good. Where are my happiness feelings? Am I depressed? Maybe I'm chemically depressed. Okay. That's acceptable. Chemically depressed is quite hip within my circle of hyper professional colleagues. That's it. I am fashionably, chemically depressed.

Oh Christ. I gotta get away. I'm losin' it. It's been more than three years since I've taken a personal time out. Where's Barry? Why the hell can't he take one night off? It's all his fault. He isn't fun any more. I married him for fun. Why am I not having any fun? Where is my fun boy?

Just look at all the smiling couples sitting around here. I'm part of a couple. Where's my other part? Shut up, depressant brain. Smile anyway. There we go. I'm smiling. Wheeee... I'm having such a good time. I wonder if all the smiles I see are as false as the one I'm wearing.

I glance at Mom to see if she can read any of my thoughts. I hope not. She'd think she raised a nut for a daughter.

Oh for Pete's sake! There's food hanging out of her mouth. She's retired now, probably letting herself go. Do I have to start worrying about *her* now? She better find herself something to do with her time. I'm not going to be responsible for her too. She's cramming more food into her mouth. What about the piece stuck on her lip? If she takes one more bite before she swallows the food already in her mouth, I'm going to have to say something to her. She can't just sit there chewing with food hanging all over her face. This is embarrassing. My mother is drooling now. Great. Just Great.

Oh God. Something's wrong. Her face. There's something wrong with her face. Part of it is not moving. It's not the absence of social grace that's causing the food to hang out. She doesn't know it's there. She doesn't feel it. Oh God.

## Summer Celebrations Turn Cold

"Mom, are you okay?" I ask, scared to hear the answer.

"Yes. Why?"

"It looks like part of your face may be a bit numb."

"Well, yes, a little bit. Am I chewing funny?"

"Yes, you are. There's food hanging out of your mouth."

"Damn." She covers it with a napkin. "I had some dental work done a few weeks back. I think they used too much Novocain. I thought it'd go away by now."

Whew! Glad that's solved. My brain gets so carried away sometimes, but its all clear now. I don't know how I got myself stuck in such a funk. I'm okay now. This is a wonderful time in our lives. Mom's fine. I'm fine. Everybody in the whole friggin' world is just fine.

> I'm okay now. This is a wonderful time in our lives. Mom's fine. I'm fine. Everybody in the whole friggin' world is just fine.

It's Friday evening, a week later, and Mom's on the phone. I'm half listening while I'm trying to put a meal on the table for Barry and me.

"There's no need for you to worry, Shirleyanne..."

Worry? What's she talking about? "Worry about what, Mom?"

"Mary's taking me to the hospital."

Worry time. "Why is Mary taking you to the hospital, Mom?"

"Oh, I had a little seizure an hour ago. Mary dropped by about then, and she caught me."

"Caught you?"

"Yep. She caught me stumbling around, slurrin' my words. She thought I'd been nippin'." She chuckles.

Mom's practically a teetotaler. No chance she's been caught nippin' by herself and her friend Mary knows it.

"Mom, give the phone to Mary. I want to talk to her."

"Hello, Shirleyanne."

"What's going on?"

"I dropped by and found your Mom like she says. She said she'd had a seizure. She told me it was the second one this week. This was worse than the first one, she said. It shook her partial loose. I told her I was calling my sister. She's a nurse."

"What'd your sister say?"

"She said I should take your Mom to the hospital. Could be serious."

"Let me talk to Mom."

"Mary's taking me to the hospital as a precaution," Mom says. "We have

## Promise I'll Stay for Mother's Day

to find out what's causin' these fits." She chuckles again. "No need for you to come. They won't be doing anything tonight, anyway."

I'm not chuckling. Seizures aren't funny, and neither are fits. "Promise me you'll give them my phone number, and you'll call if anything changes. All right?"

"Yes, Shirleyanne. Nothing to worry about. Gotta go now. Bye."

"Bye Mom."

I hang up and tell Barry what's going on. He groans. I'm sorting out what I should do next. Should I go to the hospital? No, Mom's right. They won't do anything tonight. She seems to be okay; the seizure is over. If she has another one, they'll call me.

Could the dream have been about Mom? What dream? This is crazy. I'm really losing it if I think a dream has anything to do with any of this. But I did dream about Dad, and I did have a random thought that the boat was piloted by Chiron crossing the river Styx. But I dismissed it. I don't believe that for a minute. I was worried about Dad because he was sick; I have not been worrying about Mom. She's as healthy as anyone; she hasn't been sick in years. It would never have entered my mind that she's sick. There's a reasonable explanation for what's happening, and it isn't about a boat crossing over to the other side, whatever "the other side" means.

But I have to think about the possibility of her being sick. Right now she's checking into Highline Hospital. I have to at least consider it. We've traveled through troubled waters before and we've always survived. We'll weather whatever storm might be approaching. But our leader has fallen. That's right. Our leader. Anyone else who claims leadership is just a pretender.

The pilot says we are on course, and I need to believe him. Beyond the dark seas there was sunlight. If my Mom is going to die, how can there be light?

CHAPTER 19

# A Tough Diagnosis

When I arrive at the hospital late Saturday morning, Mom is resting from a morning of reporting family medical histories and undergoing blood tests and x-rays, including a CAT scan, all ordered to try to determine the cause of her seizures. She's also talking to herself, verbalizing her internal reassurances.

"I'm just fine," she says. "I haven't had any more seizures, so there's nothing to worry about." She's obviously worried. "I'm sure it has something to do with that dental work I had done back in June. I haven't felt right since then. But they have to run these tests, to find out for sure. I understand that. We have to know what's causin' these fits."

As she spits out the word "fits", she sees me and grins. I can't help but laugh, but I'm thinking this is the third week of August and she's trying to say this is caused by dental work done in June. Who's kidding whom?

Dr. Siverling comes into the room perplexed. He says he tried to get the test results for us today, but the technicians he wants to interpret them don't work on Saturday.

"But don't worry, Lois, I'll see that someone gets working on them right away.

I don't want you worrying about this all weekend."

"Why can't I wait this out at home?" she says. "Keeping me here while they fart around is a waste." She sighs. Having to lie around all weekend in the hospital waiting for someone to interpret tests is not what she wants to hear. "Oh, I suppose they're afraid I'll have more fits if I go home, but its not home that causes these fits . . . "

Sunday morning, while Mom and I are having breakfast, Dr. Siverling comes into her room again, with no test results to discuss. He doesn't like having his family of patients treated casually. He's been our doctor and friend for more than twenty years. He took over Dr. Jacob's patient list. The fact that it's Sunday morning carries no significance with him.

## Promise I'll Stay for Mother's Day

"Lois, I'm sorry. I'll have the test results for you before dinnertime," he says, as he storms out of the room to get the action started.

As promised, just before dinner is served, a new doctor walks in and starts right in with the results of the tests.

"The tests reveal a very small spot on your brain, Mrs. Wilson, behind, and a little above your right eye. This spot is the cause of the symptoms you've been experiencing. The spot has bruised your brain and caused it to swell. It's the swelling that has caused your seizures."

"Where'd the spot come from?" Mom interrupts. "And what are we going to do about it?"

"We don't know yet what the spot is, exactly when it appeared, or where it came from. We need to find the answers to these things before we make decisions about treatment. It is a very tiny spot."

I can't tell by looking at the new doctor what this means. The message as he presents it, seems mixed. The spot is very small, he says, so that reduces concern. But the spot is on the brain. A new spot on Mom's brain causes me to be very concerned, even if it is very tiny.

And another thing, what does he mean when he says he doesn't know where it came from, and why did Mom ask that question. Where could it come from? Then he said they have to find out what it is. What could it be? Is it something solid they will have to cut out, or is it something like a cyst or a blood clot that will dissolve and go away? If it's solid, is it a tumor? Does Mom have a brain tumor? I better stop speculating and just listen.

"A spontaneous spot on the brain usually comes from some place else. The nature of your seizures indicates a spontaneous reaction to a new condition. We would like to find out where this spot came from. I'll order more tests to begin tomorrow morning. We'll start with a lung series."

Lung series, he says. The spot on the brain may have come from her lungs. How can that be? It sounds like he's expecting the spot to be more than a blood clot. If I understand what he's saying, he thinks it could be a piece of lung tissue that's somehow landed on her brain. This is new territory to me. I don't understand it.

Mom's expression hasn't changed. She doesn't appear to be affected by what the doctor is saying to us. She has to be thinking something. Either her years of presenting positive appearances are serving her well, or the apparent seriousness of her "no need to worry" facial seizures hasn't hit her yet.

"I'm pretty tired," she says at last. "I think I'll take a nap now. You go on home, Shirleyanne. There's nothing more we can do today. Both of us ought to get some rest."

## A Tough Diagnosis

There is a tone of resignation in her voice that I've never heard before. Does she know more than she's letting on? She likes to talk, but she's not talking right now. I've never heard her say she's tired before, either. And the grin has disappeared.

I need to gather my thoughts and figure out the next step. What do I need to do about this? Is there anything I need to take care of? Should I call Gene? No use getting carried away. We don't know for sure that this is serious. Yes we do. There's a spot on Mom's brain. It probably came from a spot somewhere else. This has to be serious.

What about her family? Oh yes. The family. They're all coming to Seattle next weekend for a family reunion. Oh my gosh. What are we going to do about that?

Every year the Thompsons make it a point to gather for a family reunion at one of their homes. Mom goes to all of them, but she's never had the reunion at her house. This year was to be the first time. It'll have to be postponed. Even if Mom's tests are finished and she's released from the hospital before next weekend, she won't have time to put together the kind of celebration she'd been counting on. If Mom can't be in charge and in top form, she'll be dissatisfied with the results. This year was to be her show. At last it was her turn, the end to all hard feelings. What a disappointment this will be for her.

I'm not going to make phone calls tonight. I'm too tired and there are too many unknowns. Besides, I can't call Gene. He doesn't have a phone. He marches to the tune of his own version of Walden. I'll call him at work tomorrow, after we know more.

It's Monday morning; Mom calls me at work. I didn't expect to hear from her this early. "I just got back to my room," she says. "They took me downstairs early this morning, to get started with the tests. The tests are done for now. They found what they were looking for."

"What'd they find?"

"There's a tumor in my left lung."

Oh dear. NO! "I'll be right there."

I hang up the phone and sit in my office wondering again what to do next. What is the next step? One step at a time. Call Gene. He's at work. I can call him at work.

"Mom's in the hospital. She had a couple of facial seizures last week and checked into the hospital on Friday to find out what was causing them. They did a series of tests on Saturday, and found a spot on her brain. They ran more tests this morning and found a tumor on her lung. That's all I know right now. I'm going to the hospital. I'll call you again, when I know more."

"Call me tomorrow," he says. "I'll come down on Friday."

Gene lives in Bellingham, where Shannon is attending school. He settled there in the early seventies after he completed his degrees in Chinese and Japanese at the University of Washington. After serving four years in the Air Force, he chose not to re-up even though the government promised him a degree, on them. He decided to get degrees on his own, and then decided not to pursue work related to his study of Asian languages.

He's a warehouseman at Payless Drug Stores. In his leisure time he plays the banjo and deejays a couple of bluegrass and old-timey radio shows, and speaks around the Pacific Northwest about what is now called Traditional Music. The kind of music that Pop taught us, the kind of music we still play whenever the Thompsons get together. Unloading trucks at Payless is his vocation; music his avocation. He opted to let the genius rest and live his life simply, doing only what he wants to do. My brother is an individualist, and a success, in every sense of the word. He's my best friend. I don't know what I'd do without Gene.

I arrive at the hospital, walk into Mom's room and sit down beside her. We look at each other cautiously. I want to hold her and tell her it's going to be all right, but I can't do that. Control. We must maintain control over our emotions. Emotions are running very deep, and we can't let them get away from us. So we don't touch and we won't cry. If we start now, we'll drown in our tears, and this boat of ours has to sail on for a while longer.

The test doctor comes in to tell us what the tests revealed.

"There is a mass on your left lung, Mrs. Wilson. The nature of the mass is unknown. We will have to run more tests to determine whether or not the mass is malignant, and if it is malignant, what kind of malignancy it is. We can't be sure of our diagnosis or treatment until we have more information. I have to be frank with you. We do expect to find a malignancy. The symptoms up to this point would indicate a malignant condition. We can't be sure of course, but the indications are . . . "

For God's sake! Why doesn't he just say it. This futzing around with the truth is hard on us. Okay, okay. He doesn't know us. He doesn't know we can accept truth in its rawest form. But the M.O. around here is to make sure they are absolutely certain of their diagnosis, so we'll wait again. A few more days might help us too. I must be patient with their methods.

"How big is the growth?" Mom asks.

"Very big."

## A Tough Diagnosis

Of course there is hope. As long as there is life, there is hope. But we both clearly understand the probabilities. Mom is a smoker. She has a large tumor on her lung, and a piece of that tumor has broken off, traveled to her brain, and attached itself there. It's called metathesis. The spot on her brain will grow into a mass, just like the mass in her lung.

"Well, it's my own damn fault," she says. "I've been smoking these stupid things for over fifty years, and I knew they weren't good for me. They killed my husband."

It's a typical, straight-forward Lois kind of statement. Sure, we'll have more tests, but we know they only allow us to accept the truth in stages. Tuesday morning they will do the rest of the tests they need to do. They'll stick a tube with a light and a snipper on it into her lung, and take a tissue sample. Then it will be a day or two before we know the results of the new tests. We'll probably have the results on Thursday.

"You better go back to work, Shirleyanne. That's all we'll get out of them today.

I suppose we'll have to cancel the reunion. Have you called Gene?"

"I talked to Lide last night. We decided to postpone the reunion until you are up and around. And yes, I called Gene too. He'll come down on Friday."

"You better go."

Mom obviously wants time to herself to think about what she's been asked to accept. Reluctantly, I leave her. I stop on the way out to tell the doctor I want to be here when they give her the results of the new tests.

"My Dad was told he had cancer without having family with him for support. I don't want that to happen to my Mom. Do you understand?" I want no mistakes this time.

Thursday morning, the doctor calls me. "We plan to see your mother at ten o'clock."

As I drive to the hospital, there is no sense of anticipation, no fear, and no dread. I know what I am going to hear. My mother has cancer. All I can think of is, how can I help her today. What can I say or do to make this easier for her. I can't think of a thing. Hearing that you have cancer has got to be a terribly personal, awfully lonely piece of news. What can I do to help Mom today? Just be there, I guess. It seems so small.

Dad was fifty-four when he died; Mom is sixty-six. Both of them good, decent people, both of them called to death by lung cancer. Nasty way to go for such good people.

Besides the awful reality of Mom's mortality, this poses an unsettling

## Promise I'll Stay for Mother's Day

truth for me. In the natural order of the great master plan, I'm next up. What are my chances for longevity? I don't smoke, but I grew up with parents who were smokers, and I had asthma while I lived in their home. I have an elevated cholesterol count, and I take pills every day to control my blood pressure.

My Mom's mother died of cancer, her brother, Dick, had cancerous lymph nodes removed. Dad died of lung cancer, and his brother died of brain cancer. A long and healthy life does not appear to be a slam dunk for me right now. When my last parent dies, my turn will come around. When Mom leaves, there will be no going home again. I will be the home and I will be the next to leave.

> Some things can't be changed, and the natural order of life to death is one of those things. I don't quite know how yet, but this new realization of my own temporal existence is going to affect how I approach the rest of my life.

Some things can't be changed, and the natural order of life to death is one of those things. I don't quite know how yet, but this new realization of my own temporal existence is going to affect how I approach the rest of my life. How long do I postpone joy to get the work done? It seems to me right now that time is a wastin'.

Hello bad dream. You've arrived now, and your validity is confirmed. But the story has just begun. Our game of life looks pretty bleak right now, but I'm going to use your warning to make the final out a win. I'll take you on and fight you to the end. Something good is going to come from this. No use being forewarned if you don't use it to affect the outcome.

Once again I walk into Mom's hospital room. This time there will be no more delays. We know what is coming. This time we will hear the beginning of the end, and then we will plan our pursuit to that end. I don't know what the plan will be. I do know it will be our plan, and we'll be in charge.

"Hi Mom. How ya doin?"

"Hi Shirleyanne. I'm fine."

Dr. Siverling walks in. "Lois, you have lung cancer. I'm sorry."

So there it is. The mass in her lung is large, and it has metastasized to her brain. The spot in her brain is lung cancer too.

I look at Mom all the time he is talking. She lies there listening. Nothing visibly registers in her face. What could she be thinking? How does a person accept this kind of news? Is there acceptance? I don't think so. I don't think there's even a true acknowledgement. How can there be. One day in your life, could be any day, a doctor walks into a room and says, "Good morning, Lois,

## A Tough Diagnosis

you have cancer." What's the response supposed to be? "Thank you, Doctor. Thank you for stopping by."

Sorry. This is too much for me to accept right now. My mind is resisting lucidity.

Dr. Siverling continues. "I've spoken to Dr. Bob Levenson. He's an oncologist. He specializes in treating symptoms like yours. He'll discuss treatment choices with you. The treatment options, should you choose to have treatment, will include radiation and/or chemotherapy. Surgery will not be a consideration. The cancer is inoperable. I'm sorry."

After a few more minutes of discussion, Dr. Siverling leaves. He's very sad. This is hard for him. Doctors are not merely medical dispensers. They're human beings as well. Sometimes, as we count on them to see us through our personal health issues, we forget that.

Mom begins to talk, slowly. "My life has been good, Shirleyanne. I got to see both my kids grow up. My son graduated from college and chose to return to his roots, playing the banjo—gaining his renown as a traditional American music specialist. I finally accepted that.

"It's my daughter who became the successful business executive. I don't know why I wanted those choices to be different. Your Dad and I set the example, and it worked for us. I wasted a lot of time pushing Gene to be an engineer, and grooming you to be Suzy homemaker, didn't I?" She laughs.

She doesn't expect an answer. I watch her, looking for signs of distress. There are none.

"I've even had the joy of watching my granddaughters grow up to be beautiful young adults. Your Dad never saw any of that. He never even got to meet Rebecca and Shannon." Then she added, "Of course, I had hoped to know Rebecca and Shannon a little longer."

It's such a simple, stunning statement. The tears are very close now, for both of us. Push them back. We don't cry.

Mom continues, "I'm going to fight this as long as I can. This probably means I won't be traveling to China next spring. I was looking forward to that."

She stops talking and we look at each other silently for a few moments, trying to comprehend what has just happened, or what has been happening inside her body, without our knowledge. This didn't happen this week. That damned disease has been chewing its way through her body for quite some time and we didn't even know it. We need time, silent time, to try to understand all of this before we speak again.

A woman enters the room. She identifies herself as a social worker. "Is there anything I can do for you?" she asks.

Damn it! Couldn't she have waited for a little while? Do we have to greet this messenger of good will so soon? Leave us alone. Calm down, Shirleyanne. She's doing her job. Some people need immediate support from professionals schooled in helping people who've received bad news. Mom and I have each other. We can handle it.

"Thank you. Not right now."

She leaves the room and we realize that the word is out. Mom has become one of the dying. I wish we'd had more time to adjust to this by ourselves. We would have liked to work through our feelings before sharing them with others. We appreciate the concern and we may welcome help at a later date, when this thing grows beyond our ability to take care of it. But right now, please, we would rather keep it to ourselves.

Mom and I are discovering for the first time that we are more than mother and daughter. We're in this life together as friends and life partners as well. No more directing from the top and acquiescing from the bottom. Forget past roles. We truly care for each other as equals. I'm grown up now. This is the way it's supposed to be. Life evolves. We never understood that before, but we understand it now, don't we, Mom.

It's about time.

CHAPTER 20

## *Medical Decisions*

TUESDAY WE HAVE our first appointment with Dr. Levenson. Mom and I have agreed that we will attend her appointments together. We'll have a better understanding of the discussions and ask more useful questions if both of us listen and ask. Also, Mom can't drive while she's on the anti-seizure drugs. She'll need a driver.

Most of us have opinions as to what we'd do if a serious medical diagnosis were handed to us. It's easy to say we'd decline treatment if it would not result in long-term survival; easy to say if it were only hypothetical. But what does long-term survival mean? A month, a year, or must long-term survival be defined as five years or more? What is the definition and who defines it? There are too many questions and no easy answers when we're talking about a personal situation with a real diagnosis. I wonder what we'll say.

At first glance Dr. Levenson looks pretty young to be working against a possible death sentence for a senior citizen. But he quietly establishes himself to be both mature and caring.

Mom starts talking. She talks about herself, her family, her travels, her everything; everything, that is, except her illness. She's stalling for time to gather herself for what she must face to survive the next chapter in her life. Dr. Levenson shows no clinical impatience. He lets her speak for as long as she needs to before he begins his part of the discussion.

"The x-rays show a large lesion in the lung, with a related spot on the brain. The prognosis is not good, but I feel treatment will be beneficial."

"Well, my life has been good," Mom says, "and it may be nearly over, but I want to fight this thing. Shoot the works."

So there you have it. Shoot the works. But of course.

She rambles on, shoving "this thing" aside. She doesn't say cancer. Cancer in her book is a synonym for hopeless. She has yet to experience a win over cancer. She's talking about her trip to Kenya last year and her planned trip to China next year. She talks about her future great grandchildren; she talks

## Promise I'll Stay for Mother's Day

about whatever she can think of that has a future attached to it. Dr. Levenson smiles and waits again for her to finish.

When he gets another chance to speak, he suggests that we treat the brain disease first, since it's the cause of her current symptoms. He places a call to Dr. Welch at the Swedish Tumor Institute. Dr. Levenson has to convince Dr. Welch to accept Mom as a patient.

"Yes. It is advanced, but I believe we can relieve the conditions she is experiencing with aggressive treatment . . . Yes, I'll ask . . . thank you Dr. Welch." He hangs up the phone and begins to set out a plan.

"First, Mrs. Wilson, you will have radiation for the lesion on the brain, under the care of Dr. Welch, at Swedish hospital. There will be twelve-to-fourteen treatments. The exact number will be determined by when we feel we've achieved the results we are looking for. When the radiation is complete, you will return to my care for chemotherapy for the lung disease."

Dr. Levenson begins to explain the consequences of the chemical treatments. "You will feel fatigue and experience bouts of nausea after each treatment, and more than likely your hair will fall out on your pillow one night, all at once."

"Will it grow back?" she asks.

"We can't say for sure. Sometime it does; sometimes it doesn't."

It's my turn to ask a question. "Why will there be radiation for the brain and chemotherapy for the lungs?"

"Chemotherapy does not reach that part of the brain where the lesion is located."

"What other side effects are there," I ask. "And what will be the long-term result of her treatments?"

It feels a little strange that I am asking these pointed questions, but Mom talked and talked and did not seem to want to include the medical situation in her conversation. And we have to know certain things.

"Sometimes we hit a home run, and the patient will survive three years, or more. With the brain involvement, it will be difficult to accomplish this."

"Does a home run mean you will eliminate the brain cancer?"

"Here, the home run means we will arrest the growth for a while. Radiation will not destroy the malignancy."

Here we are now at the how much treatment versus the how much time crossroads. Dr. Levenson made it clear we are only buying time. How much time? Perhaps three plus years, the doctor says. That would make sense, three more years. Or perhaps less. How much less? I don't want to know that today. Besides, Mom said to "Shoot the works." And she's the boss.

"Should I stop smoking?" she asks. "I know the cigarettes caused this."

"Not unless you want to. You'll have enough stress dealing with the disease." It's another telling answer. Long term is a fading reality.

"How often will I have chemotherapy?"

"We'll determine that as we go along. It will depend on the results of what we are doing. At first I would anticipate a treatment every four-to-six weeks."

She's ready to ask the time question. "My granddaughter is getting married in March. Do you think I'll get to go to the wedding?"

"I think you can plan on that," he says.

She starts jabbering again about her life's adventures and her family's accomplishments. Dr. Levenson listens again. Little does he know how much listening he'll get to do over the next few months.

"These are not experimental treatments," Dr. Levenson explains. "There are no good treatments or bad treatments. They all work some times, but not all times."

"What about the chemotherapy?" she finally asks. "Is that going to be day trips, or will I stay overnight? I have to think about transportation. Since I'm taking these pills for my fits, I can't drive."

"Transportation will be no problem, Mom."

Dr. Levenson gets to talk again. "There are various kinds of chemotherapy options," he says. "I will determine the exact treatment schedule after your radiation is completed. Treating cancer is very difficult and complex. The disease has many unpredictable tendencies, and each person reacts differently to treatment, depending on individual physical liabilities and emotional limitations. I'll have to analyze your specific reactions before I can prescribe further treatment. We don't want the results of treatment to be worse than the disease itself.

"Mrs. Wilson, would you be willing to have your treatments contribute to cancer research?" So that's the question he told Dr. Welch he'd ask to get his acceptance for her radiation treatment. They're going to get something from this too.

Her response will be affirmative. She's no longer one little person trying to take care of her little disease. She will become a player in a much larger arena. To become part of a team that fights something as big as cancer will be seen as an irresistible opportunity. She says yes.

"These are not experimental treatments," Dr. Levenson explains. "There are no good treatments or bad treatments. They all work some times, but not

## Promise I'll Stay for Mother's Day

all times. The point of this research is to find out why specific treatments work and when they work, so that eventually, we will know what to prescribe for each individual. Right now, deciding which of the proven treatments is best for each patient is more or less a crap shoot."

So. Dad died twenty-five years ago and treatments were a crap shoot. Has there been no progress in a quarter century? The papers Dr. Levenson hands us actually says that treatment today is still a crap shoot. It must be true. Still, Mom is ready to go with it, and it's her call.

> "Mom has a high tolerance for pain and discomfort and her will is strong. Would a peaceful exit be better? What's peaceful? Is it a so-called gracious acceptance of an ungracious disease taking away a proud life? I don't think so."

"Either of you may call me at any time," Dr. Levenson assures us. "Our next visit will be in about eight weeks, after the radiation therapy with Dr. Welch. Good luck."

On the way out we stop at the front desk to ask how the billing will be handled. She assures them she is well insured. Paying the bills is an important item for her.

Are we doing the right thing? The treatments are going to be rough, perhaps even rougher because of the research participation. Mom has a high tolerance for pain and discomfort and her will is strong, but even for her, this is going to be a very tough battle. Would a peaceful exit be better? What's peaceful? Is it a so-called gracious acceptance of an ungracious disease taking away a proud life? I don't think so.

On our way to the car, Mom says, "Well, at least there is hope. They wouldn't be doing anything is there wasn't hope."

Hope is the eternal instrument for working on life's difficulties. Mom is walking with more determination and pride than she has since the diagnosis of this relentless, ugly disease. She's been handed a shred of hope from the medical profession. She can now address this business of living once again, rather than accepting the inevitability of dying. Her body may have pulled a fast one on her, but she can combat its trickery. When her earthly battle is over, Mom will have faced another enemy and prevailed once again. She will march to her judgment day with determination and an eye on the future. She will always have hope and a plan and, therefore, a future.

"I don't want all this to interfere with your work, Shirleyanne."

"That won't be an issue, Mom. I've worked for Fisher Broadcasting long enough to have flexibility in my daily routine. We'll make this work."

When we're hit with a major crisis, we initially confront only the crisis, as if our daily lives can be put on hold while we attend to the responsibilities of special needs. Then we find out it's not that simple, even with flexible schedules. We cannot abandon our daily lives. We have to find a way to insert these new challenges into this multi-layered sandwich we call life.

*Shirleyanne, 1981.*

CHAPTER 21

## *Sandwiched*

WOULDN'T YOU KNOW IT? Mom's first chemotherapy is going to occur while I'm on a business trip. I have to get on with my fall travel. Texie has a pharmacy degree. She will take Mom to her first treatment and she'll relay the information to me as to the effects and expectations of treatments in words I can understand. It's better that she'll be the one attending the first session. I'm rationalizing to cover my guilt.

It takes only a few hours by air to distance myself from the stress at home. I didn't realize I was feeling stressful until I landed in Chicago and found myself remembering how much I enjoy traveling by myself. I have time this evening to dine at the original Morton's Steak House and stretch out in a luxury hotel on State Street, paid in full by my employer. Tomorrow I'll conduct a sales meeting with consummate professionals in the media rep business and go on sales calls to the big ad agencies, Campbell Mithun, NW Ayer, BBD & O, etc. I have the privilege of working at something I do well, knowing exactly what to say, hear, and do at every stop. No uncertainties, no second guessing, no self recriminations. It's a good day of calls.

After Chicago it's Detroit. The people there surprise me with a birthday apple pie and the afternoon free to explore the city. I use the time to buy a new outfit for my weekend in New York City. There's no better place to spend a weekend than in Manhattan, where I'll undoubtedly begin with a Manhattan at a mid-town bar.

I scan the New York Magazine to check out my choices. It looks like it'll be a weekend of shopping on Fifth Avenue, brunch at The UN Plaza, where I'm staying, and a couple of trips to the theater. But let's start with the shopping. Pretty clothes and more pretty clothes. Would you believe a red knit dress and a black leather trench coat? Love red. Love leather. Then it'll be dinner at Smith & Wollensky. That's where I'll get the Manhattan, along with a steak medium rare, baked potato with butter, sour cream, bacon, chives. And a baked, creamy New York cheesecake. Bring on the cholesterol!

## Promise I'll Stay for Mother's Day

The evening theater selection is a Pulitzer Prize winner I know nothing about. But Pulitzer Prize must mean something. How can I go wrong?

I can go wrong. Glengarry Glenross is a play about dirty rotten sales people and their dirtier, rottener sales manager. The men in the audience are roaring with laughter while the women, for the most part, smile politely, wondering what the hell is so funny. I sit quietly in my seat, glad that no one knows I'm one of the dirtier, rottener folks.

It's raining when the play lets out so I set out to hail a cab. There are more people than cabs, of course, so I step in front of three nice old ladies and take their cab. As a dirty, rotten sales slime-ball I can do this. When in New York...

I get a Sunday wake up call from Barry, wishing me a happy birthday. I don't like birthdays. I don't want to be around people wishing me a happy one. I never know whether birthdays are supposed to be endings or beginnings, so I don't know how to act. I do know I prefer to act alone, thus the travel at birthday time.

"Do you have a reservation, Ma'am?" I'm trying to get a table for brunch.

"No, but I'm staying here at the hotel, and I'd like to have brunch." I smile sweetly and look him straight in the eyes.

(Sniff.) "Certainly. Would you like to sit in the lounge until we have a table for you?"

"Certainly."

I sip champagne in the lounge for what I consider to be a decent length of time before I walk back to the sniffy one and say, "I'm ready to be served now."

Only one eyebrow shoots up as he turns to show me to a lovely table for one, next to the grand piano. Perfect. In New York, being a pushy broad works. I take my time, eating a sumptuous brunch, listening to the music, flirting with the pianist and writing myself a self-satisfied birthday letter.

After a leisurely brunch I stroll back to the theater district—it's a nice day—and I see Tommy Tunes and Twiggy in "My One and Only." It's a gloriously happy play, leaving me singing as I leave the theater. "Let the music start ... Let the band roll out ... Strike up the Band!" What a great birthday!

Back in the hotel room, I kick off my shoes, pull out the earrings, take out my self-written birthday letter and plop myself down on the bed to read my letter to me.

"Today's my birthday. I am 45 years old. I know it's my birthday because I got a call from my husband in Seattle. He said, 'Happy Birthday.'

"Today ought to be an important day. Turning 45 is more like a milestone than a plain ol' birthday. More than 40, certainly, and maybe more than what 50 will be. At 50, I'll be all set, with my life outcome already determined, everything in place and working toward retirement. I do get to retire someday, don't I? Long ago, I thought 30 was the age when life was all set . . . or was it 21? I don't remember.

"Whether it was 21 or 30 doesn't matter. Neither was a milestone. Neither determined anything. Forty is most everyone's milestone, I guess. If things are going well, we proceed with the rest of our lives, thinking positive thoughts, holding our heads high with self-satisfaction. If life is not as we dreamed it would be, then it's mid-life crisis time, society's all-purpose excuse for screwing around and messing with everything we've accomplished up to that point. Whatever crazy crap we pull during our mid-life crisis is to be understood and tolerated. People we hurt during our crisis, well, they must understand too. At 40 we've earned the right to spread a little grief.

> Today's my birthday! I'm 45! Somebody congratulate me for being here, for surviving. But nobody knows it's my birthday. I'm afraid if I stay home where everybody does know, I'll still be alone.

"I was in fine shape at 40—good job, new husband, kids growing up nicely; 40-to-45, a different story. Much tougher. Big-time success: high-stress job, kids with growing pains, new marriage going sour (is it really?), terminally ill parent, financial strains no matter how much I earn. Add in the quintessential high blood pressure and elevated cholesterol. And Voila! All the coveted trappings of success are mine.

My God! I planned to have it all together by age 50, and the 40-45 half-decade brings it all down. No, it's not down yet. But it's tumbling. How do I stop it? How do I know what to stop? You have to know what's important to know what to stop and what to keep, and I don't know what's important any more.

"Is money important? Sure. Family? Of course. New challenges? I have that. Then what's wrong? Nothing stays put. Work going well? Family is jealous. Mom IS sick? I neglect work. Go to work? I neglect Mom. Take care of Barry? Becca and Shannon are pissed. Take care of Becca and Shannon? Barry's bent out of shape. And, by the way, how do I get my piece of the Shirleyanne action? That's easy. I take a trip by myself to The Big Apple. I pretend Seattle's not there. Bottom line, I run away. It's a family coping system that goes way back.

"I'm sitting here by the piano listening to the lovely music in a fantastic setting eating marvelous food, and the musician person is flirting back. What's my problem? I don't know. But the music doesn't offer its usual balm.

## Promise I'll Stay for Mother's Day

I'm feeling sorry for myself. This is horse crap. Get over it, Shirleyanne. What do you want? Do you even know?

"Yes, I know. I want arms. Today's my birthday! I'm 45! Somebody congratulate me for being here, for surviving. But nobody knows it's my birthday. I made sure nobody knows. I do this every year. Why? Because I'm afraid if I stay home where everybody does know, I'll still be alone, because I'm strong; because nobody thinks I need them, because I've put on this stupid hero's cape to cover my needs.

"I do have needs. I just don't show them. Why should I have to show them? Why can't they see? Sure, I'm strong. And I'm capable of taking care of my needs. But *all* of them, *all* the time? Do I have to fail to get hugs? Do I have to fall on my ass to find arms? Damned if I will."

End of note. As you can see, I'm having a marvelous birthday.

After two solid days of sales calls it's time to head home. I call to see what's happening out West. Becca answers the phone.

"I'm ready to head for the airport. How're things?" I ask.

There's a pause. "Gran' didn't want you to know. She was feeling weak so Dr. Levenson put her in the hospital yesterday, for a couple pints of blood. She'll be home, though, when you get here."

The respite is over. But it was cathartic, and I'm ready to return and do my share. Barry meets me at the airport. He looks good. I'm always surprised to see how handsome he is.

During the flight home I began to look forward to seeing him. When we're apart I remember the things about him that I love. His openness, his laugh, his energy. He works hard. He really tries to please me. If he could just take time to be with me more, to have Sunday breakfast with me. I'm so tired of eating alone on Sunday.

"Missed you honey," he says.

"Missed you too," I say back. If we miss each other so damn much, why don't we spend more time together?

We drive by Mom's house on the way home. She looks better than I expected, considering what she's been through. The blood transfusions must have done what they were supposed to do. She wants us to stay a while and watch the vice-presidential debates. Geraldine Ferraro is holding her own. I'm trying to imagine a woman V.P.

The vision is cloudy. I think it's too soon. We're not quite ready for a woman to be the Vice President of the United States of America. Female Mid Life Crisis? Oh yes. Female VP? Not yet.

Back in the car Barry brings me up to date on the home front.

"Shannon came home from school this weekend, but she came to our house instead of your mother's. She didn't tell anyone her plans, of course, so no one knew where she was. I was at work all weekend, when I wasn't getting my car fixed. I need some money to get new brake pads."

"Anything else need fixing, Barry?"

"Yeah. The downstairs toilet is backed up. We need to get that fixed too.

"Anything else?"

"No, that's all."

"Say welcome home, Honey."

"Welcome home, Honey."

*Shannon, Becca, Lois, and Shirleyanne, Christmas 1984.*

CHAPTER 22

## *Christmas Past and Present*

It takes Mom a week to ten days to fully recover from a chemotherapy treatment. She's had three now, and as predicted, each one affects her more than the one before. In addition to the weakness and nausea, her skin has broken out into a fiery red rash, another reaction to one or more of the chemicals they're dripping into her body. She's also losing her appetite. The chemicals take away saliva, leaving her mouth dry and sore. Who'd want to eat with that going on?

And yes, she is bald. Her hair fell out all at once, as predicted. She's decided having an assortment of hats to wear will suit her better than wearing a wig every day. Her favorite chapeau is a dog's (or "dawg") head. We're fans of the University of Washington football program. Its fall and its football season, and we wear "dawg" hats.

"WOOF!" she says, as she slaps the hat on her head and laughs. "WOOF!"

Covering her bald head is easy, and carries a certain amount of merriment. Making sure she has enough nourishment to continue her fight is more problematic. We're going to have to work on that.

The holidays might help. We're nuts about holidays around our house, especially Christmas. There's a lot of good food to eat at holiday time, and a lot of family to overcome whatever may us keep us down. It'll be a challenge this year, but we've had challenges before. As a matter of fact, when Gene and I were kids Christmases were a little weird.

It started about two weeks before Christmas. Dad and Gene and I would begin to speculate about where we were going to get our tree, and where we'd put it. As if there'd be a change from the previous Christmas. We buy our tree at the same IGA store parking lot every year and put it in the same corner of the living room that had been mysteriously cleared to make room for a tree on the morning of tree-getting day. We get our tree on Friday because Mom works Friday evenings. She doesn't do trees.

Dad gets home from work early and the three of us go pick out the tree and buy new icicles, also available at the IGA store. We're pretty fussy about which tree will be ours. It has to be a fir, 6' 3" tall; high enough that Dad has to stand on a chair to put the angel on top and low enough to clear the ceiling when he does. And it has to be perfectly straight; no leaning to one side. We turn it around and around to make sure.

When we get the tree home and in the stand, we dig out the decorations from basement shelves, and Dad methodically begins to string the colored lights. When he finishes, Gene and I begin hanging the decorations. There isn't a lot of variety, just red, green, blue, silver, and gold glass balls. Some silver balls have a contrasting hot pink or dark green stripe around the middle. There are different sizes. We hang the smaller balls up high on the smaller branches, gradually adding the larger balls as we decorate the larger bottom branches. Gene and I exchange smiling glances throughout the annual routine, keeping our internal glee at bay. This is serious business. Dad has standards.

Each year we help him fulfill his vision of the perfect Christmas tree.

Then we hang the icicles, one strand at a time. Dad insists that each one is to be draped perfectly on each side of the branch, top branch to bottom branch, inside branch to outside branch, just like the glass balls. This takes one-to-two hours.

Every fifteen minutes or so Gene and I have to break loose. Laughing, we take turns at grabbing a hand full of icicles and throwing it at the tree in a wadded up glistening glob. It spoils the perfect picture. The thrower is officially scolded by the Arkansas Tree Sergeant and we go back to one strand at a time until fifteen minutes later, when the other one of us tosses another icicle glob . . . and is scolded again by the ATS.

Finally it's time for the angel to be put in place. That done, Dad turns off the room lights and turns on the tree lights.

It's a dazzling sight! We step back from the tree and stare at our masterpiece, the three of us finally grinning at each other in annual satisfaction, with colored lights and shimmering icicles reflecting in our eyes. We pulled it off one more time. It's probably our most satisfying evening of the year. The drifter's home is once again defined as he imagined it. How do you measure satisfaction? Take a look at Dad's big, big smile.

Mom gets home late on tree-trimming Friday. She passes through the room, nods, walks into her bedroom, takes off her coat, walks back out, turns the room lights back on and sits down on the beige living room sofa to read the evening newspaper.

One morning each year between the tree-trimming evening and Christmas

Eve we wake up to a fully decorated Christmas house in shimmering holiday splendor. This year it's a Thursday morning. It must be Santa's elves who sneak down each year from the North Pole to decorate while we sleep. No one else owns up to it. We crinkle our eyes and grin at Mom when she walks in to make sure we're ready for school. She ignores us.

The week before Christmas, packages begin to arrive from Milton-Freewater and they, along with one package each from Mom and Dad, are placed under the tree. We're not to touch, comment, smile, or ask questions, about any of them lest we appear greedy. Christmas is not discussed at the dinner table or anywhere else among the four of us. Of course Gene and I do all these things between the end of the school day and the time Mom and Dad arrive home from work. We laugh, shake, rattle, and guess. We can hardly wait for Christmas Eve when get to open them all!

Christmas Eve has its own ritual. After school I work like highly paid help to make sure the house is sparkling clean and I prepare dinner to as near perfection as a young girl age 10+ can get it. Dad helps me put the finishing touches on dinner. Gene plays in his bedroom with his balsa-wood airplane kits. He spends a lot of time in his room while chores are being done.

Mom arrives home later than usual on Christmas Eve, and literally runs her white-gloved fingers over the black lacquered living room floor, looking for dust I may have missed. We sit down to the kitchen table and eat in relative silence before we move to the living room when dinner is done. Gene and I sit on the big beige sofa looking at each other sideways, grinning inconspicuously (we think), knowing the waiting has to be over soon. Mom and Dad discuss the day, blah, blah, blah, and finally Mom says, "All right you greedy kids, I guess it's time to open presents."

And we do, and the presents are wonderful. Then we go to bed. We know Santa will come in the night and Christmas Day will bring a whole new glorious world. The lights are on, the house is warm, and delicious aromas waft their way into ourbedrooms to wake up our noses and the rest of our bodies. Gene wakes first, comes to get me and we rush into Mom and Dad's bedroom, jump on their bed, throw back their covers, pull them up out of bed and drag them laughing into the living room. We knew they'd already been up because the house is so warm and the smells are so delectable.

We don't have to wait for a thing. Presents first! We don't even have to unwrap them. Santa doesn't wrap presents at our house. He displays them around the tree.

They're always just what we told Santa we wanted. Not extravagant, of

## Promise I'll Stay for Mother's Day

course, because we know Santa is not wealthy. But they're perfect for us and perfect for our household. Mom and Dad exchange their presents for each other on Christmas morning too. Dad always finds just the perfect piece of jewelry for his beloved wife. Mom is adored, and she knows it.

Then we have a wonderful breakfast and a day of playing with new toys, and laughing and singing carols all day, until it's time for our Christmas dinner which is simply splendid. Dinner is served on fine, French Havilland China set on a Belgian lace table cloth, draped to cover the living room table. The cold wintry gloom of the days leading up to Christmas Day is gone. A new day of celebration arrives just in time to fulfill our version of a traditional family Christmas.

> "You know what I'd really like, Mom? I'd like for you to write each of them a letter. I don't know what kind of letter, nothing sad, but something they will keep and read every year."

It wasn't until I learned about Christmas Eve, 1930, that I understood our strange Christmas saga. When I first learned of Mom's twelve-year-old Christmas Eve, I wished I'd known the story earlier. But then, I'd have missed an important lesson of acceptance. Sometimes we just need to accept what each day brings. There was a reason for our odd Christmas rituals. If we take the time to look, we may find there's a reason behind every human story. We were blessed because we knew that, come Christmas morning our veil of gloom would magically lift. That assurance doesn't happen for everyone. Veils of grief hang over large segments of the world's population with no hope for relief.

The holidays changed with the arrival of Rebecca and Shannon. Christmas preparations begin the day after Thanksgiving. It's become very important that we have lots of presents under our tree. In fact the year their father moved out, the girls and Mom and I began a new tradition. The first weekend of December we check into a nice hotel in downtown Seattle for a weekend of fine food and shopping, shopping, shopping. We go more than a little overboard, but we're making up for lost time.

"What shall I get the girls this year?" Mom asks me.

She doesn't usually ask. Left unsaid is the thought that this could be her last Christmas with us. She wants to give them something special.

"You know what I'd really like, Mom? I'd like for you to write each of them a letter. I don't know what kind of letter, nothing sad, but something they will keep and read every year."

I had in mind some sort of personal "try-hard, do-good-work, make-me-proud" kind of message. I should have known better. Much too ordinary. Mom cocks her head to one side, like she does when she's thinking about something that's about to become important. Then that signature grin of secret knowledge spreads across her face, and I know she's decided what she's going to write.

"I know just what I'll write," she says. "I'll tell each of them about the first time I ever saw them.

"I remember when I walked up to the hospital nursery window and looked over each of the new babies. My eyes stopped at the prettiest one—a perfect little round head with strawberry blond hair. I looked at that little baby and turned to Lloyd and said, 'That's ours.' He wanted a boy, you know, but he couldn't help but be proud of that pretty little thing. I had a bet with his dad that I'd get me a little red-haired granddaughter, and I got her. That was Rebecca."

She doesn't call her "Becca" like the rest of us. It's always Ree-beck-a. She chose the name for its Biblical beauty, and she doesn't care for the shortened version.

"Then when Shannon was born, that poor little tyke, she was yellow and she had a frown on her face. And her dad said she had a big nose. She looked at me as if to say, 'Granny, it's not going to be easy for me. I'm going to need your help.' And she did, didn't she?"

To share her feeling of the moment she first saw them is a gift no one else could give. It's honest and unique. But most of all, it's simple. No matter what is happening to her or going on around her, she manages to discover the one simple need of the moment and focus her heart and mind on fulfilling that one need. I've become so scattered, trying to do everything at once, I barely reach the surface of my relationships. I must reach for her kind of simplicity.

Mom is scheduled for another chemotherapy session. As I'm getting ready to go pick her up, the phone rings. It's Becca.

"Mom, Gran' is dreading this treatment. She doesn't want to go, but she thinks she has to, because she's not ready to give in yet. She doesn't want us to be disappointed in her. Do the treatments have to be so strong, every time?"

Mom is still playing brave soldier with me. She wants to remain the leader of the clan. I'm still the child and she's the parent, and parents are supposed to be braver and stronger than their children. Parents pass the torch reluctantly to their children and she's not ready to hand it over. She's not about to tell me she's hurting and wants to lay back a bit in this fierce struggle against odds that clearly are insurmountable. She's still the matriarch and I can't fault her for her pride in that, but the tone of Rebecca's message has let me know that I need to take a more decisive role in Mom's care. We can't leave everything up to the

## Promise I'll Stay for Mother's Day

doctors. Mom deserves more than a medical crapshoot. I need to talk to Dr. Levenson before tomorrow's treatment. I pick up the phone.

"Dr. Levenson, Mom told my daughter that she is dreading the treatment tomorrow," Not knowing how the conversation will be received, I pause before I continue. He waits, so I begin.

"The last one was pretty rough, and she's afraid of what this treatment will do to her. I don't think we can get by with doing nothing. But is there . . . I don't know how to say this . . . I don't want to offend you, or ask you to do anything that is medically unethical . . . but can we hospitalize her and just give her a nutritional boost, or at most, a dramatically reduced chemo treatment this time? She's pretty drained."

"Have we discussed time yet?" he asks.

"No," I respond, "and maybe we should. I don't think Mom wants to know about time, but the family would like to have more information. Maybe it's time for me to step into a more decisive role on her behalf. Does this make sense? Is it appropriate? Is it all right for the two of us, you and me, to make decisions about her treatment without her input?"

"There usually is someone in a serious family illness who has to walk the line between patient and doctor and family, and who ultimately will have to make very important decisions, alone," he says. "It appears that, in this family, you are that person. Don't be concerned about our discussions. Our conversations and decisions will be held in confidence, and in these circumstances there are no wrong decisions. You mustn't second guess yourself. Whatever we decide for your mother will be the right decision, given the particular knowledge and circumstances at the time. It is an extremely difficult position to be in, but I will help you."

"What about time?" I ask.

"It's hard to predict how much time she has, because this disease is unpredictable. In cases like your mother's, when both the lung and brain are involved, the average time left after diagnosis is six-to-ten months. I feel Lois will fall somewhere in that average."

"And we're in the fifth month right now . . . " I pause to calculate . . .

"Yes, that's right," he says.

This news is stunning. I don't know why, because I knew it wasn't going to be a long time, but I hadn't established a clear time frame. At best, we're buying only five more months and, at worst, two more. Two more?!? She may not even be here for Mark and Becca's wedding. That would be just awful, to come so close and not make it.

Well, she sure as hell won't make it if we keep pouring poison into her veins at the rate we're going now. Two-to-five months is not enough time for her to have to bravely tolerate this self-imposed wretchedness. I doubt that she fully understands the affects of the treatments, or the short amount of time she has left. It really is time for me to take a more decisive role in her care.

"Dr. Levenson, I'd like for you to alter the treatments. Is that possible?"

"There's always a medical reason for the treatments I prescribe," he says carefully, "and it may be a good medical decision to re-evaluate what we are currently doing."

I fumble on, trying to excuse my request. "This is a very important season for my family. We love the holidays. I'd like for Mom to enjoy them as much as she can, and I'd like for the rest of us to enjoy her too. Can we continue to treat her with that in mind?"

Dr. Levenson answers, "If there were no brain involvement, we would be more aggressive in fighting the lung disease, but we are only treating the symptoms at this point. I think she should enjoy the season, too."

"Thank you Doctor. We will see you tomorrow."

I hang up the phone and sit here, trying to comprehend what has just taken place. It appears that I have made a decision to shorten my mother's life so we can have a happy holiday season. Is that what happened? Can I do that? Can I make a decision like that about someone else's life? But this is not life as we've known it. All it really is, is squeezing out a few more weeks for us to be with Mom. But she would want this too.

Right? That's what people always say when they make choices for other people, without their consent . . . "She would want it this way . . . " Is this just a cop out, or would she really want it this way? I don't know. But this is my decision, and I am the parent now. There is to be no second guessing. Dr. Levenson said so.

At this stage every treatment is difficult and this treatment has taken its toll. She's not talking very much. Her silence is more telling than words. I'm beginning to miss her talking. Never thought I'd miss that. But as the days pass, she seems to be regaining some strength. Dr. Levenson and I have not had further conversation, so I don't know if there was an adjustment in the chemotherapy dosage, and I don't need to know. She's feeling better.

But she's decided she won't be able to make the weekend in town with

## Promise I'll Stay for Mother's Day

us. It was last year I realized how important this now traditional excursion had become. Details have become rituals. We must drive into town Saturday morning, have breakfast along the way and check in with two reservations rather than four.

When we first began this trip, money was very scarce so we had to cut corners to carry this off. Becca and I walk up to the reservation desk while Mom and Shannon stand behind a post, smuggling a sleeping bag inside a shopping bag, giggling at how clever we are. Once we're checked in, the girls race each other to the elevator and wrestle over who gets to push the buttons. When we're in the room, Shannon pushes and pulls every room button and knob, and opens and closes every drawer, looking for who knows what. We dump our stuff, leave the room and shop for a couple of hours, and go to the same restaurant every year for lunch.

"I'll have a B.L.T. and a soda", I say to the waitress.

"No you won't," the girls say together. "You will have a cheeseburger and a chocolate shake, just like every year. We're talking tradition here, you know."

At dinner I decide to order mince pie for dessert. It's not often you find mince pie in a restaurant. It won't be as good as Lide's home-made elk mincemeat, but I think I'll give it a try.

"No you don't", says Shannon. "You'll have burnt crème, like you always do."

That was last year. Because Mom cannot join us, tradition is suspended this year. It's not the same, but we have to learn to go on without her. We're sailing into the dark waters now. If there is a light ahead I'm not seeing it.

Taking care of Mom has left me very little time to take care of Barry. Except for last weekend when we put up our tree, we've shared practically nothing for weeks. We're living in the same house, but days go by when we don't even see each other. I don't understand why I'm allowing this isolation to occur. I rationalize that I'm simply taking care of family and Barry is taking care of business, traditional roles that all families have. But we've never been bound by traditional roles. We've crossed lines before to get what we want. We're not crossing lines these days. We're passing each other on different sides of an imaginary line that separates us. We should be sharing, but we're not. This will pass, I insist to myself and to Barry. When this is over, we can share. When the store is on its feet we will share. When Mom's illness is over, we can share. Some day we will share again.

Who am I kidding? This is the ultimate family sharing time; this is life and death time. If we really want to, we'll find the time to share this now. The question is, do we want to?

## Christmas Past and Present

Christmas Eve has arrived, and family and friends are knocking at the door. Barry gets home from work just in time for dinner. How considerate. While I'm preparing dinner for seventeen people, including his parents and kids, and while I'm setting up tables and hauling chairs, Barry is nice enough to come home, and climb the stairs to our bedroom to be "alone for a while." When he gets his fill of alone time, he comes downstairs.

"Why are my parents sitting by themselves?" are the first words from Barry following his descent from the bedroom. "You're not making them feel very welcome. It's only your family you care about. Obviously, my family doesn't count."

"Why don't you talk to your family, Barry. And on your way over to them, it would be nice if you could set up a few chairs."

My icy retort brings me an even icier glare. But he's joined the party. The man has arrived. Now the party can begin.

Long skirts, festive sweaters, candlelight, fabulous food and a shameful pile of presents . . . the whole thing. Everything in excess. Wonderful no-holds-barred extravagance, straight from the pocket books to the heart. There shouldn't be a direct connection, but sometimes it just works out that way.

I watch Mom more intently than usual. Again, I wonder what she is thinking. I unwrap her gift to me. It's her cameo pin. Nearly forty years ago, I helped Dad pick it out for her. Forty years! Where did they go? We must treasure the moments, for we have only moments. Years pass too quickly to treasure. Becca and Shannon open their letters. Becca quietly leaves the room.

Barry just opened his gift from his Dad. It's a small electric train set. Barry always wanted an electric train and never got one as a kid. He is noticeably touched. There! That's the spirit!

When it's time for people to go home, I go through the usual "Merry Christmas, thank you for coming." Mom and Gene are approaching. They're going back to her home to sleep. We'll see them again tomorrow.

Mom walks over to me and puts her arms around me. Is that a hug? Did my Mom just give me a hug? It's our first hug. Maybe it's a new tradition. Maybe we'll hug every year in our next lives. Merry Christmas Mom, for all our past Christmases, for this Christmas, and for the anticipation of Christmases to come, somewhere on another plane.

Time on this plane is running short.

CHAPTER 23

## *Another Damn Divorce*

I PROMISED MYSELF I would hold on to my marriage, for Mom and for Becca. I've obviously lost control over my own needs, but I could at least try to keep my marriage together a little while longer, for them. Mom shouldn't have to worry about my marital problems when she has enormous problems of her own, and Becca doesn't need to witness her mother's marriage falling apart when she is happily putting her own marriage together. I promised myself I'd wait out this awful disintegration, but I'm going to have to break my promise.

One would think that people could live together without talking all the time. There's no need to talk. We know what's happening. Why can't we peacefully co-exist until all this over? Because we're not supposed to merely exist. Human beings are supposed to share feelings and help each other get through times of turmoil. Life is full of "supposed to" moments. They mean nothing, unless you live them honestly.

I'm not talking; Barry's not talking. Neither of us is talking, feeling, or sharing. We're pussy footing around the house doing our best to avoid each other. This stupid cat-and-mouse game we're playing inside our home is depleting the energy I must count on to get through these next few months. Barry and I have to talk.

"I need time to myself, Barry. I have to have emotional space to work things through my head. I don't want a divorce, but I don't know how to live with you any more. We don't laugh, we don't make love, we don't talk."

"No, I take that back. One of us talks. You talk. You call me on the phone and talk to me while I'm at work. You call me to bitch and complain, about the store, about the customers, about my daughters, about money, about everything. What do you want me to do? Do you want me to magically solve all our problems by myself? Is that it?"

"Am I the magic fixer of all things? I'm sorry if you feeling I am ignoring you, but I can't solve all our problems by myself. And for that matter, I am sick to death of talking about problems all day, every day. Either help me with some

## Another Damn Divorce

of this or keep your criticism to yourself. Either we're going to share a few warm, peaceful moments, or we're going to stop sharing all together. I need an oasis from this pressure. I need to come home and rest. I need a smile now and then. Get off my back and give me a little support, or this marriage is over."

I hate ultimatums. Barry's transferring his frustrations to me by bitching, and I'm transferring them right back with ultimatums. This particular outburst couldn't have come at a worse time. Our new store is in financial trouble and Barry is, literally, sick from worrying about it. Now I've handed him the possibility of losing his wife as well as his business. Nice going, Shirleyanne.

> I promised Shannon I'd be there for sure, but I've broken promises before. This time it'll work out . . . I promise.

I feel guilty for this outburst, but I have to have some relief from someone. Something has to give, or I'll lose my ability to function. What is it that will have to give? Is it the marriage? Do I have to give up on my marriage? I don't want to give up on my marriage.

I don't want to give up on anything. I'll have to prioritize my responsibilities. I'll make a list. Mom, Girls, work, Barry. Which item goes to the top of the list. Shall it be my husband, my mother, my daughters, or my work? What about me? Am I on the list?

I can manufacture all the lists I want, but life is going to hand me its own list right now. Its Christmas vacation and the girls are home. Aside from Mom's medical needs, the girls have minor but pressing medical problems we've decided to take care of while they're on break.

Tomorrow Mom needs to go to Riverton Hospital, in Burien, for a blood transfusion. It's time for another energy lift. The day after tomorrow, Shannon is checking in to Overlake Hospital, in Bellevue, for surgery to remove the steel plate from her arm . . . the plate they put in the arm she broke last January in a car accident. Turns out it's too big. Friday, I meet Becca at the Mason Clinic, in Seattle, for a medical consultation about her chronic circulatory problems. She has engorged veins in her legs that cause big, sore red bumps. It's called arethema nodosum, which means red bumps.

It's not life threatening, but it hurts and it looks ugly, so we're exploring treatment options to take care of it. I'm taking a week's vacation to cover these things.

It'll be a little tricky getting Mom home from her hospital and getting Shannon to her hospital at the right time, and trickier still to meet Becca's doctor and be back at Shannon's hospital before she goes into surgery. I promised Shannon I'd be there for sure, but I've broken promises before. This time it'll work out . . . I promise.

## Promise I'll Stay for Mother's Day

I broke it. Not everyone had the same tight schedule. Other people had their own priorities. Got Mom home; got Shannon registered; got to Becca's appointment. But then the wheels rolled to a stop. Becca's doctor forgot to check our time table. He was late. I spun out of there as soon as I could and raced back to Overlake to find Shannon's room empty. I'm on time. I'm not late. Where is she? I whirl myself out of her room and run to the nurse's station.

"Where is my daughter, Shannon Anderson?" I demand nervously.

"They took her into surgery at two o'clock," is her curt reply. The reply comes with a frown of disapproval.

"They weren't supposed to take her until four forty-five", I offer lamely. "Her sister was at the Mason Clinic for a consultation. I thought I could make it."

"She will be coming back from surgery soon."

I walk back to her room, my heart bursting with guilt. Shannon is wheeled in, wide awake and wanting to go home. I look at the doctor.

"I see no problem with taking her home as soon as the anesthetic wears off," he says.

I see a problem. Thinking everybody would be settled and taken care of I scheduled a client meeting for tonight. You know, the ol' what you can't get done during the day, you tack on to the end of the day routine. Not gonna work. I call my client. No answer. Too late. So. Barry can take care of Shannon, family effort and all that. Right. Fat chance. Oh yes. I haven't checked in with Mom since I took her home. Hey Mom.

How ya doing? Fine, I hope.

Take out that list. Who goes to the top now? Who comes first, and who's on second? I chuckle. I can here Mom say, "No, Shirleyanne, it's who's *on* first, not who comes first. And who's never on second. *What's* on second." She's laughing at me. I can almost hear her.

Even when she's not around, her humor keeps my mind in balance. Today is not a tragic day. Today is an outrageous day. You can't do anything with an outrageous day, except laugh. Everything I do is wrong. Nothing works. There's no list; there's no choosing; there's no prioritizing. I try to do everything and I accomplish noting. No one is satisfied. Everyone is either slightly or really pissed. I'm laughing. No. It's not laughter. The Village Idiot is crying.

Tension at home is mounting. It's been a week since that disastrous day. Barry says, "I want you to imagine yourself as a third person in this room."

This room is our bedroom, and Barry is lying next to me, asking me to pretend to be someone other than his wife.

## Another Damn Divorce

"Be my counselor," he says. "If you weren't my wife, what advice would you give me to help me keep my wife?"

If I weren't his wife?!? But I am his wife! How can he possibly expect me to remove myself from this marriage bed and give him a counselor's objective opinion? He's serious. I have to try.

"If I were your counselor, and I knew you wanted to have your wife back, I would advise you to do as she asks. I'd ask you to give her the time and space she's told you she needs, so she can restore her emotional energies and have something to give to you again, when this is all over. She needs for you to be self-reliant during this crazy time. Please help her if you can. If that's too much to ask from you, give her the space she asks for."

> If I were your counselor, and I knew you wanted to have your wife back, I'd ask you to give her the time and space she's told you she needs, so she can restore her emotional energies and have something to give to you again, when this is all over.

Barry doesn't answer immediately. The air is so oppressive I try to hold my breathing, so I won't run short of air.

At last he says, "I can't do that. I can't stand the rejection. I need my wife now."

More silence. Now I'm the one who can't stand it. I have to cut through the atmosphere in this room. I have to find a way to respond.

"Would it be easier for you if I left the room?" I ask, as his wife.

"Yes, it would," he says peevishly.

That's not the answer I expected. I thought he'd put his arms around me and say, "No, honey. That's what he calls me. Honey. Let's work on this together. Let's sleep now and talk more in the morning. I really don't want you to be my counselor. I want you to be my wife."

That's what I want him to say, but he remains silent. I get out of our bed and walk down the stairs to sleep in the guest bedroom. I can't sleep. This is not my bed.

Suddenly I hear crashing sounds. They're getting closer. Barry is crashing into the guest room. The lights go on. My eyes slam shut. I feel his hands grabbing my arm, pulling me out of bed. I manage to get to my feet. He still has hold of me. He's pushing me up the stairs.

"You are going to watch me move out. I'm moving out now, and you are going to witness what you've done to our marriage. I'm not going to go through this pain alone."

I'm mute. I'm being pulled into the kitchen to watch him sort through the

## Promise I'll Stay for Mother's Day

silverware and the pots and pans. I'm being dragged back down the hall to watch him load his car with this and other things he's pulled out onto the porch.

Our next door neighbor is outside, walking his dog. Wouldn't you know it. Ralph is watching us. It must be about midnight. What's he doing standing there, watching us? When will this stop? How long is this going to go on? Should I ask for his help? What good would that do? Ralph is watching us and he's doing nothing to stop it. Can't say I blame him. Who'd want to get mixed up in this mess.

I hear Barry asking me, over and over, if I am sure this is what I want. No, for Christ sake! This is not what I want. This is what *you* want. I didn't ask you to leave, and I didn't drag you out of bed. You did this, you sniveling idiot! You created this night. *You* did this.

I'm afraid to speak. I can't answer his questions, and I'm not going to ask him to stop packing. If he stops, this night could come again, and I don't ever want to go through anything like this again. I want to tell him to stop; I want to tell him I don't want this to happen. I want to tell him I think this is stupid, that we can settle this and get back on track. I want to tell him a lot of things, but I can't talk. The fear that this will happen again keeps me silent.

Finally, he calms down. He takes my arm and leads me into the family room and puts on a record. He takes me in his arms, and we are crying and dancing to the same music we laughed and danced to on our wedding day. That was one of the happiest days of my life. After more than eight years of managing a family on my own, I thought I had a partner to share the responsibilities, to lighten the load, to dream with, to laugh with.

How did I manage to let it get away this time? I didn't pay enough attention to the relationship. That's how. I let other things, other people get in the way. I should have stopped the boat and got off when we were safely sheltered in the covered bridge. I should have refused to sail on.

Months ago I vowed that something good would come from this impending death in the family. If something good were to come along, I wouldn't even recognize it. I'd let it slide away. I don't want my Mom to die and I don't want my husband to leave, but it looks like I'm going to get both barrels, straight on. And I'm ill-equipped to stop it.

Barry's gone and I'm sitting here in the dark, alone. Another damn divorce coming up. Promises broken.

CHAPTER 24

## *Today I Marry My Friend*

I STILL BELIEVE IN WEDDINGS, marriages even. My mother's was for life, and my daughter's will be for life too. Becca and Mark are friends. Their wedding invitation says, "Today I marry my friend." They would like each other even if they were not in love with each other. Ultimately, friendship is the necessary ingredient for a lasting marriage.

So we're in high gear preparing for a celebration. Hundreds of people are coming to this happy event, and the mood is joyous. People I knew when Rebecca's father and I were newly married are coming. New and old relatives, friends and colleagues are all coming. Lloyd has married a wonderful, intelligent, warm-hearted woman, Barbara, who brought another daughter into our midst.

The dresses are almost finished—always the glutton for over deliverance, I made a few of them in my spare time—the band is reserved, the food has been ordered, and the presents are starting to arrive. Do we need this now, or what!

There are about forty people in our home for the rehearsal dinner. We're putting all of them to work folding programs, wrapping groom's cake, finishing hems. Mom is feeling wonderful and in her glory. Not all her brothers and sisters are coming, but Hazel and Don are here. And so is Natalie, Barry's daughter. She is one of seven bride's maids.

It's not going to be a small event. Natalie doesn't know if Barry will come to the wedding, but we hope so. In spite of all that has taken place, we are still married and maybe it will work out. Stranger things have happened within this family unit.

"Mom, can you come downstairs? I want to show you something." It's Shannon.

When I get to her room, she thrusts a piece of paper into my hands and says, "Is this stupid?" It's a poem she's written about her sister and herself.

"This is a story about two little girls,
One with straight hair, the other with curls.

## Promise I'll Stay for Mother's Day

One played with dolls, the other wrote on walls..."

I am more moved that I can safely express. It's a poem of sisterly contrasts, with Shannon deferring to Becca, depicting Becca as the "good" sister. Shannon doesn't need to do that. Different is neither better nor worse.

"Shannon, life is not a competition. Becca's strengths are not your weakness. You have strengths of your own, not the least of which is a warm and vulnerable heart. Your poem is far from stupid. It's absolutely wonderful."

Finally it's time for our beauty sleeps. Hazel and Don take Mom home. The rehearsal is over. We're ready for the real thing. Tomorrow, March 23, my first born will be married. We are sleeping under the same roof as a threesome for the last time. We've been through a lot, Rebecca, Shannon and I, but it's been good. We've never glossed over the tough times. We've hammered them out with as much honesty and energy as we have the good times, and we are as close as we are because we lived it that way. You're a couple of gutsy kids. You supported me at least as much as I supported you.

Much is written about idiot women like me who think they can do it all. If the truth were told, we would pay homage to the terrific kids who pull us through the messes we create. Without them, there would be little reason to put up with our most trying times, and no rewards for having done it.

Their Granny, my Mom, was always nearby as a roll model for blazing trails and following them to the end. I have to say, though, that I think her trail was easier than mine. No, I didn't have to find a place to live on my own when I was thirteen. No question, my childhood years were easier than hers, but my adult years are not. She had the benefit of a lifelong partner in marriage. She had my Dad standing just a little behind her, smiling his blessings and supporting her every decision and deed. You had Dad, Mom. I've failed to find a friend to marry. If only there were two Tom Wilsons in the world, one for your generation and one for mine. Dad, are you going to be with us tomorrow?

Dear Becca, how can that pretty little red head in the hospital nursery be old enough to become someone's wife tomorrow? It doesn't seem possible, but you are old enough, and ready enough to be married. Bless you, sweetheart, and your new husband. I close my eyes tonight feeling very good, very satisfied, and perhaps even happy.

This is the day a new marriage will begin, a new marriage that will last a life time.

How can I be so sure? Sometimes you just know.

About noon, bridesmaids and dresses, flowers and a hairdresser arrive. I'm still sewing. Noon was to be my cut off time, but I'm still sewing. I've

Today I Marry My Friend

*Lois, Shirleyanne, Rebecca and Shannon, March 23, 1985
at Rebecca and Mark's wedding.*

made a couple of bridesmaids' dresses. There's no bad luck in that. And I made Mom's dress. I just remembered that I made Mom's dress for my wedding. This generation's version is an ankle length dusty rose silk tone-on-tone print dress, with long sleeves, rolled collar and matching sash, tied in back. I would have finished my self-imposed deadline on time, but at the last minute we noticed that Becca's slip needed more shortening, so I extended my sewing time to one o'clock.

My dress is drop-dead gorgeous. Shannon picked it out. It's an understated, elegant peach-colored satin and crepe chemise, with a large flat bow on the left hip. For months I had Becca worried that I'd wear something white, black, or red, and flashy. Whenever we'd pass a dress rack with some off-the-shoulder sexy black frock, or a shiny red frou-frou, I'd stop and exclaim, "Ohhh! Mother of the bride . . . it's ME!" But thanks to Shannon, I'll be properly subdued for the occasion. You should know by now, Becca, I can play any role that's sent my way. Today it's a peachy role. Hold the red. Your mother is ready for this.

Four o'clock we are due to leave for the church. Emilio is doing a yeoman's job of coiffing eight women. He's a master. And he's finished right on schedule. We're almost ready.

## Promise I'll Stay for Mother's Day

"Mom, I can't wear this bra." It's Shannon. "It makes me look flat in this dress. I have to go to Nordstrom and get another one."

"No, Shannon, there's not enough time."

"I have to. It won't take long." She's gone.

"Where's Shannon?" asks the Bride. "I need help with my dress."

"She's at Nordstrom tryin on bras."

"What?!?"

"Let me help."

"I'm still flat, Mom. Nothing works for me." She's back.

It's time to get to the church. The church scene is as hectic as the home front. It's picture time. With extended family, getting the right pictures with the right people together is a little puzzling for the photographer. More than once the attempt to couple the Father of the Bride and the Mother of the Bride slowed things down. Hasn't the photographer heard of "modern" families?

The order of procession is forming in the lobby. Most of the guests are in their seats. I glance around the room in time to see Barry slip in the side door and head into the sanctuary. I break away from the crowd to go get him.

"Come Barry. Walk with me. Sit with me."

He's reluctant at first, but other people come forward to shake his hand. I put my arm around him and pull him toward the door with me. We're genuinely happy that he's come to be with us.

Mom appears stronger and happier than I've seen her in a long time. She's helping, she's laughing, and she is having herself one heck of a good time. We've truly been handed a special gift of life on this day, and I for one, am very, very grateful.

I hear the organ and the beautiful sounds of Donna singing, "Ave Maria", and I think back to Mark and Rebecca's engagement party last July, when Mom was healthy and Barry and I were living as husband and wife. It seems so long ago. Then I look around and see all of us together again, for one more, happy occasion. We have moments of happiness. Why not months? Why not years?

Becca and I share a warm embrace. Then we get in line. People ahead of us slowly walk down the aisle toward the altar. Mom is just ahead of me. She gives me a triumphant grin before she takes the arm of her usher, Mark's friend Mike, who asked for the honor. He supports her shaky shuffle to the front pew.

At last it's my turn. I take a deep breath and feel the tension of this past year roll off my shoulders, down my arms and fall away from my body. My usher arrives. Feeling genuinely relaxed, I stroll down the aisle with him, smiling to all the people seated on either side of us. Happy faces, happy people. As

## Today I Marry My Friend

we approach the altar I pause and throw a smile toward my new son-in-law just in time to catch a return wink and a Snickers bar flying in my direction. I hear laughter from those who saw it coming and a few claps for my swift, one-handed catch.

The procession of the bridesmaids follows, all of them sniffling and shaking as if this were a death march. Lighten up girls. It's just a wedding. The ring bearer and flower girl are picture perfect. They almost steal the show. We're all in our seats now; the organ pauses.

Father Paul looks at me and nods. The beginning strains of Lohengrin's Wedding March ring out. I rise and turn to see my daughter standing at the back of the church beyond the candlelight, in a white dress and veil. Does anyone hear me gasp? I don't think so. Attention is focused on the bride. She is breathtakingly lovely.

Passages. We are all just passing from one stage of life to the next. There is life before life, life during life, and life after life, and each part has its passages. Rebecca is passing from childhood to womanhood. She is leaving me to be with another. It is right, it is natural, it is good. Mom will be leaving me soon, too. Will someone be waiting to meet her? Is her leaving going to feel as natural and good as this leaving? Will I turn around and see her beyond the candlelight? Will I feel as fulfilled then as I do now?

So many questions are yet to be answered. I want us to be ready when Mom's passing comes. I glance at her. She's restless. She has waited for this moment. This is what the treatments were for. She made it to the wedding. But she is restless. She has something else on her mind. A new family has begun, and she can move on.

I am beginning to understand how this all works. We are a part of eternity even while we are here, passing each other inside and outside of our boat of life, occasionally going inside to sit behind the Pilot to check our progress. Are we on course? Oh, I think so. We've finally turned this boat around and we're headed in the right direction.

My eyes leave Mom's face and they turn toward the altar. Is it just the candles' glow... or is it a special sunlight that I see?

CHAPTER 25

## *Easter Deliverance*

I'M A MEMBER of the Seattle Executive's Association, a group of business men and women that meets once a month for lunch to discuss their respective businesses and to trade business leads. It's been three months since I've attended the meeting. I miss both the business and the companionship. Today's speaker has drawn me from my absences. I'm very much looking forward to hearing what he has to say.

It's the Wednesday before Easter, and Dr. Dale Turner, minister of the University Congregational Church, is the guest speaker. I've occasionally attended his church services. He's an extraordinary human being and an outstanding inspirational speaker. I could use a dose of his inspiration today.

Dr. Turner steps to the podium, looks at this assemblage of high-powered executives and says, "I am going to try something a little different today. We're going to talk about poetry. Did you know we have a marvelous world of poetry available to us to help us through our days of turmoil? Do we become so busy earning a living and getting ourselves through rigorous daily routines that we forget to access poetic imagery to add value to our existence? We're not put on earth to earn *a* living. We're born here to learn *of* living, before we go on to our next plane of existence. So today, this Wednesday before Easter, we are going to take about twenty minutes to consider what the wonderful world of poetry might have to offer us."

Dr. Turner begins to recite poetry from memory. He starts with early hymn composer, Isaac Watts, and moves forward to twentieth century humorist, Ogden Nash; he takes us from John Keats to Robert Frost; from Alfred Lord Tennyson to Dylan Thomas, weaving his message through our minds and emotions, revealing life as it could be, as it should be. Through poetry we expand our world from mere reality to unlimited possibility.

His message takes me home. So many times our family read together from "The Treasury of the Familiar," a marvelous book of short stories, essays and poems. So many times I listened to my Mother recite her favorite rhymes:

## Easter Deliverance

"A bunch of the boys were whooping it up . . ."

"I think that I shall never see a poem lovely as a tree . . ."

"Oh Captain, my Captain, thy fearful trip is o'er . . ." and Mom's personal call for doing battle, "The Charge of the Light Brigade":

"Theirs not to make reply, Theirs not to reason why, Theirs but to do and die . . ."

Oh my! The memories! I'd forgotten our family's love for fine literature. How could I forget something so important? Mom and Dad read to Gene and me when we were growing up, and Mom reads to my children, still. We give books to each other for holidays and birthdays. I make sure I have quiet times with the books I receive. Quiet times keep me functional. When did I last share the fruits of my quiet times with my family? Have I forgotten how to share poetry and quiet times?

So many important elements of our lives are no longer a part of our daily existence. We've put music and poetry and sunsets and flowers aside, as if they are just fluff, to be gathered in when the so-called important stuff is taken care of. Why? Beauty never used to be fluff. It used to be essential. It *is* essential. We must bring these essentials back into our lives before you go, Mom. We should have been sharing these poems all along. I am missing their presence. I am missing you.

Dr. Turner ends his discussion with a story about a famous poet.

"One day, Alfred, Lord Tennyson, and his son were walking in the woods. Lord Tennyson was in his eighties, nearing the end of his life here on earth. His son asked him to write a poem just for him, on this day. Lord Tennyson sat down on a fallen tree there in the woods and wrote a very simple poem, quite unlike any of his other poems. His son thought the poem was trite, too simple. He was disappointed in the poem his father had just written. But this poem soon became Lord Tennyson's favorite, of all the poems he had written. He stipulated in his will that any published collection of his writing must include this poem. This was Alfred, Lord Tennyson's favorite poem . . ."

"Sunset and evening star,
and one clear call for me . . ."

Oh no . . . no. Of all the poems in all her books, this is my Mother's favorite. He's reciting this poem for her! This is another spiritual message, meant for me to understand. The meaning is clear. No . . . Please . . .

## Promise I'll Stay for Mother's Day

"May there be no moaning at the bar,
When I put out to sea . . . "

I begin to cry. Sitting at this table in a room full of business associates, tears are streaming down my face. It's Mom's favorite poem, and its message is about the acceptance of death.

"May there be no moaning at the bar . . . " She's accepted her impending death. It's time for me to accept it also.

"Crossing the Bar" is the poem Mom selected to be printed in Dad's Memoriam. I am hearing these words aloud for the first time, since he died. I am also feeling his presence in this room. Are you here to help me, Dad, to let me know you're waiting for her? Are you asking me to let her go? Why today, Dr. Turner. Why did you choose to recite poetry in this room, on this day? You are a messenger from a God I'm not sure I know.

My yesterdays have returned today in the form of poetry. I've received another message from another world to prepare me for Mom's leaving. Dad's been waiting more than twenty years to see her again. He's taking her from me. A sense of sadness washes over me as I realize how soon she will go to him, but there is a sense of peace as well, knowing she will be with family. I don't consider myself to be a deeply religious person. So how do I explain this to my plain, earthly sense of existence.

"But such a tide as moving seems asleep,
Too full of sound and foam.
When that which drew from out the boundless deep
Turns again home."

I feel so very much alone. How can I turn again home, when there is no home, when no one outside of family has ever understood my full range of senses, when my family keeps leaving me. It takes blood to understand blood. What will I do when my family's life blood is gone?

Today is Good Friday. I've gone to several bookstores in the past two days and haven't found any books with Mom's favorite poems in them. I'll keep looking. In the meantime, today we're going to chapel together.

Mom looks really pretty today. She's trimmed her wig and she's actually wearing it. She says she wishes she'd trimmed it before the wedding, which is the only other time she's worn it in public. Wolf hats definitely are not wedding or chapel garb. She's chosen to wear a bright pinkish-red skirt and vest, with

## Easter Deliverance

tennis shoes to match. Her lipstick is the same cheery shade as her outfit. People will be surprised to see how pretty she can be, and she's tickled at the prospect of this.

Looking good helps with feeling good. Part of the looking good can also be attributed to a new variety of chemotherapy. So far, no side effects.

Texie arrives about the time Mom's treatment is finished. We're the first ones to arrive at the chapel. The chaplain greets us and Mom immediately launches into lively conversation with him stopping briefly to explain to us that he used to work on a special assignment for his church in Laos. Mother! We're here for Good Friday services.

Sometimes I wish she'd settle in to a given moment, but such a wish is futile. She's going to cram every moment with every opportunity to learn and grow, until the moments run out. More people arrive. The Chaplain has to move on to greet them. He's been rescued.

> Good news will come on Easter Sunday, he says, a day of promise and restoration. Will it? I can relate to this day of suffering and loss, but I may need a nudge toward the promise of restoration.

The chapel fills to standing room only. I'm surprised to see so many people at a hospital religious service. The sermon reminds us that Good Friday is a day of sorrow, a time of loss. I must interject, at least in my mind. Loss is not limited to Good Friday. Good news will come on Easter Sunday, he says, a day of promise and restoration. Will it? I can relate to this day of suffering and loss, but I may need a nudge toward the promise of restoration. Please don't let my mother suffer. She doesn't deserve it. She's accepted everything that's happened to her with such grace and good humor. Come on, whoever is watching over us. Give her a break.

Easter Sunday is here. I'd planned to go to Sunrise Services, but I can't quite make myself get out of bed. I was awake at sunrise with plenty of time to get to the service, but I'm staying in bed to take advantage of a seldom used opportunity for solitude. At times there is more spiritual revelation in reflective personal thought than in the external words of someone else. This morning is my personal Easter. It's my day of restoration.

I don't remember what we did last Easter, but it most certainly was different from this Easter Sunday. Today is a holiday, and neither Mom nor I will be fixing food. Brunch will be at Mark and Becca's apartment, and dinner will be at Mark's parents' home. I suppose I should feel a little guilty and left out of the loop with this holiday's fixins, but I'm more than ready to be waited on today.

## Promise I'll Stay for Mother's Day

It's quite a nice spread at the young Suryan's residence. The works. They've prepared fresh fruit, bacon, ham, crepes, eggs and sweet pastries, all beautifully served. Not only is my daughter bright, beautiful and accomplished, she's married well and she sets a fine table. I willingly pass the holiday torch to our new generation. Is this world ready for another Wonder Woman?

Mom, Gene, Shannon, Cliff Perry, and a few other friends have joined us. Champagne pours freely. Mark and Becca have thought of everything to make this repast a delight.

The champagne tastes mighty fine. Is it all right for me to get just a little bit tipsy this Easter Sunday? It has been a very long week, and I really would like a little more champagne, please.

CHAPTER 26

## *Traveling Handicapped*

THE PROBLEM OF NUTRITION remains. Mom is not eating enough. She says her mouth is so dry she can't swallow. The hospital dietitian suggests we try sour foods. Drink lemonade or grapefruit juice, chew sour gum, imagine delicious meals; try anything physical or imaginary that will send sensory messages to the brain to stimulate the flow of saliva. The mind will respond to a suggestion as much as to an actual physical contact. There must be something that will get her juices flowing.

No need for illusion when we know where the real thing exists. We need to put her in a kitchen where the succulent smell of real juices simmering in a roasting pan will grab hold of the olfactory senses and tune up that saliva gland. A call to Dr. Levenson tells us there is no reason we can't take a trip across the mountains whenever we want to, if its turkey we're after and if that's where we need to go to get it. Milton-Freewater, here we come! The town name changed in 1951 when they incorporated the town of Freewater.

Gene is driving her pickup truck these days. He has no car and she has no use for her truck. Friday, he and Cliff will drive over the pass straight from Bellingham. Mom and I will take the 5:15 evening flight to Walla Walla, then ride home with them on Sunday. We'll have a predictable time frame for getting there Friday night and we'll fix a bed in the bed of the truck for our ride home. Friday's the day. I'll call Lide.

Friday morning the phone rings. It's Mom. "My legs gave out. I can't walk."

"What do you want to do, Mom?"

"Well, we're going to have to get a wheelchair. Can you get that done?"

The travel agent says a wheelchair will be waiting for us at the airline's check-in curb outside the terminal. This side is handled. I'll ask Lide to take care of her end.

"Lon's planning to pick you up. I'll ask him to get a wheel chair. Are you sure you should make the trip? Won't it make her weaker?"

"She wants to go to Milton one more time, and we can't wait. Making this

## Promise I'll Stay for Mother's Day

trip won't make a bit of difference in her condition. She'll be getting weaker anyway. We're not in a turn-around situation. We'll see you at the Walla Walla airport about six-thirty."

Rebecca is with Mom when I arrive to pick her up. She meets me at the front door and fills me in.

"Gran' can't walk, Mom, but she keeps trying and she falls down every time. Are you sure you should take this trip?"

"Yes, we *need* to take this trip."

Mom's neighbor, Richard, arrives to pick us up. "I'm worried about Lois. I saw her walking to the grocery store yesterday. Her legs were wobbly and she fell down in the street. I don't think she should be left alone any more, even for a short time."

"I'll get someone when we get back from our trip."

"Next week is spring break," Becca says. "I can take care of Granny for a week, while you find someone."

Mom comes tottering out of her bedroom, dressed and ready for travel. She's on her feet, but she's holding on to something all the way to the living room—the counter, the refrigerator, the table. Her mobile home is laid out pretty well for someone with limited faculties. She is voicing no hesitancy about making the trip, nor does she offer any complaints about this turn of events. She sees me and nods.

"Let's get rollin'," she says.

Richard picks up her overnight bag and helps us get her into the car. Then he hops in. He'll drive her car home for us. I grab a couple of hats.

"Have a good trip," Becca says. We're off.

When we stop at the travel office to pick up the tickets, I discover that the ticket price is twenty dollars more than the quote.

"This is not the price I was quoted."

"That's the price of the ticket. Would you like me to call a manager?"

We haven't got time to call a manager. What's the choice here? Pay the price or go home. We pay and move on.

A look at the ticket itself brings another surprise. We'll be stopping in Pasco to change planes. I start to say something then look at Mom sitting in the car, patiently waiting for me to take care of business. She has only one thing on her mind, and that's to get to Milton-Freewater. Nothing else matters. I'll follow her lead and keep my mind focused on the important issue of the day.

When we get to the airport, there is no sign of anyone waiting at the curbside with a wheelchair, like the travel agent said there would be. Count to ten.

## Traveling Handicapped

One, two, three . . . Okay. I'll get out and find one. Inside the terminal there's a wheelchair in a corner behind the check-in counter. I grab it and wheel it to the car, park it and lock the brake. With some effort, Richard and I lift Mom into it. We say goodbye to Richard, I release the brake, turn her around, and we're on our way.

Her luggage and mine are piled on her lap and my purse, still on my arm, is banging against the wheel, fouling up the works. Pushing a wheelchair, fully loaded is no easy task. It's damned heavy. We wait in line at the counter to get our seat assignments. I ask which gate and the airline attendant points. No offers of assistance. We must look like we know what we're doing. Not likely. I think people are purposely steering clear of us for fear of being run over. To hell with 'em.

> For some sick reason, I keep picturing myself as a little girl playing house, pushing my dolly in her buggy, while the dolly sits there with a sweet smile on her face, letting me do anything I want.

Mom sits there in the wheelchair, letting me push her, saying nothing when I jam the wheels for the ninety-seventh time. Her quiet resolution is amusing. For some sick reason, I keep picturing myself as a little girl playing house, pushing my dolly in her buggy, while the dolly sits there with a sweet smile on her face, letting me do anything I want. God! I hope I'm doing the right thing. It's too late to be wondering about that. I'll keep plundering along, doing whatever I think needs to be done. It's not my first turn at unchartered ignorance.

When the nurse put my baby daughter in my arms for the first time, I looked at the nurse and asked her what to do. The nurse poked the bottle into my baby's mouth and fortunately that smart little baby began sucking like she was supposed to. She seemed to know she was dealing with inexperience and her well-being was going to require a lot of patience on her part. Here I am again, playing the part of novice caretaker, with no friendly nurse standing by. But I luck out again. The person I am caring for understands exactly what she's dealing with, and she has patience to spare.

We finally arrive at the boarding gate and a young man walks over to us. He looks at Mom, then at me.

"Can she walk?" he asks me.

Of course she can walk, you idiot. That's why she's sitting in this wheelchair. She's crazy about wheelchairs. She asked if she could ride in one just for the fun of it. But why ask me. Her brains aren't in her legs, you know. They're in her head, and they're working at full capacity. Go ahead. Ask her if she can walk. I can hardly wait to hear her response.

## Promise I'll Stay for Mother's Day

I didn't say that, of course, but I wanted to. "No, she can't walk," I said.

"We cannot board her in that wheelchair," he says, nonchalantly. "Follow me."

He turns and walks away. I turn her around and take out after him. We follow him into an elevator and ride down to ground level then continue outside to where a group of small planes are parked. Where the heck are we going? Heaven forbid someone should tell us anything. We push on around the building. I see a little plane with little propellers sitting on a little runway. We seem to be heading toward it. I hope they're not planning to put us on board that vehicle. If they are, the young man is right. We are not going to get up those little stairs leading to the plane's door in this wheelchair.

> Mom, of course, is cracking jokes about her being escorted onto an airplane by two handsome young men.

Adjustment time. I'd forgotten about little airplanes with little propellers. I'd pictured us boarding a jet plane with a ramp attached to it from inside the airport. I thought we'd just wheel her through the ramp, right up to the door of the plane. But I see we may have a problem.

We continue onto the runway, over to the little plane. When we get to the bottom of the stairs, another man brings over a weird looking, skinny little chair. That'll work. I hope there's help coming to get her into that. This man and the man we've been following pick Mom up out of the wheelchair and strap her into the skinny chair. Then they pick her up again, chair and all, and walk her up the stairs backward.

I can't believe what I'm seeing, but everyone else seems to think this is business as usual. It would have been nice to have known what the drill would be before we started this return home. Mom, of course, is cracking jokes about her being escorted onto an airplane by two handsome young men. Who am I to protest?

And what's to protest? We're on our way to Milton-Freewater. There's just a bit more to it than I anticipated. Driving would have been easier, perhaps, but we'd have missed all this adventure.

We're experiencing a very small slice of what it's like for people with physical handicaps to get through what others regard as routine procedure. The tasks get done, but my anxiety could have been eased with a few advance explanations. They knew what they were doing, but we didn't. The biggest rub for me was their not addressing the person they were assisting. Physically handicapped people are not stupid. I guess that's what my mind is protesting. But this is not a day for protest. Fixing how society approaches basic handicap procedures is for another time.

When we land in Pasco, we wait for the plane to empty. Two men come on board and strap her into another funny little chair and walk her down the

## Traveling Handicapped

stairs, across the runway to another little plane. If I was surprised by the size of the first plane, I am astonished at the size of this one. We are escorted to the two seats right behind the pilot and co-pilot, one of us on each side of the aisle. There are nine similar two-seat rows in the plane, eighteen seats total. A netting separates us from the men piloting this air ship.

Mom, fortunately, is oblivious to all the fussin' going on inside my head. She's yakin' to the pilot about something. Probably her trip to Kenya—there's this trip connection, making for a story connection. All it takes is a small connection for a saga to begin. To look at her smile and her anticipatory posture, you'd think we were on a luxury trip headed for some exotic land. I'm still trying to learn this business of knowing when to fight for the ideal and when to gracefully accept what's been handed to us. I need to settle down and take a cue from her. There's something about a silk purse from a sow's ear. Now that's just plain silly.

The baggage compartment is a stack of luggage pushed behind the netting between us and the co-pilot. It keeps tumbling down and rolling into the aisle. This won't do. We wait while another man comes on board and walks out with the luggage that's rolled into the aisle, which includes both our bags. Hey! They can't take that away. Thinking we had carry-ons, I left my medication in my bag. Have I mentioned my medication? I had my day at the doctor too.

Firemen were doing cholesterol screenings at a shopping mall. When they read my numbers they started backing away almost shouting, "Don't touch that walking cheeseburger!" Then they took my blood pressure and called for back up. That's a bit of an exaggeration. But I am on meds. And I can't lose them.

"Where are you taking those bags?"

"We're putting them in the nose of the plane. They'll be traveling with us."

As we approach the Walla Walla airport, Mom starts rummaging in her knitting bag. Off comes the turban and on goes her wolf hat. She doesn't say a word. She just puts on the wolf hat and sits there looking straight ahead as if all ladies wear wolf hats. A few people notice her change of chapeau and smile. They seem to understand this is a special flight. When we land, they stop to compliment her on her choice of hats and wish her a safe journey. It's our turn to depart. Another nice-looking young man comes on board. Mom flashes me a see-who's-going-to-carry-me-down-the-stairs grin.

"You must be the special person a group of people in the airport are waiting to see." That she is.

We strap her in and head down the stairs. I look toward the terminal and see Gene and Cliff, Lon and Freda, and Lide and Peck. They see us and laugh, which is exactly the reaction Mom wanted. What she didn't want was a reflexive response to how the disease has changed her face and body. She and her wolf hat made sure that didn't happen. The wheelchair is waiting.

We wheel to their cars, get in and drive to Milton-Freewater, fifteen miles away. Along the way I recall a whole lifetime of trips to Milton-Freewater. During the war we saved our gas ration stamps and drove across the two-lane mountain pass in our 1939 Ford—we graduated from the Terraplane in 1944. With it went the floor-board gear shift that Dad loved to pull out and hand to astonished passengers while he was driving.

It took seven-to-eight hours to travel the three hundred miles from Seattle to Milton. The trip usually required a stop in either Ellensburg or Yakima to put a patch on a tire or two, to keep us on the road. Every trip was a major project. With that perspective, today was not so bad.

There were many other times after the war, mostly in the heat of summer, when we made the trip across the pass from Western Washington to Eastern Oregon. The long, hot drive seemed to go on forever, but the discomfort of the journey was always forgotten as soon as we arrived, because the getting there was so good. Family was waiting for us, and we love our family.

Throughout our childhood, Mom seemed driven by a seemingly inexhaustible need to prove herself as a sophisticated woman living in an urban world. I watched and listened to the well-dressed, hard-working, tough-talking career woman, who happened to also be my mother on certain days. It was only in Milton-Freewater where she could relax and poke fun at herself. She seldom laughed or played in Seattle. Dad and Gene and I laughed and played while Mom worked. Dad and Gene and I went to ball games and book stores and listened to music. And Mom worked.

When she retired from work and had time on her hands away from the city mainstream, the bibbed overalls crept out of the closet on the west side of the mountains, and she began hanging out with Gene and his Bluegrass musician friends. She learned she could be accepted by almost everyone, without trying so hard and asking for so much attention. Big city affectations were dropped, and the irresistible charm of a good lady, being true to herself, came shining through.

She still carries feelings of guilt for having left her family and her mountain culture behind, all those years ago. I'm hoping that one more welcome home from these good people will take care of those useless feelings forever, for this will be our last trip home. There will be no more.

I never imagined there would be a last trip. We never do.

CHAPTER 27

## *Crossing the Pass Leaves Spring Behind*

Driving up to the back door of Lide and Peck's house, I'm still lost in my personal reverie. Memories skip over the past thirty years as if they never existed. I'm remembering only my childhood with my Mom and Dad, and all the aunts and uncles who were younger then than I am today. They were healthy and happy, working in the wheat fields and canneries, riding horses and hunting, and singing and laughing, accepting each other's presence as if it would last forever.

Why can't it last? Why does it have to wind down? Why do people have to get old and tired and sick. There just has to be a reason for life to have to end this way. The only reason I can think of is it must feel so good when it's finally over. Is that it? Is life meant to be mostly pain with a few laughs thrown in to make us continue to struggle for something better? Who knows, and what's the use of wonderin'? That's the deal we cut when we are born.

The rest of the family comes out to greet us. The look on Hazel's face tells me she's shocked by the look of Mom's face. It's only been four weeks since the wedding, when Mom was dancing the night away. In Mom's time frame, four weeks is a long time. I'm not sure we have four more.

Dinner's ready. We sit down to the table together, as we have for years and years, enjoying fine home-cooked food and home-style laughter. It feels so good, and I'm so glad we came. I'm not the same tired, frustrated, angry person who headed for the airport this afternoon. Whatever any of us may have felt inside ourselves earlier today has been overcome by this feeling of family. Mom knew we needed this gathering. She could have called it off at any time for any number of reasons, including, "I can't walk", but we needed this and she knew it. Who's going to call us together when she's gone?

After dinner, Mon insists that Gene play some of the tapes from old-time artists he's brought to give to Jack. The first set of tapes he plays is a selection from "The Two Black Crows", a comedy team of the 1930's. We laugh at the corny jokes as if we'd never heard them before. He follows the Crows

## Promise I'll Stay for Mother's Day

with music from early Carter Family recordings. It's an evening of jokes and tunes from another era of American culture, still living in the back hills of our hearts.

Now it's time for our own music, live, right here in this living room. Mom has her list of favorite songs and she wants to hear them all. Who's going to make us listen to the same ol' jokes and the same ol' songs over an' over when she's gone? There's that "when she's gone" question again. Life will continue for us when she's gone. It doesn't seem possible, but it will.

Mom's getting tired and she should go to bed, but she doesn't want to miss anything, so we take the mattress out of her pickup and lay it on the living room carpet, behind Peck's big chair. We make it up for sleeping, get her ready for bed, and lay her down right there, so she can drift off to sleep hearing her favorite tunes. A smile spreads across her face as her eyes close to the strains of "We'll all have chicken 'n dumplins when she comes . . ."

Cliff comes to sit beside me. He hands me a piece of paper with words he wrote this afternoon as he and Gene were driving across the mountain pass, on their way to Milton-Freewater. "I brought you something," he says.

"Time turns tail to winter again.
Crossing the pass leaves spring behind
As if dog days were skipped over
and fall fog evenings never felt.
Pores shivering in frozen white,
the mountain shoulders slowly shrug
to say there's just no way to tell
when crocuses will bloom for good.
Still, plums with foolhardy faith
show full white petals to any bee
desperate to fly over ice."

There's no way to tell when crocuses will bloom for good. Are we the foolhardy plums, or the desperate bees? Crocuses were not meant to bloom for good. Let go. Let go. No, I can't. Not yet. We are still desperately trying to fly.

It's time for bed. I get the guest room all to myself and take advantage of the solitude to rethink the events of the day. I recall my thoughts of the career woman I thought I knew as we grew apart in my adult years. Mom's done a complete about face. I wonder if it was a gradual process of change I failed

## Crossing the Pass Leaves Spring Behind

to notice, or if some specific revelation occurred to bring forth the happy memories of her early years, so she could enjoy their influence at the end of her life. Was it the shock of the "Good morning, Lois, you have cancer", day that brought her life full circle? Do I have to have to wait for a day like that myself, or can I recapture the spirit of my roots through the journey we're on right now.

At the beginning of this journey, I vowed something good would come from it. Until recently, it seemed to be a long trip to nowhere. Maybe the something good is finally happening and maybe I *can* learn from it. Right now, however, the something good is the comfort of a warm bed, and it's been a long day. G'night, Mom.

Oh dear. Mom's in bad shape this morning. I was hoping a couple of good days would come together. She seemed so much better last night, compared to yesterday morning. This morning she can't even roll herself up to sit, and she's wet her bed. Cliff helps me get her up and into the bathroom where I wash her and help her change her clothes. Then, with a fresh start, Cliff comes back to carry her to the big chair with the high, firm back and sturdy arms. We prop her up with pillows and blankets and bring her morning coffee and cigarettes. No use denying her these nasty pleasures at this point.

Lide and Hazel are fixing breakfast and the boys and I are making music. Mom's pensively watching and listening. Breakfast is ready. Mom's too tired to join us. We put a pad on her mattress and bed her back down. All we can see of her is her little bald, gray-skinned head above the covers. It doesn't look at all like Lois Thompson-Wilson.

After breakfast I put on my jacket, grab my camera and walk past the barn, past the corral, to the banks of the Walla Walla River. I look around at these quiet rolling hills and suddenly feel rooted to this ground. I take pictures of the hills, the corral, the orchard, the barn, pictures I've been carrying deep in my heart for many, many years. Nothing has changed. Here lies my childhood, waiting for my return. There is patience in these soft, silent hills. Their continuity and their silence are calling me. I must find my way home.

Cliff has also spent the morning outside, on the other side of the river. He climbed the hills and gave in to his own moments of collecting his soul. Another poem came to him, acknowledging our closeness with nature and the fundamental, orderly passage of youth to age, to death. Today's poem is more pointed than yesterday's writing, with the ominous entrance of a new player who's arrived to make sure we don't forget the real reason we are here.

"Everyone knows why we are here.
That damned rascal stalks the orchard,
scythe slung loosely, almost whistling.
We hear his song again and again.
Fresh grass shivers in early spring,
knowing new green fades to fodder,
knowing winter stores begin here,
knowing blossoms turn fruit to fall,
knowing these trees must bear sturdy
their weight of years, before falling.
Thus known, our silence whispers to us now."

That damned rascal stalks the orchard. We hear the grass shiver and feel the weight of years bending the branches of our sturdy tree to the ground. Play louder, Gene and Cliff and Jack! I am not ready for his song.

It's dinner time again. One more sit down. Mom's up, rested and feeling much better. More people arrive. Tommy brings a jewel for Mom's turban. We're enjoying lots of people, mounds of food, rounds of laughter, and a few quiet moments during our repast.

A move to the living room brings music.

"My grandfather's clock was too large for the shelf,
so it stood ninety years on the floor . . . "

"Joe can't come to dinner, I'll give you the reason why.
He blowed his nose in the corn bread, and called it pumpkin pie . . . "

"When springtime comes to the mountain
and the wildflowers scatter o'er the plain . . . "

When springtime comes again, one of us will have returned to the mountains forever. Springtime won't be the same.

It's Sunday morning and Mom is ready to play. She gets up off her bed by herself and walks into the bathroom. When she comes out, she is so tickled with herself.

"Hey! Look at me! Watch me walk!"

She lurches straight across the living room and WHAM! She runs smack into the wall next to the kitchen. She shakes her head, turns and heads in

## Crossing the Pass Leaves Spring Behind

another direction. She's undeterred. We watch, horrified, not knowing what to do. We don't like seeing her smack into the walls, and we don't want her to fall down and hurt herself, but her spirit is so high, we can't offer a discouraging word, or get out of our chairs to stop her.

Fortunately, she heads in the direction of the big chair and sits herself down. We all stare at each other in amazement. Then the room spontaneously erupts into relieved laughter. Mom looks at us and grins, still tickled with herself.

It's been a wonderful weekend, but now it's time to go. Slowly, we gather our belongings with dread and begin to load the pickup. Last night Hazel told me she is going to have to get help with this. She thought our good life would go on forever. Mamie understands what is going on and she watches quietly as we pack. Lide comes to me by the back door.

"I don't think I can go out there and see her leave."

"Sure you can, Lide. Come outside with me."

"Just don't let her suffer."

If there is any justice in the universe, this lady will not suffer, and I still have some confidence in universal justice. I know her leaving will be relatively pain free with a certain measure of dignity. We've come this far, and we're not about to let it get away from us now.

"Take care of Ma," Jack whispers.

The truck is miraculously loaded with everything we intended to get into it. We've got the overnight bags, Mom's bed, musical instruments, sandwiches, apple pie, chips, beer, and whatever else we've seen fit to poke inside. It's time to boost her into the back of the truck. Her legs are hanging over the tail gate, and she's looking around. It's such a picture, I have to take it.

There she is, sitting in the back of her pickup, this former big-city career woman, who has returned, full-circle to her beginnings. Does she fully comprehend what's happening, that we are saying goodbye to our family trips to Milton-Freewater? She's not showing any signs of regret or sorrow. Is it that easy for her to leave us, or is she giving out with her brave soldier routine to keep us from surrendering? I aim my camera.

"Flash me a big one, Mom."

The biggest grin you ever saw begins to spread across her face. CLICK. It's a beauty. This is how I will remember her.

Time to go. We turn toward home, leaving home behind. But not for long. I just figured out her grin. She knows we'll be returning to the Blue Mountains of Oregon before this year's new green fades to fodder. This was not our last trip home.

CHAPTER 28

## Awakened By a Loud Thud

WE BEGIN THE FIVE-HOUR trip back across the mountains, with Gene, Cliff, and me sitting in the cab, filling our time with country songs and silly games. We put Mom in the pickup canopy by herself, hoping she will lie down and go to sleep. Our plan doesn't work. Today is an awake day. She's rummaging around back there, getting into things, smoking cigarettes, and drinking coffee. I pray she doesn't either scald herself or set us all on fire. Oh well, if the truck is going to blow up on us today, I suppose we'll hear the bang on our way out.

It's a rough trip all the way. We stop a few times to stretch our legs, and chat with Mom. We encourage her to get some rest, but she doesn't settle down. I scold her a bit when we get home.

"Mom, you need to sleep when you have the chance, to conserve your energy for the rough times ahead."

"Couldn't sleep," she says. "The banjo kept falling on my head." Sounds like our life story.

It's obvious she can't be left alone for even a little while. I ask Cliff and Gene to stay with her while I go home to repack my suitcase. I'm moving in with Mom. Tomorrow I'll call the transitional team to cover the days. It's late when I get back to Mom's, and she's in bed. I get right into bed with her and fall asleep instantly.

I awaken to a loud thud. Damn! She's not in bed. Where the hell is she? I throw back the covers and walk quickly to the sound of the noise. Mom is sitting on the floor in the living room. I crouch behind her and lock my arms under her arms and around her chest, and pull her into a chair.

"How come you're not in bed, Mom?"

"I was hungry."

I fix her a sandwich and we talk for a while before we get back into bed and fall asleep right away. BAM! Oh for God's sake! Why won't she stay in bed?!? She's on the floor beside the bed. It's not easy for me to pick her up. I haven't learned how to do it yet, and she doesn't know how to help me. It feels like I imagine moving a hundred pounds of gelatin would be, for all the control I have.

All too soon morning arrives and it's time for me to get up and get ready for work. I get dressed and go to the bathroom to put on my makeup when I hear Mom rustling around in the living room. Better go see what she is up . . . CRASH! Now what!

I take off toward the living room and see her sitting on the floor between the love seat and the teacart. The teacart is on its side. She's sitting there, with a funny little smile on her face, lightly rubbing her head. There's no sign of blood, or even a bump or a bruise. I breathe a sigh of relief. This falling all over the place clearly doesn't bother Mom at all, but it's a bit of a chore for her daughter. Getting her up out of this position she's in requires moving the furniture. I don't know how she got stuck in there in the first place.

> Jesus Holy Chri . . . . ! Guess who's sitting in the street beside the garbage can!?! I gotta give her credit. She has her cane with her. How in God's name did she get out there? What am I going to do with her! I can't tie her down.

"Mom, you simply must use your cane or call me when you want to move around. I'll come and help you. You could hurt yourself real bad if you keep falling like this."

"Okay," she says.

I put her in the loveseat and place her cane beside her. I sit down at the table in the chair closest to her and begin to look over the paperwork I started working on a few days ago. I'm trying to get her affairs in order, as they say.

Pretty soon Mom gets up with her cane and wobbles back to the bedroom. I hear little noises in the bedroom and I begin to relax a bit. When I go to the kitchen to pour myself a cup a coffee I peek around the corner. She's getting dressed. All's well. I take my coffee into the living room and scan the morning newspaper. Not much news today. I put the paper down, stretch my arms, and glance out the window.

Jesus Holy Chri . . . .! Guess who's sitting in the street beside the garbage can!?! I gotta give her credit. She has her cane with her. It's lying in the street beside her. How in God's name did she get out there? What am I going to do with her! I can't tie her down. I take a deep breath, walk out the front door, down the porch steps, and approach her.

"What are ya' doin' down there?" I ask teasingly.

She smiles and shrugs, and says, "Emptyin' the garbage."

"I can see that. You shouldn't be doing that by yourself, Mom."

"Okay."

How can I be angry? She appears to be unhurt and she is so sweet. Once we get back in the house, which is no easy task, she wants to sit down and take care of her bills. She's writing checks and cussing, and writing checks and tearing them up. She becomes confused and puts statement heads with the wrong checks. A check for the gas bill is in an envelope with the phone bill; the rent check is in with the water bill; the Visa bill has no envelope. She realizes that things are in disarray.

"Shirleyanne, you better look at these. I'm all goofed up."

I sort through all that she has done and get it straightened out. She finds the missing Visa envelope and goes over her bills with me. She points out that the Visa bill is paid in full when she dies, so I should not make any payments after she dies.

"I guess you have to live at least another month, then, because we just paid it," I say to her.

"We better go by the office to make sure my lease papers are all okay", she says, "and we should drive to the bank and have checks made out with both our names on them."

"We can do that tomorrow, after we see the doctor."

Becca arrives and I leave for work.

I diddle around at work until almost seven o'clock. My delay today isn't fair to Mark and Becca, but I needed a little extra time to finish my work and recharge. It may appear that I take all this crashing and falling lightly, but that's not the case. Mom takes her bumps calmly and I mirror her behavior so as not to upset her. It's not easy for me to be picking her up off the floor and off the street, but there's no reason for me to burden her with my over reacting. But it's not easy. So I take a little extra time getting home.

Dinner is ready when I arrive. Mom doesn't want to eat. Mark says she thinks it's morning.

"She keeps asking me when I'm going to leave for work. I tell her I just got home from work and she says, 'Oh.' Then she says, 'When are you going to work?'"

Mom totters into the room, sees me and says, "What are you doing here?"

"I'm home from work and I'm ready to sit down to dinner with Mark and Becca. Come sit down with us."

"Well that's what Mark kept telling me, but I didn't believe him. Seems like morning to me."

Mark has certainly proven his mettle as a new family member. He joined our family about the time the lid blew off. He not only seems to accept that all these difficulties are a part of living and dying, he also goes along with our way of dealing with them. We're lucky to have him.

When Mark and Becca leave for the night, Mom gets up and starts walking around. By now I know enough to watch her. I catch her near the back stairs and ask her where she thinks she's going.

"The garbage man comes in an hour," she says, I have to take the garbage out."

"You already took the garbage out this morning. It's not morning time now. It's night time, and we need to get ready for bed."

I hope she gets that message pretty soon. She and I are going to have to be on the same day and night schedule, if I am to get any sleep at all.

She hasn't got the message yet. About eleven o'clock, I manage to get her to bed, but she brought a can of Ensure to drink and a cup of coffee, and she's decided to have another cigarette. And she talks and talks and talks. She settles down about three in the morning. It's all right, though. I'm tired, but she is so good natured, I can't discourage her. There will be enough time for sleep later.

Dr. Levenson wants Mom to stay in the hospital for a few days, maybe until Friday. He wants to run tests and give her more blood to build her strength up again. We check her into the hospital.

Mom does not like this turn of events at all. I assure her that she will go home as soon as she is feeling stronger. But she's not sure we will let her go home again. She knows that at some point she will not get to return home, and she's not ready for that. She wants to make certain we know she's not ready yet. I have to admit the thought of her sleeping in the hospital and me sleeping alone in my own bed at home for a few nights sounds enticing, but for no more than a few nights. I know that.

Wednesday morning, after just one night, Mom is antsy. She's had two pints of blood and she's feeling good, and she wants to go home. I tell her she must stay in the hospital for a few more days.

"I don't want to," she says firmly.

"We'll discuss it with Dr. Levenson tomorrow morning," I say, just as firmly.

Thursday morning I arrive to find Mom fully dressed with her jacket on and her overnight bag sitting beside her on the bed.

"I'm going home now," she says triumphantly. "Dr. Levenson has released me, but he wants to talk to you first."

I am furious. So you want to go home, do you? Well, good for you. I would

## Promise I'll Stay for Mother's Day

like to go home too. My home. Have you thought of that? What choice did Dad have twenty years ago, when you put him in the hospital and left him there for the better part of four months? Why did you do that, huh? I'll tell you why. You did that because you either couldn't or wouldn't take care of him yourself. Well, you're not so easy to take care of either. No wonder you're in such fine spirits. You don't have to do anything you don't want to do. I'd be in pretty damned good spirits myself, if I could do whatever I want to do, whenever I want to do it. I'd be cheery as hell. Fine. We'll go home, but you better start eating and using your cane, and you better figure out when it's day and when it's night, because I cannot go twenty-four hours a day indefinitely.

> No wonder you're in such fine spirits. You don't have to do anything you don't want to do. I'd be in pretty damned good spirits myself, if I could do whatever I want to do.

Fortunately, that was only my idiot brain talking, not my mouth. I just nod and leave her room to find Dr. Levenson.

"I wanted her to stay another night," he explains. "But when I arrived at seven thirty this morning, she was all dressed, with one foot out the door. I can't keep her here, if she wants to go home."

I'd planned to take tomorrow off, to give Becca a break, but I guess I can stay home both days. Tomorrow, Mom and I had already planned to begin to take care of the business side of dying.

Tonight Mom sleeps. My little internal outburst has simmered and died. I have no right to be angry. It's not me who is sick and in pain and saying good bye to all I know and love in this world. It would help if I could unload some of my emotions onto someone else just for temporary relief. If someone would take them from me for just a few minutes, I would take them back again. Oh hell, why get into that again? I don't know how to release my emotions to someone else.

This morning we drive to the Trailer Town office to change the lease agreement for her mobile home. We put both our names on the lease, and we change from an annual agreement to a monthly fee. Then we get a new will witnessed and notarized. Then on to the drugstore to get her more pills and to the bank to get my name added to her checks.

No one asks questions about what we are doing. No need. Mom can hardly walk, she can't turn around, and she can't sit down or stand up without help. She's also that terrible shade of greenish-grey, and she has a difficult time keeping her thoughts together. And her writing is shaky, at best. All the people we see today are very kind and patient.

When we are finished with our errands, I ask Mom if she wants to stop and visit with Becca on our way home.

"No, Shirleyanne, I'm just too tired. I need to go home and go to sleep. I wish I could just close my eyes and have it be over."

I let the remark pass. We calmly begin the chores of getting her personal and financial affairs in order today, as if this were a part of our normal daily routine. It's just not sinking in. We're taking care of this business because Mom is going to die. Soon. Where is the emotion? This is not business as usual. Why are we acting this way?

Where are the tears? She said she wishes she could close her eyes and have it all be over. If that's what she wishes, then it's time for her wishes to be granted. Her tiredness tells me we're no longer fighting to beat death. We're preparing to meet it.

Mom and I have not discussed the possibility of a deity, or whether there is or isn't a god watching over us, making judgments as to what happens after we live our lives on this earth. We've spent our years going to church, and felt the spiritual comfort of religion. We just haven't put a structure to our beliefs about the possibility of life beyond this plane. It's enough for us to know that continuity exists, and there is something better for us than the life we are experiencing right now. I believe she is reaching out for whatever it is that is better. I believe she deserves it, and I believe she is ready to grab on to it very soon. And I want it for her.

It's time for me to let go.

Or is it? Am I suddenly embracing all this acceptance crap because I'm tired? Is this some sham I've conjured up because I'm tired and I feel inadequate, because I don't like picking her up off the floor and changing her clothes?

Questioning my motives has become a moralistic exercise I put myself through every day. Are my decisions for her or are they really for me? But why would I want her to leave? Who loses when it's all over? Mom is traveling on to something better. She gets to enter into an eternity of only a spiritual existence, and I'll be stuck here, very much involved with the physical pain of getting through this life, a life that will be missing her guidance and humor. How can I possibly think her leaving will be a relief for me?

It won't. Why would I want her to go? I don't. She's the one who wants to go. Why are you so anxious to go, Mom? Why must you leave now? What's your hurry?

Gene thinks Mom is in pain, awful pain. Miraculously, we've been able to

## Promise I'll Stay for Mother's Day

control pain, until now. Most of our lives we fight for some measure of control and most of our battle is against pain, either physical or emotional. Mom's dispute now is with physical pain, my struggle is emotional pain.

"Where do you hurt, Mom?" I ask.

"Oh, my neck and back, a little. I took some aspirin. I should feel better soon."

"Do you want something stronger; do you need more help?"

"No, not yet."

A stronger pill would ease her pain. There is no relief for my aching heart. I put her to bed and putter around the house looking for something to do. How about solitaire?

Red jack on black queen, black eight on the red nine. I can handle that.

This morning we'll be meeting a new nurse, specifically trained to take care of a person in Mom's condition. I decided we need professional help to make Mom's days easier and safer. Mom's decided to get herself dressed for the occasion. She comes out of her bedroom wearing her Wilson athletic sweatshirt, jeans and tennis shoes, all in shades of pink and gray. And her underpants are on top of her jeans.

"Are you sure you want to be dressed that way?"

She looks down at her pants and says, "Oh, I know it. But I did it and I'm not in the mood to change."

If she's not concerned, I'm not concerned. Who are we trying to impress, anyway. She fixes herself a large bowl of hot cereal, adds spoons full of brown sugar, pours on thick cream, and eats every bite. This has become her favorite meal. When she is finished, she totters back into her bedroom and changes her clothes. Her underpants are underpants again. I'm glad I didn't make an issue of it.

Mom is asleep when Joan arrives, and we go over Mom's current state of health. Some days she sleeps almost all day; some days she's awake and wants company. Some days she can walk; other days she can't. I want to make sure Joan understands how dramatic the swings are, from being able to take care of herself to being nearly moribund. Joan is the true professional I'd hoped for. She understands graciously, and I feel very comfortable leaving Mom in her daily care. Having Joan here is a satisfying relief.

Mark and Becca are watching television when I arrive. "How're things?" I ask.

"Oh fine," Mark says. "She thinks it's morning." Aargh!

"Hi Mom."

## Awakened By a Loud Thud

"Hi! I better get rollin'."

"Why?"

"Time to get up and get rollin'."

"No need to hurry, Mom. It's seven o'clock Monday night."

"Monday night?"

"Yes..."

"I don't believe you."

"Well, it is. Mark and Becca and I are here after work, and we are about to have dinner. Want to join us?"

"No. If its night, I guess I'll go back to sleep. The lady was nice. I like her. Tomorrow I'll have a bath while she's here."

Mark and Becca go home around nine o'clock and I check on Mom. She hears me and opens her eyes.

"What time is it?"

"Nine o'clock at night."

"Gotta get rollin'. Have to be at the doc's in an hour."

"No, you don't. The appointment is for tomorrow morning."

"Isn't this morning?"

"No, it's still Monday night."

"Well shit then." Her language is getting a little salty these days. "I guess I'll sleep another hour."

Let's hope it's longer than an hour. Gene told me yesterday that Saturday night she turned the light by her bed on and off every five-to-ten minutes, all night. I lie down beside her and fall asleep.

About two in the morning, I awaken. Something is up. She's fussing and coughing and groaning. Her breathing is labored and irregular. I can tell her pain is enormous. Is this another temporary shut down, a part of the familiar roller coaster? I don't think so. I can't explain what it is, but this is different. She moans, she tries to move, she wets the bed. I get one towel to wipe her dry, another to put under her on the sheet. This will do until morning.

"Can I help you, Mom?"

She doesn't answer. I decide not to make any calls. I'll wait until morning. Whatever happens, I can handle.

At last it's morning. Mom tries to get up. She wants to go to the bathroom.

I try to help her get there. We can't even get her into a sitting position. She hurts so bad! Every move is torture. Why, oh why, does she have to go through this pain and humiliation! I was sure we'd be spared this.

There's no pain medication in the house. Isn't that strange. I've never

## Promise I'll Stay for Mother's Day

thought about it before. For nine months she's been treated for lung and brain cancer without pain medication at home. That says something about the woman who is suffering. But we need something now. I call the Visiting Nurse office and ask if Joan, or someone, can come right now with pain medication. The answer is no. I cancel Joan's visit for today and call Mark and ask him to come help me get Mom to the hospital. I call the hospital to notify them that we're coming in.

"Do you want us to call an ambulance?"

"No thanks, but I'd like to talk with Dr. Levenson, if he's there.

Dr. Levenson says he needs to see her before she has any medication, so he can better evaluate what is happening. Mark and Becca arrive and we get her to the hospital. A couple of hours later, she is feeling much better.

Professional care makes such a difference. Dr. Levenson says he will keep her in the hospital for a few days to run more tests to determine the exact cause of her discomfort and confusion. Excuse me, doctor . . . I believe she has cancer. What's the mystery? I keep the sarcastic thoughts to myself. He's a fine doctor, doing a fine job.

The tests reveal that the lung blockage has grown and caused secretions to back up, thus the coughing and breathing difficulties. She's developed a fever. They plan to do a CAT Scan to check on the brain disease, and another x-ray to see if the lung disease has metastasized into the surrounding area.

Wednesday morning the tests confirm the expectations that the cancer is growing again in her head, and it has spread from her lung to her ribs. Two primary reasons for her confusion and pain. Dread disease . . . spread your misery!

Dr. Levenson tells Mom, "We are going to keep you in the hospital until your condition stabilizes. I don't want to come in here tomorrow morning to find you dressed, with one foot out the door. This time I won't allow the other foot to follow."

She grins and says, "Okay, I'll follow orders, Doctor. How is Mr. Carlisle? He didn't look very good the last time I saw him. Are his treatments still working?"

I see the first sign of impatience from Dr. Levenson. "Lois, our only concern now is for your well being. I don't want you concerned with what we are doing for other people. It is *your* pain that we want to take care of."

God! It must be rough sometimes, always working against time in a futile struggle to hold off death. Obstetricians bring new life into the world, orthopedic surgeons mend bones, and oncologists wage a losing bet with death. It takes a very special kind of person to handle that battle, day after day. Dr. Levenson is testimony to just how special.

Wednesday evening Mom is feeling better and receiving visitors. Friends and relatives stop by to offer support and good cheer. Mom is holding court and loving the attention.

Thursday, there is a turn for the worse, much worse. I can't see that we'll be taking her home again. Each rally is more short-lived, and is followed by a bigger let down. I don't know how much further down she can go. Her temperature is down to near normal, but the pain is still present. She's smoking cigarettes continuously, as if she's hoping they will hasten her exit.

I call our family to let them know of the progress of the disease. Progress, do I say? Progress toward what, the other side? Progress toward death? Yes, that would be progress. It's time to redefine progress.

Earlier today, a friend of mine asked me how things are going with my Mom. I told him things are getting pretty bad. Nick's brother died of lung cancer last fall. Nick told me that when things get real bad, the doctors can change the kind of medication they give her to ease the pain. The medication takes care of the pain, and eventually, the disease as well. It is a humane and accepted way to rid the body from the pain of the disease, and release the soul to see a better world.

*Shannon, Lois, Shirleyanne, and Becca. Grant's Pass Oregon 1980.*

CHAPTER 29

## *I'll Stay for Mother's Day*

Friday, May 10, Mom and I are waiting in her hospital room to see Dr. Levenson. We intend to ask him what to expect in the near future. It's showdown day.

As he enters the room he's met with a straight-out question. "Dr. Levenson, what are we going to do about the brain disease?" she asks.

"Lois, you have had all the radiation you can have. Our efforts right now are going to be directed toward controlling your pain."

She quietly looks at the doctor for a few minutes and nods. "I now understand the condition I'm in, and I don't want to put my family through any more of this."

Dr. Levenson replies, "I don't think your family is concerned about what they are going through. We're all concerned with what you are going through, and we want you to be as comfortable as possible. I'm going to prescribe a change of medication for your pain. You will be feeling less pain very soon."

She nods again. Her eyes draw away from us. She turns her head and quietly looks out the window, staring beyond the adjacent scenery. Dr. Levenson and I step outside her room to allow her private time to consider what she's just been told.

"We'll begin morphine this afternoon to relieve her pain," he says to me. "It will cause her to sleep more and more. I will prescribe it for her at regular intervals, until things begin to get grim. Then we will increase the doses until there is no more pain."

"I will want to know when we get to grim," I respond.

"I will not alter treatments without first consulting you."

We both understand what is being said and we both hope her ordeal will end soon. We know this is not the way she would choose to live. She's always lived so well. Much more of this would truly be unfair.

I walk back into Mom's room and sit down with her again. My thoughts

## Promise I'll Stay for Mother's Day

return to that day last August when we first knew we were beginning the end of our journey on earth together. The end has come too soon.

Mom turns her gaze from the window and looks at me. "I don't want to live like this any more."

"I know you don't, Mom, and you don't have to."

No more time for pretending, or alluding to some future date with death. The time is now, and I want this time to be remembered with clarity and dignity. These next few days will be our most important time with each other. I've just given her permission to leave this life, and she has responded with a look I will never forget.

> Fasten your seat belts, folks! Lois Thompson-Wilson is beginning her final ascent into a heavenly life, and she is movin' in high gear.

With the simple statement, "I know, and you don't have to," she and I have reached a universal understanding that comes to a parent and child only once. It comes at that moment when the child allows her parent to become eternal.

"I'll see to it," I say, as I look into her eyes. She smiles and nods.

We both understand the meaning of our agreement and my promise, and we accept it. She has entrusted me with her final days of this life, so she can prepare for her first steps into the everlasting days of green pastures.

All the years of our lives we wonder about that final bend in the road. We know it will come, but we don't know when, and we don't know what will happen to us when we reach it. More than anything, I think we're hoping for some measure of satisfaction. What a disappointment it would be to finally reach the point where we can look beyond the bend only to discover there is nothing ahead of us. If I truly thought there would be nothing, I couldn't let her go so easily.

We sit together in silence, each of us pursuing our own thoughts. I speak first. "I feel Dad preparing a pink room for you."

"You remember that day?" she asks.

Remember? How could I forget. Childhood revisited. It's Mom and Dad and Gene and I, headin' down the road to find Ma a pink room. Dad got to the land of pink rooms first, and he's been waiting all these years for Mom to catch up. She's on her way, Dad, and she's as excited as I've ever seen her.

"I do it my way", she says over and over, almost singing the refrain. As death approaches, Mom is coming to life. Fasten your seat belts, folks! Lois Thompson-Wilson is beginning her final ascent into a heavenly life, and she is movin' in high gear. She's laughing and talking and giving orders, telling me

## I'll Stay for Mother's Day

where everything is, one more time. She says she will miss not being here to great her great grandchildren.

"You're going to have to take my place as 'Granny', you know." She laughs at that one. Yeah, right. Me as Granny. That's a real hoot.

Is death supposed to be this easy? Is life the struggle and the pain? Do we only endure life so we can feel the rapture of death? Something very special is going on here. I've never experienced anything even closed to the euphoria I'm feeling right now. It probably has something to do with the lady that's leaving. She's always grabbed for the best part of every moment, and her last moments are going to be her most gratifying.

"I feel better now," Mom says. "I was worried about you and Gene having to deal with my incapacities. Now I know there won't be any. You won't allow them to keep me around that long. And I won't have to die at home. My Mother died at home, and it was horrible. You and Gene shouldn't have to go through anything like that. What if Rebecca and Shannon were there when it happened. I don't want them to remember me dying. I want them to remember how I lived.

"Now I can close my eyes tonight, and not have to wake up in the morning."

Wait a minute. Tonight?!?

"Not tonight, Mom. Not yet. You're still having one heckuva good time. Soon, but not tonight."

"You don't know what it's like, Shirleyanne, to have a pain that feels like a hundred big, long, hot needles, pushing their way through your body, attacking and expanding their painful territories, one space at a time. I want to be free from this pain, before it captures my spirit as well as my body."

It's the first time Mom has spoken to me of pain, and it's not offered in a complaining tone. She wants to be set free from the pain of death so she can keep her spirit alive. Pain is a companion that will defeat her, unless we defeat it. And we will defeat it. This afternoon the pain will begin to leave, but to eliminate her pain, we must also eliminate her life.

Pain or death? What a choice to have to make, but we've made our choice, and in doing so, we have won. We've taken charge of both the pain and the disease. So retreat, you sons 'a bitches. We're in control again. You will not win this one. We are going to welcome the end of this life, our way.

Becca enters the room and Mom looks at me knowingly, as she smiles at her granddaughter. "We made some decisions today," she says. "I do it my way,"

Becca looks at me, puzzled. Mom starts talking to Becca about her future

## Promise I'll Stay for Mother's Day

great grandchild, and about what wonderful granddaughters she and Shannon have been. She sails on and on with her glorious rhetoric...

"I think we better go back to school and work, Becca. She's not going to get any rest as long as we're here... bye for now Mom, we'll be back around dinner time."

We leave Mom to her exciting thoughts of transition. When I try to explain to Becca what's taken place today, I become concerned. Mom is so convinced that today is going to be her last day, I begin to wonder if she might find a way to help it along. I stop at the nurses' station to express my concerns. I want no giddy enthusiasm for her new life to cause Mom to make unwise decisions about getting there. I ask them to watch her a little more closely. Becca and I leave the hospital together, not knowing what evening will bring.

When I arrive at the hospital after work, I find that Mom has been moved to a room directly across from the nurses' station. Gene is in her room and he and Mom are having a very animated discussion.

As soon as Mom sees me she lets fly. "Gene's not buying into our plan."

"What plan, Mom?"

"Well, you know. I'm leavin' tonight. I told you I don't want to live like this, and I won't let the two of you hold me up any longer."

"I know you're in pain, and none of us want that," Gene says. "But the doctor is going to be taking care of the pain, so you can enjoy the time you have left. And with the pain gone you might want more time than you think."

"If you make me stay, I'll stop taking the medication, and I'll stop eating."

"Now that's ridiculous..."

Gene and Mom are going at it, tooth and nail. This is good. We get to live like we live, right up to our last breath. If we always agree, one of us is unnecessary, and until her last moment, Mom's input is going to be as necessary as any of ours.

Finally, Mom say, adamantly, "I don't want to live like this any more. I'm satisfied with my life and I don't want to wake up tomorrow to another day of pain."

Gene shot right back. "You are still alert enough to take me on, and if you'd take your medication you wouldn't have any more pain."

"It's just not time yet, Mom," I offer.

"Why isn't it?" she demands.

Just to stop this silly arguing, I blurt out, "Because Sunday is Mother's Day, and we want to have our Mother around for that."

As soon as I said it, I knew I had given her a real time to depart. Sure enough...

## I'll Stay for Mother's Day

She smiled her sly grin of triumph. "Okay. I'll stay for Mother's Day."

End of argument, end of life. That answers the last question I had about this disease. Mom is leaving on Monday. "I'll stay for Mother's Day," she said. But can even this determined lady move to the next level by willing it to happen? She's going to have to, because she's getting no help from me on this one. If it's to be Monday, Mom is going to have to ring down the final curtain all by herself. Anyone want to bet against her?

Mom simply won't settle down. I've never seen anyone so excited. The only thing Dad ever said about his impending death was, "I'll be bug dust soon." When he left, he went quietly. Let me tell you, this woman is not going to go quietly. She's never been a real quiet person anyway, but I've never seen her quite this noisy. She can hardly wait to get the last part of this journey under way. She wants to make sure, one more time that everything is taken care of, so she can get movin', or as she says, "Gotta get rollin'." What is she so all-fired excited about? It's for sure she's not excited about being bug dust. She's not shutting down, she's packing her bags. She's on her way to somewhere.

> Let me tell you, this woman is not going to go quietly. She's never been a real quiet person anyway, but I've never seen her quite this noisy. She can hardly wait to get the last part of this journey under way.

While I feel there is something down that eternal road, I'm still searching for a form I can put into my head. Green Pastures has always served as a useful painting in my mind. The basic laws of physics state that energy, once created will continue. The Bible teaches that there is life after life. Physics says that energy continues; the Bible says that life continues. Physical laws and spiritual theories both say there is more. Hey Dad, I feel you waiting for Mom, and if you were only bug dust I wouldn't feel a thing. Mom thinks she's going someplace and she thinks she's going to see you when she gets there. She's excited about it, and you damn well better be there for her.

Finally, about nine thirty, Gene and I get up to leave. If we don't leave, she won't go to sleep and she won't have the strength to make it through to Mother's Day. When she sees us stand to go, she stops talking. Her eyes are misty, as she looks at us.

"You've been wonderful kids. I'll miss you."

I step closer and take her hand. She pulls me closer and gives me a good night kiss. It's our first kiss. Good night, Mom. Please stay with us a few more days.

I'm taking my time getting to the hospital this morning, puttering around, restless, not knowing what it is I need to do. Finally it comes to me that I must try again to find the poetry of Mom's life. I've been casually looking for a collection of Tennyson's poems for over a month now, without success. There's a book store near the hospital. I'll try there.

The last try is the best try. Not only does this store have Alfred, Lord Tennyson, but there is a large volume of collected works that contains many more wonderful pieces of fine literature. The next couple of days I'll read to Mom some of the beautiful and humorous poems she read to me "when I was sick and lay abed I had two pillows at my head . . ."

With book in hand, I enter Mom's room. Since I'm limited in the medical vernacular, I can't professionally identify Mom's actual physical condition, so I will just say she is in a deep sleep, but a very busy sleep. Changes in her facial expressions as she sleeps indicate a very active mind. If only I could know what that mind is thinking right now.

I sit down and begin to read.

"Oh Captain, my Captain
thy fearful trip is done . . ."

"Yea, though I walk through the valley
of the shadow of death, I will fear no evil . . ."

Beautiful words for a beautiful lady about to embark on a fabulous journey. Once in a while her eyes open and we connect, but we speak no words. We've said them all and her mind is on to other things now. I stay with her until early evening, then return home to get a good night's sleep.

Today is Mother's Day. I put on a new outfit I found yesterday while I was looking for poetry. It's a bright rusty red linen skirt with a matching red and white polka dot blouse and new ivory earrings. Mom has told me more than once about the time she walked into Dad's hospital room looking less than her usual best.

"You spending so much time running up here you have no time to take care of yourself?" he said, visibly disappointed in her appearance.

I'm not about to make that mistake today.

Mom's mind is racing. Her hands are moving, she says a name now and then . . . "Hazel and Don" . . . "Jack" . . . "Mabel" . . . is she saying goodbye?

Mark and Becca come in. Gene and Shannon arrive from Bellingham. Cliff calls.

A nurse brings Mom's lunch tray, containing a can of Ensure and a bowl of cream soup. It looks putrid.

"Doesn't this look good!" the nurse says to her nearly comatose patient.

I don't know what that nurse is thinking. Mom's not going to eat, much less taste that lunch. I look at Mom and her eyes flutter in a sort of conscious recognition. Then that slow, familiar, gotcha grin is spreading across her face. A word is beginning to form.

"Bullshit," she says.

In other words, cut the crap. Don't try to get me to eat that awful smelling lunch by telling me it looks good. I'm through eating and you know it. Save it. It's bullshit.

Late afternoon, Shannon and Gene get up to return to Bellingham. I could tell them this is her last day, but my mind still has this small seed of doubt that even she can pull of her final choice. I should tell them to stay, but what if . . . oh, I don't know. I'm no prophet. Let it ride. Let them go.

I sit down with my book to read more poetry. The pages fall open to . . .

"Twilight and evening bell,
  And after that the dark!
  And may there be no sadness of farewell,
  When I embark . . . "

It's time for me to go home, Mom. You said you'd stay for Mother's Day and you did. Thank you. I'll leave you now, so you may go ahead and wait for me, as Dad has waited for you. Have a safe journey to wherever it is you're going. My Mother's Day here with you has passed.

## CHAPTER 30

## *Our Separate Journeys Begin*

It's seven thirty in the morning. The phone rings. "I've just been with your mother," Dr. Levenson says. "Her vital signs are still there, but there has been a dramatic change in her condition."

"She said she would stay for Mother's Day."

"That's all we can expect."

The weather is pleasant as I drive to the hospital, but the cheery sun that shined on my previous drives toward destiny is not taunting me today. Clouds are approaching.

The curtains are drawn around her bed. A nurse hurries over to me and touches my arm.

"She's gone. She passed away peacefully at 8:20 this morning. She's ready for you."

Mom died twenty minutes ago. I feel cheated of a glorious moment, but Mom made it clear she didn't want witnesses. She wanted to encounter her moment of death alone. That moment has to be one of life's most exquisitely personal experiences. She wanted that moment of glory to belong to her. I hope she wasn't disappointed.

I walk into her room and pull back the curtain. There I see a human being very much at peace. She could be asleep, except for the supreme stillness. No one alive could be so still, so peaceful. I search her face for some sign of cognizance. There is none. Yet, when I speak to her softly, from my heart, I know she hears. Her heart has stopped pumping the blood of life, but her soul is alive and listening from somewhere in this room. I've heard it said that life leaves not suddenly, but gradually like a delicate handkerchief being lifted from above. I must call Gene.

The affects of a death in the family do not begin or end with the death itself. Death is simply an episode that forces people to make changes in their lives, changes that would take place eventually, but happen to occur at a particular time, due to the emotional upheaval of the impact of death.

Barry and I were withdrawing from each other before Mom's illness. It only served to accelerate our separation. We propelled our activities into a pace

## Our Separate Journeys Begin

that prevented our relationship from stabilizing past the first rush of romance. Our marriage dissolved because it had not fully bonded before the arrival of her illness. Her death facilitated the inevitable separation of our two lives.

Tuesday morning brings messages of condolence and support. Comforting words, but I want to be alone. There is so much left to do . . . always so much to do.

Gene and I are hosting a picnic at my house on Sunday, to celebrate Mom's life. There'll be food and music, of course but I want some sort of simple commemorative piece to give to people. I'll have to put something together today and get it to a printer. I also need to clean the house. Boy, do I need to clean the house! And tomorrow I must go back to work. So today's the day to get organized.

The memorial piece will be on pink parchment paper with "Crossing the Bar" on one side and some sort of biography on the other. How can I possibly put Mom's life on one side of a piece of paper. Just do it. Becca came to help with the organization. Most of the day is a blur. I know we got to the printer, but I don't remember anything else. Was she here for lunch? Did we have dinner together? I don't remember.

I do remember that, when I lay my head down on my pillow I said good night, once more to the two people who have left me. "Good night to you, Mom," and "Good night to you, Barry." I wish you both love and Godspeed. Our separate journeys are underway.

It's tough to settle down. For nearly two years my days have been long and my hours full. My mind and body have become accustomed to constant activity. They don't know how to be still. They keep darting here and there, with no regard as to order or good sense. I learned how to take care of problems, now I need to find fulfillment in routine. I want a real life now. I want it right here, right now. I don't want to wait for my own trip to those far off green pastures. I'm not going to pass over the time I have left with an expedient smile. I want more. I want to laugh out loud and sing and cry, if I need to. But I don't know how. I need help.

With good recommendations in hand, I set an appointment with Dr. Byrde Hill.

"Why have you come to see me?" she asks.

"I need reassurance that I'm okay."

"Are you okay?" she asks solicitously.

"Don't start in with your practiced tone," I snap back.

"Okay then, why don't you just begin to tell me what would make you feel okay."

## Promise I'll Stay for Mother's Day

That's better. Now I can talk. I bring her up to speed on the chaos of the past couple of years. Then I hear myself say . . .

"My Mom's death was the most powerful, exciting experience I've ever had. I know it'll take time for me to fully understand all that I've learned from her and her passing, but frankly, right now, I am riding on a very high plane. I feel wonderful and excited about moving on with the rest of my life.

"Mom's final days were glorious. She was so satisfied, so happy, so ready to travel on. I wish everyone could experience such a beautiful passing. It was exhilarating! Is it all right to feel this way? Am I all right? Will this continue, or am I experiencing an unnatural high that will crash when I least expect it? I've never experienced this kind of peaceful euphoria before. I want it to continue."

"People who survive tumultuous events like you have just described," she says, "are those who are able to find a positive outlet for their feelings, some release mechanism for the stresses of coping. You seem to have a good understanding of your feelings. You may not express them to other people, but I would surmise that you've found some way of expressing them to yourself."

"Yes, in this world of exposing every blip, burp, and bathroom trip, there are some people left who express their feelings to themselves. I am one of them. I not only have feelings, I am aware of them, and I choose to parcel them carefully. Because you don't feel my heart pounding doesn't mean I have no heart; because you don't see tears streaming down my cheeks doesn't mean there are no tears. Because you hear no screams doesn't mean there is an absence of outrage. Pain is a private emotion for me. I don't need my pain ratified by strangers. It's my pain and I'll do with it as I please.

"And while I'm on this little rant here, let me also say that love can be as personal as pain. Dad and I used to sit together in a row boat for hours on the pretext of fishing, seldom speaking out loud, but always sharing our silent worlds of private emotions. Not passive emotions . . . private emotions.

"Gene and I did not have to discuss ad nauseum how we would take care of our Mom. We knew how we'd do it, because we cared about doing it. Our behavior grew from caring, not from words. That's just the way we are.

"Mom and I shared a full hug for the first time six months before she died. I defy anyone to say we never loved because we were never seen hugging.

"Nothing seems to bother you," people say to me. That is so assumptive, so ignorant, so disrespectful."

When I've finished my rant, Dr. Hill has a few words of well-spoken advice.

"You came here asking if you are okay. I will affirm that you are indeed okay. But try to slow down, and learn to be more patient with yourself and with other people. Not everyone has the same need for emotional privacy as you do. Some people do want to share out loud. Give them their due.

"I'd like for you to allow yourself more latitude. Because you've always done things your own way doesn't mean it's the only way. Gift yourself the opportunity to give birth to a new happiness. Let the euphoria last a while. It's okay. Follow your mother's example of taking herself less seriously in your later years. From what you've told me, she exited laughing. You can learn to laugh out loud as well, and with ease. It's a wonderful release.

> "Grow where you are planted." If she's to grow where she was planted, we better head for Promise. I call Lide.

"Take a true measurement of what brings you pleasure. Expand your choices. Take time to learn what makes you happy. Take a chance on personal happiness."

As weeks pass without unwelcome incident, I slow my daily routine to a pace that includes social gatherings with friends and thoughtful time with my self. My appearance begins to change. As I look at my life with more clarity, my look in the mirror reflects shinier hair and brighter eyes. I've even polished my nails. I understand now that Mom's two-hour Sunday night nail-polishing routine served as therapy to prepare her for another week of work. Took me a while to figure that out, didn't it?

The changes are noticed. It's been years since my appearance has attracted attention. A surprised, "You look great!" is a far cry from a solicitous "How do you feel?" And it's a helluva lot better than the dreaded, "I don't know how you do it, Shirleyanne", which by the way, I'm not hearing so much any more.

Life is good. But there is unfinished business.

It's early August and I'm trying to get myself ready for work but something is holding me back. It's a signal. Pay attention. I fix myself a good breakfast, take it into the living room and sink deep down into my black velvet loveseat. It's time to address what to do with Mom's ashes. The box has been sitting on a shelf in the linen closet upstairs since I picked it up at the funeral home four days after she died. It's wrapped in brown paper, identified by her name and crematorium number. She can't spend an eternity in my linen closet locked inside a box with a name and number on it. It's high time I bring closure to this.

Mom loved the soil. She liked turning it in her hands to yield pretty flower gardens and harvest backyard vegetables. She had a plaque hanging on her kitchen wall that said, "Grow where you are planted." If she's to grow where she was planted, we better head for Promise. I call Lide.

"I'm thinking we'll bring Mom home Labor Day weekend, and put her ashes in the ground, in Promise."

Lide is relieved. "That sounds good. We were wondering what you would do."

"We'll put together some kind of service, with music and readings. Would you see if there is space in the cemetery on top of the hill near the homestead?"

"I'm sure there is," she says. "I'll take care of it."

There you have it. There's one final journey to make. Blue Mountains here we come.

CHAPTER 31

## *Promise Fulfilled*

Friday, August 30, Mark and Becca and I drive to Milton-Freewater. Shannon has elected not to go with us. She hasn't yet reached acceptance of her Granny's death. Some day she will mature enough, if not to embrace life's difficulties, at least to deal with them. Gene and Cliff will meet us at Lide and Peck's house.

When we walk into the big country kitchen, we smell a dinner nearly ready to eat and I see a lace table cloth folded on the corner of the dining table waiting to be spread. Mom added lace tablecloths and fine China to her table after she moved away from her country home, but Lide has always made it her personal mission to keep her simple country ways in spite of economic prosperity. I'm deeply touched by Lide's show of respect for Mom's chosen lifestyle as she and I spread the lace cloth together.

The drive to Promise will take about three and a half hours. We'll stop in Wallowa on the way, to pick up the piece of paper that will permit us to bury Mom in the Promise Cemetery near the abandoned Thompson home site. The cemetery was established many years ago for the Blue Mountain settlers and descendents. It's maintained by the people of Willowa as a community project.

The week before Memorial Day each year, the townspeople drive the thirty-mile dirt road to the cemetery to clean up winter's waste and place flowers on the graves of settlers with no known living family. Lide and Peck make the trip each Memorial Day to pay their respects to deceased neighbors and place flowers on Teeny Thompson's grave. Mountain people have a heartfelt respect for the people who have preceded them.

Although I've heard a lot about Promise through the years, I've been to Promise only once before. When I was sixteen, the family went there to put a new stone marker over Teeny's grave. I remember feeling a strong sense of family bonding in this homage to her brief existence, even from brothers and sisters who, by place of birth, never knew her. I also remember thinking Promise is a beautiful place for eternal rest.

## Promise I'll Stay for Mother's Day

*Mark, Rebecca, Shirleyanne, Gene, August 31, 1985.*

After breakfast we pack a lunch from last night's dinner leftovers. Lide and Becca gather flowers from the garden and lay the beautiful, long-stemmed blossoms together in unstructured, natural bouquets. As we're headed out the back door, I spot a goofy hat sitting next to a pile of fresh folded laundry in a corner of the utility room. It's a straw sun hat with a plastic bird sitting on top of the crown and a bright pink flower thatched into the brim. Lide said Mom left it here last spring. I grab the hat and toss it into the back of the pickup with Mom, next to the food and flowers. It's time to get rollin'.

Cliff and I ride with Aunt Mamie on the road up the mountain. She reminisces. "Look over there", she says. "That's Valentine Hill. Pop would hitch the horses to the buggy and come down across the top of that hill on his way into town. It took him almost a full day to get there. Sometimes we'd get to go with him.

"I remember my first trip across Valentine Hill. We didn't go into town very often, just when we were desperate for supplies. We had no money, of course, so we bartered for our goods. I'd heard rumors that someone in town had a car and I wanted to see it. I begged Pop for weeks to take me with him on his next trip to town. He finally gave in and let me go with him. We looked and looked all over town for the car, but we didn't find it. I was real disappointed.

"We finally got a car ourselves and Pop drove it like it was a horse. He never was good at mechanical things. When he'd meet someone on the road, he'd push the horn and yell, 'Oooga, Oooga', and when he'd want to stop the car, he'd pull back on the steering wheel and say, 'Whoa'. It's a wonder we weren't all killed. And it's a good thing cars don't buck."

She giggles at the memory. Personal recollections of long-ago stories are passing through all our minds as we make our way back into the hills to a world with minimal signs of late twentieth century civilization. Two or three people in worn, bibbed overalls nod to us as we drive by them, stirring up dust on their road. An abandoned Harley, missing its tires, leans against a stump in the middle of a field about fifteen miles in. It's an improbable piece of machinery, testament to the unexpected turns in our lives. Not all memories are congruous with their surroundings.

The cemetery has a post and wire fence defining its boundaries. When we get to the gate we see a sign propped up against it. It's a city sign, the shape of an arrow. White, with black letters, it reads, "Dead End." This must be the place.

We pick up Mom's box, put the hat over it and walk to her burial site. Looking out over the mountains we see fields spread out in the lovely pre-fall shade of soft golden yellow, with occasional clumps of dark evergreen trees adding color and texture to the landscape. The sky above us is a deep cornflower blue. Across the valley there are only a few houses and barns still standing. Our gazes turn to the ground beneath our feet. Mom's piece of earth is next to her unknown sister, at the foot of a little laurel tree that blooms fragrant pink and lavender blossoms in the spring.

Lon and Gene pick up shovels and begin turning the soft summer dirt. They dig deep enough so her grave won't be disturbed by passing animals sniffing for a new presence in their quiet mountain field. Gene places Mom's box in the ground and sprinkles a shovel of dirt over her. Without saying a word, he passes the shovel to me. I pour my shovel of dirt and pass it to Hazel. We pass the shovel all around, until everyone has a chance to return earth to earth, covering Mom's ashes. We give one of us back to the earth, and it feels good.

Our first song is "Little Annie."

"I will wait for the leaves to return to the trees.

I will be waiting when the springtime comes again . . ."

*Grave site, Lois, 1986.*

I speak.

"The only thing in her life that Mom didn't talk about was where her final resting place would be. I think she wanted us to figure it out, perhaps a kind of test to see if we really knew where her heart was. It wasn't a difficult choice. She loved these Blue Mountains of Eastern Oregon. This is where her life began and it's right that this is where she would return, to live forever.

"We were lucky she paused in her eternal journey long enough to give us her love and unique perspective as to how to spend our time on this earthly plain. She taught us well, and now it's time to give her back to the more important task of discovering the wonders beyond this existence . . . "

Hazel interrupts. "You mean there is something more important than being here with us?"

"Oh Lord, I hope so," I laugh in reply.

Another song. "The Master's Bouquet"

. . . "Beautiful flowers that will never decay.

Put there by angels to show us the way,

Beautiful flowers in the Master's bouquet."

Texie steps forward to read her chosen poem, then Cliff begins a letter he has written to Shannon, to help her understand Mom's legacy.

"I was lying there in my bathtub with me head back, drifting away in thoughtlessness, when I heard a voice laughing somewhere near my left ear.

I recognized the voice, of course, and I knew that wonderful, almost harsh laugh—the kind of laugh that enjoys watching people with their pants down, and I say her name out loud. 'Lois'.

"And I begin to chuckle as I lay there listening to the laughter in my head, and soon I was laughing out loud for no good reason, other than the contagious quality of Lois' laughter. And then my laughter turned to tears as I realized how much I would miss her whole approach to life, her blunt opinions, the sharpness of her vision, her quick wit, her delight at human foibles, her sense of humor about herself, her ability to roll with some pretty hard punches, her stubbornness, her courage, the whole of her life and love.

"And I cried for the huge cavern that her death has left in my heart and in the hearts of dear friends. But as I lay there bawling like a baby, she seemed to speak to me through the mist in a kind of grumble, something like, 'Aw come on now. Don't waste your tears on me. That's what life is all about. And she laughed again, and pretty soon I was laughing in spite of myself, and singing the damn Doodlebug Song we all loved so much.

"One of the things Lois showed me was how to look square in the face of that bastard, death and say, 'I know you will have me in the end, but I will choose the time and the place. I will make the preparations and take care of the details. I will provide for family and friends; I will choose the day and the way.'

"There are not many people on this earth who are able to do this, who have the courage and foresight necessary to deal with it, who have the opportunity to do it, who have the sharpness of mind to even see the possibility, who have the humor and love to savor the days, who have the guts and the will power to carry it off. But Lois had all of this and more.

"She also showed me another thing, and that is this. Until the very moment you die, it is possible to live completely, to laugh, complain, teach, listen, joke, give, gripe, love and all the rest of it. This sounds so simple today, but she actually did it, and did it well, which makes all the difference.

"If any one of us can do half as well, without bitterness and anger and sorrow, we would do Lois proud. To me that is her legacy. She gave me the rare opportunity to experience this precious gift of life in the midst of death."

Cliff hands me the rest of the letter to read.

> "Lois, Mom, Aunt Ma, Granny, remains alive. She lives in Rebecca and Shannon, and in Shirleyanne and Gene, and in all her family and friends whose lives were touched by her generous hand.

"Lois, Mom, Aunt Ma, Granny, remains alive. She lives in Rebecca and Shannon, and in Shirleyanne and Gene, and in all her family and friends whose lives were touched by her generous hand. She's the one who makes us laugh at some of the dumb situations we find ourselves in, when we could feel hurt or hard done by. It's then that we stop and laugh at how ridiculous we must look. Laughing at oneself is the hardest thing to do, but it's great balm for the soul. Life's like a hunt for doodle bugs. When you find yourself stupidly bending over with your butt out and your arms stuck out behind you, it's no big deal. It is to laugh!

Finally, we sing "The Doodlebug Song" all together.

"Doodle-oodle-oodle, up, up, up.

Doodle-oodle-oodle, up, up, up.

Oh the Doodlebug jumped and looked all around,

And doodled back in the ground . . . "

We cross the road and spread our picnic food. Pretty soon I'm aware that someone is missing. I look around and see Mark kneeling over the grave site. He is working on something. I walk back across the road to see him put the finishing touches on a three-foot cross he has just made out of fresh tree branches, tied together with a light-weight rope.

There stands the laurel tree, and under it sits a straw hat with a plastic bird and pink flower on it. Several bouquets of fresh flowers in coffee cans blanket the fresh-turned ground from the hat to the little cross, crafted from plain materials by loving hands. It is the finishing touch this beautiful spot of ground needed.

We all walk the quarter mile to the site of the old home site. The house is long gone, but Mamie shows us where it stood, and where the garden was, and the root cellar. We look back across the dell and see the cross, sitting line-of-site from the exact spot where Mom was born.

Peace at last. We're standing here together, one, two, and three generations from Bress and Annie Thompson, looking out over the crest of the Blue Mountains, remembering our journey with their seventh born. We went through many long, hard seasons with her, including days when I wondered why we had to take on so much change and pain, days when I questioned if we'd ever make it to this bend in the road and feel again the warmth of late summer sun.

Peace seldom comes on its own. It requires the conscious and constant companionship of people forcing and responding to change as they search for a better way to live with themselves and others. The seasons of change will

## Promise Fulfilled

always bring uncertainty and pain, along with a sure and steady process of loss before giving way to the birth of another spring followed by bountiful summers of fulfillment.

We are all changed from having been a part of Mom's rebirth and joy as she lived through her final season of pain and passage. Through your last season, Mom, I rediscovered poetry, music, laughter, love, and pain. It was worth the pain to recapture the joy.

Our world did not tumble or crumble. It just seemed that way for a while. During a brief period of our life, the banjo kept falling on our heads. That's all. When a big ol' banjo keeps bustin' us on the head, how can we possibly see the light beyond the dark sea?

We stand up, shake off the hurt, open our eyes and look for it. And when we finally see the light, we allow a big grin to spread across our faces. Then we let the grin erupt into full-blown, knee-slappin' laughter. The sun is always there. All we have to do is look for it and move ourselves to the warmth of its presence.

Thank you, Mom, for providing our light and our laughter for so many years. We will carry on your legacy.

"Doodle-oodle-oodle, up, up, up . . ."

Life is to laugh. Rejoice and let go!

*Crossing the Bar*

*Sunset and evening star,*
*And one clear call for me!*
*And may there be no moaning of the bar,*
*When I put out to sea.*

*But such a tide as moving seems asleep,*
*Too full for sound and foam,*
*When that which drew from out the boundless deep*
*Turns again home.*

*Twilight and evening bell,*
*And after that the dark!*
*And may there be no sadness of farewell,*
*When I embark;*

*For tho' from out our bourne of Time and Place*
*The flood may bear me far,*
*I hope to see my Pilot face to face*
*When I have crost the bar.*

Alfred, Lord Tennyson